2015 ALMANAC FOR KIDS

Scholastic Inc.

Copyright © 2014 by Scholastic Inc.

Scholastic 2015 Almanac for Kids is produced by J. A. Ball Associates LLC, 801 Second Ave., Seattle, WA 98104.

President and Editorial Director: Jacqueline A. Ball
Design Director: Ron Leighton
Designer: Mathew McInelly
Writers: Lynn Brunelle, Jim Brunelle, Delia Greve, Monique Peterson
Research: Brianne McInelly

ISBN 978-0-545-67949-7

10 9 8 7 6 5 4 3 2 1   14 15 16 17

Printed in the U.S.A.   40
First printing, September 2014
Cover design by Jessica Meltzer

Due to the publication date, statistics are current as of June 2014.

CONTENTS

ANIMALS

CAPTURING A "GHOST CAT" ON CAMERA

The endangered snow leopard is so secretive it is sometimes called the "ghost cat." It stays out of sight for good reasons. Hunters want to kill it for its beautiful fur. Farmers want to kill it because it preys on their livestock. It is losing habitat to livestock pastures, and to make matters worse, some species of its prey are endangered too. Fewer than 6,500 snow leopards remain in the wild.

As part of a three-year study, scientists from Norwegian Life Sciences University decided to use camera traps—cameras mounted on poles—to "capture" snow leopards in northern Pakistan. The cameras would neither hurt the animals nor scare them away by invading their space. After many weeks, the researchers' work paid off in close-up pictures of one snow leopard. The images could tell them a lot about the animal's habits and activities.

YOUR TURN

If you were an animal, which state would you like to call home? Every year the Humane Society of the United States ranks the 50 states and Washington, DC, on the way it treats animals. In 2013 California was the top-ranked state for the fifth year in a row.

The ranking was based on laws and policies providing for humane treatment of companion animals, farm animals, exotic pets, and wildlife. Where does your state rank? Go to humanesociety.org and look for the interactive US map.

Match each of these names to the correct animal group: bale, drove, trip, troop. (See p. 29.)

THE ANIMAL KINGDOM
Detailed Classification

- Porifera SPONGES
- Cnidaria COELENTERATES
- Platyhelminthes FLATWORMS
- Nematoda ROUNDWORMS
- Mollusca MOLLUSKS
- Annelida TRUE WORMS

Cnidaria
- Hydrozoa HYDRAS, HYDROIDS
- Scyphozoa JELLYFISH
- Anthozoa SEA ANEMONES, CORAL

Platyhelminthes
- Turbellaria FREE-LIVING FLATWORMS
- Monogenea PARASITIC FLUKES
- Trematoda PARASITIC FLUKES
- Cestoda TAPEWORMS

Mollusca
- Polyplacophora CHITONS
- Gastropoda SNAILS, SLUGS
- Bivalvia CLAMS, SCALLOPS, MUSSELS
- Cephalopoda OCTOPUSES, SQUID

Annelida
- Polychaeta MARINE WORMS
- Oligochaeta EARTHWORMS, FRESHWATER WORMS
- Hirudinea LEECHES

Arthropoda
- Insecta INSECTS
- Chilopoda CENTIPEDES
- Diplopoda MILLIPEDES
- Symphyla SYMPHYLANS, PAUROPODS

Insecta

Collembola, SPRINGTAILS
Thysanura, SILVERFISH, BRISTLETAILS
Ephemeroptera, MAYFLIES
Odonata, DRAGONFLIES
Isoptera, TERMITES
Orthoptera, LOCUSTS, CRICKETS, GRASSHOPPERS
Dictyptera, COCKROACHES, MANTIDS
Dermaptera, EARWIGS
Phasmida, STOCK INSECTS, LEAF INSECTS
Psocoptera, BOOK LICE, BARK LICE
Diplura, SIMPLE INSECTS

Protura, TELSONTAILS
Plecoptera, STONE FLIES
Grylloblattodea, TINY MOUNTAIN INSECTS
Strepsiptera, TWISTED-WINGED STYLOPIDS
Trichoptera, CADDIS FLIES
Embioptera, WEBSPINNERS
Thysanoptera, THRIPS
Mecoptera, SCORPION FLIES
Zoraptera, RARE TROPICAL INSECTS
Hemiptera, TRUE BUGS
Anoplura, SUCKING LICE

Mallophaga, BITING LICE, BIRD LICE
Homoptera, WHITEFLIES, APHIDS, SCALE INSECTS, CICADAS
Coleoptera, BEETLES, WEEVILS
Neuroptera, ALDERFLIES, LACEWINGS, ANT LIONS, SNAKEFLIES, DOBSONFLIES
Hymenoptera, ANTS, BEES, WASPS
Siphonaptera, FLEAS
Diptera, TRUE FLIES, MOSQUITOES, GNATS
Lepidoptera, BUTTERFLIES, MOTHS

Mammalia

Insectivora, INSECTIVORES (e.g., shrews, moles, hedgehogs)
Chiroptera, BATS
Dermaptera, FLYING LEMURS
Edentata, ANTEATERS, SLOTHS, ARMADILLOS
Pholidota, PANGOLINS
Primates, PROSIMIANS (e.g., lemurs, tarsiers, monkeys, apes, humans)

Rodentia, RODENTS (e.g., squirrels, rats, beavers, mice, porcupines)
Lagomorpha, RABBITS, HARES, PIKAS
Cetacea, WHALES, DOLPHINS, PORPOISES
Carnivora, CARNIVORES (e.g., cats, dogs, weasels, bears, hyenas)
Pinnipedia, SEALS, SEA LIONS, WALRUSES
Tubulidentata, AARDVARKS

Hyracoidea, HYDRAXES
Proboscidea, ELEPHANTS
Sirenia, SEA COWS (e.g., manatees, dugongs)
Perissodactyla, ODD-TOED HOOFED ANIMALS (e.g., horses, rhinoceroses, tapirs)
Artiodactyla, EVEN-TOED HOOFED ANIMALS (e.g., hogs, cattle, camels, hippopotamuses)

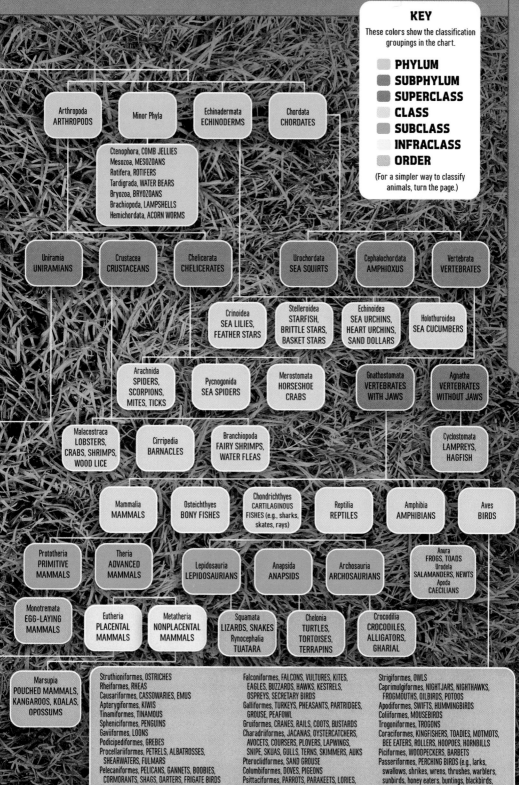

KEY

These colors show the classification groupings in the chart.

- **PHYLUM**
- **SUBPHYLUM**
- **SUPERCLASS**
- **CLASS**
- **SUBCLASS**
- **INFRACLASS**
- **ORDER**

(For a simpler way to classify animals, turn the page.)

Arthropoda ARTHROPODS

Minor Phyla

Echinodermata ECHINODERMS

Chordata CHORDATES

Ctenophora, COMB JELLIES
Mesozoa, MESOZOANS
Rotifera, ROTIFERS
Tardigrada, WATER BEARS
Bryozoa, BRYOZOANS
Brachiopoda, LAMPSHELLS
Hemichordata, ACORN WORMS

Uniramia UNIRAMIANS

Crustacea CRUSTACEANS

Chelicerata CHELICERATES

Urochordata SEA SQUIRTS

Cephalochordata AMPHIOXUS

Vertebrata VERTEBRATES

Crinoidea SEA LILIES, FEATHER STARS

Stelleroidea STARFISH, BRITTLE STARS, BASKET STARS

Echinoidea SEA URCHINS, HEART URCHINS, SAND DOLLARS

Holothuroidea SEA CUCUMBERS

Arachnida SPIDERS, SCORPIONS, MITES, TICKS

Pycnogonida SEA SPIDERS

Merostomata HORSESHOE CRABS

Gnathostomata VERTEBRATES WITH JAWS

Agnatha VERTEBRATES WITHOUT JAWS

Malacostraca LOBSTERS, CRABS, SHRIMPS, WOOD LICE

Cirripedia BARNACLES

Branchiopoda FAIRY SHRIMPS, WATER FLEAS

Cyclostomata LAMPREYS, HAGFISH

Mammalia MAMMALS

Osteichthyes BONY FISHES

Chondrichthyes CARTILAGINOUS FISHES (e.g., sharks, skates, rays)

Reptilia REPTILES

Amphibia AMPHIBIANS

Aves BIRDS

Prototheria PRIMITIVE MAMMALS

Theria ADVANCED MAMMALS

Lepidosauria LEPIDOSAURIANS

Anapsida ANAPSIDS

Archosauria ARCHOSAURIANS

Anura FROGS, TOADS
Urodela SALAMANDERS, NEWTS
Apoda CAECILIANS

Monotremata EGG-LAYING MAMMALS

Eutheria PLACENTAL MAMMALS

Metatheria NONPLACENTAL MAMMALS

Squamata LIZARDS, SNAKES
Rynocephalia TUATARA

Chelonia TURTLES, TORTOISES, TERRAPINS

Crocodilia CROCODILES, ALLIGATORS, GHARIAL

Marsupia POUCHED MAMMALS, KANGAROOS, KOALAS, OPOSSUMS

Struthioniformes, OSTRICHES
Rheiformes, RHEAS
Causariiformes, CASSOWARIES, EMUS
Apterygiformes, KIWIS
Tinamiformes, TINAMOUS
Sphenisciformes, PENGUINS
Gaviiformes, LOONS
Podicipediformes, GREBES
Procellariiformes, PETRELS, ALBATROSSES, SHEARWATERS, FULMARS
Pelecaniformes, PELICANS, GANNETS, BOOBIES, CORMORANTS, SHAGS, DARTERS, FRIGATE BIRDS
Ciconiiformes, HERONS, BITTERNS
Anseriformes, DUCKS, GEESE, SWANS, SCREAMERS

Falconiformes, FALCONS, VULTURES, KITES, EAGLES, BUZZARDS, HAWKS, KESTRELS, OSPREYS, SECRETARY BIRDS
Galliformes, TURKEYS, PHEASANTS, PARTRIDGES, GROUSE, PEAFOWL
Gruiformes, CRANES, RAILS, COOTS, BUSTARDS
Charadriiformes, JACANAS, OYSTERCATCHERS, AVOCETS, COURSERS, PLOVERS, LAPWINGS, SNIPE, SKUAS, GULLS, TERNS, SKIMMERS, AUKS
Pteroclidiformes, SAND GROUSE
Columbiformes, DOVES, PIGEONS
Psittaciformes, PARROTS, PARAKEETS, LORIES, LORIKEETS, COCKATOOS, MACAWS
Cuculiformes, CUCKOOS, TURACOS, HOATZIN

Strigiformes, OWLS
Caprimulgiformes, NIGHTJARS, NIGHTHAWKS, FROGMOUTHS, OILBIRDS, POTOOS
Apodiformes, SWIFTS, HUMMINGBIRDS
Coliiformes, MOUSEBIRDS
Trogoniformes, TROGONS
Coraciiformes, KINGFISHERS, TOADIES, MOTMOTS, BEE EATERS, ROLLERS, HOOPOES, HORNBILLS
Piciformes, WOODPECKERS, BARBETS
Passeriformes, PERCHING BIRDS (e.g., larks, swallows, shrikes, wrens, thrushes, warblers, sunbirds, honey eaters, buntings, blackbirds, finches, weavers, sparrows, starlings, birds of paradise, crows)

Show Some Spine

The simplest way to classify animals is to divide them into two groups: those with spinal columns, or backbones, and those without backbones. The bones in the spinal column are called vertebrae, so animals with backbones are called vertebrates. There are at least 40,000 species of vertebrates. There are many millions of species of invertebrates, or animals without backbones.

All mammals, fish, birds, reptiles, and amphibians are vertebrates. Invertebrates include everything else: sponges, jellyfish, insects, spiders, clams, snails, worms, and many, many others.

Vertebrates

Invertebrates

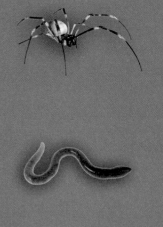

Animals with Most Known Species

Mollusks
100,000

Fish
24,000

Worms
20,000

Birds
9,600

Reptiles
8,700

Mammals
5,000

Insects and
Other Arthropods
1,000,000+

10 Longest Animal Life Spans

Animal	Maximum age (years)
Quahog (marine clam)	400
Giant tortoise	150
Human	122
Sturgeon	100
Orca	90
Blue whale	80
Golden eagle	80
Elephant	75
Sea anemone	70
Crocodile	60

For the better part of 200 million years, dinosaurs ruled the world. Yet until the 19th century, they didn't even have a name. In 1842, English scientist Sir Richard Owen concluded that recently discovered fossils of huge jaws and teeth must belong to reptiles unlike any living animals. He named them *Dinosauria* ("terrible lizards"). Some dinosaurs *were* great. *Supersaurus* could grow to a length of 130 feet (40 m)—as long as a 13-story building is tall—and weigh as much as 10 elephants. But other dinosaurs were the size of chickens. Most dinosaurs were herbivores, and most lived on land. They coexisted peacefully with mammals, most of which were small rodents.

How Big Were Dinosaurs?

Apatosaurus 75–80 ft. (23–24 m) long
Tyrannosaurus rex 40 ft. (12 m) long
Stegosaurus 30 ft. (9 m) long
Ankylosaurus 25 ft. (7.6 m) long
Triceratops 25 ft. (7.6 m) long

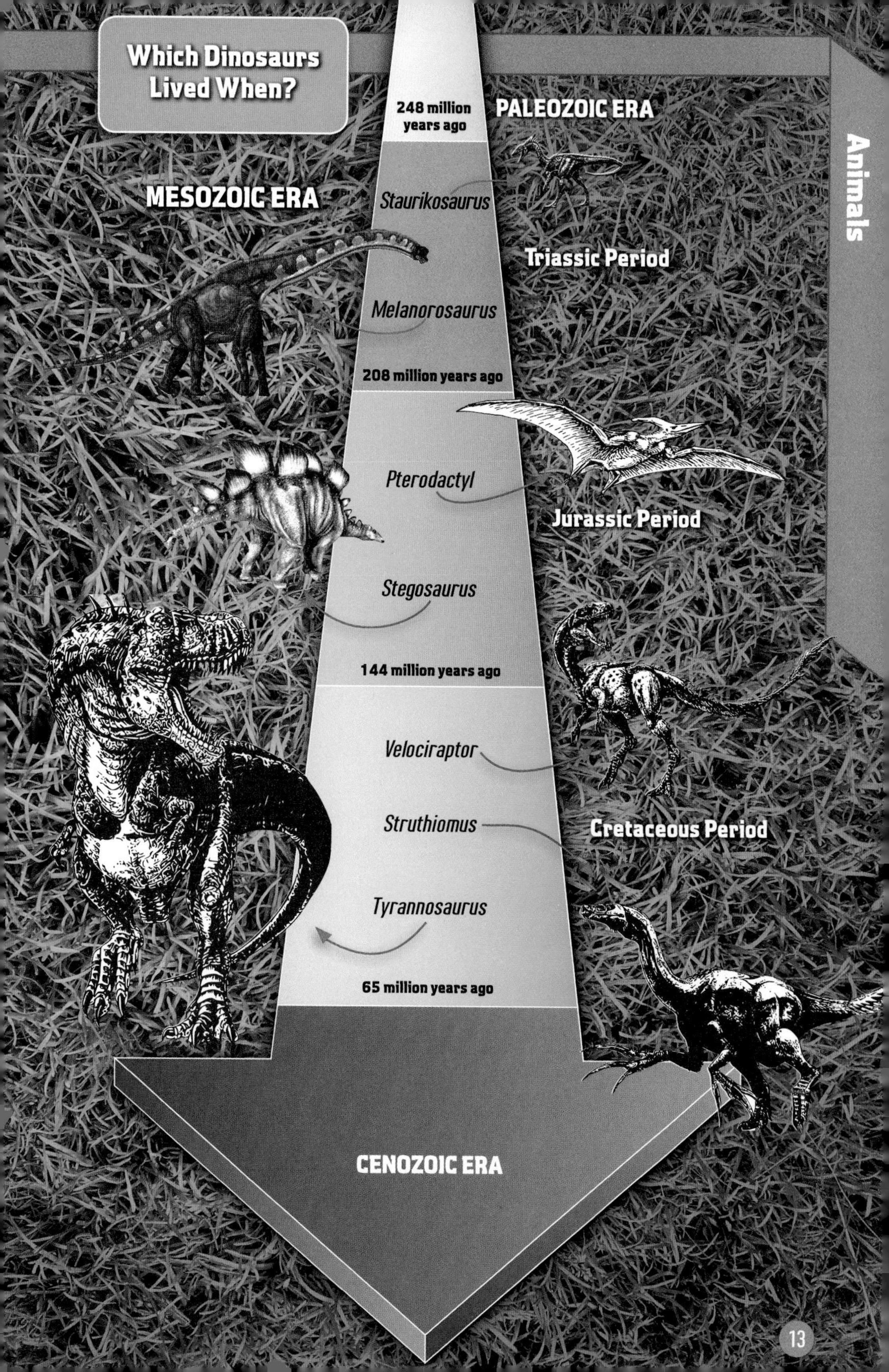

Which Dinosaurs Lived When?

248 million years ago

PALEOZOIC ERA

MESOZOIC ERA

Staurikosaurus

Triassic Period

Melanorosaurus

208 million years ago

Pterodactyl

Jurassic Period

Stegosaurus

144 million years ago

Velociraptor

Struthiomus

Cretaceous Period

Tyrannosaurus

65 million years ago

CENOZOIC ERA

Sauropods were the giants of the prehistoric world. The *apatosaurus*, *diplodocus*, and *seismosaurus* were all sauropods. These dinosaurs had long necks, long tails, and huge stomachs and chests. Big as they were, the sauropods were peaceful plant-eaters.

Theropods were the only meat-eating dinosaurs. One of the fiercest was *Tyrannosaurus rex*, but the *velociraptor* was equally ferocious. It slashed and sliced prey to pieces with the razor-sharp curved claws on its feet.

Stegosaurs' plates and spikes may have done more than keep away enemies. Scientists think blood flowing through the spikes could have been warmed or cooled by the air moving over the stegosaur's back, controlling body temperature.

Ankylosaurs were built for survival. Heavy, bony plates protected their bodies like armor on a tank. Some types had a mass of bone on their tails that they could use as a club.

Ceratopsians looked like rhinoceroses. They had horns on their faces and a curved collar of bone around their neck. Horns over a *triceratops*'s eyes could reach 3 feet (90 cm) long.

Animals

What Really Killed the Dinosaurs?

For millions and millions of years, dinosaurs dominated. Then they were gone—forever. What happened? In March 2010, after years of debate, an international panel of scientists concluded that an asteroid was to blame. They said an enormous asteroid about 6 miles (9.6 km) wide struck Earth with an impact more powerful than a billion atomic bombs.

The crash caused worldwide earthquakes, tsunamis, landslides, and fires. It sent millions of tons of sulfur, dust, and soot into the atmosphere, blocking sunlight for months. Plants died, and plant-eating dinosaurs starved to death. The meat-eating dinosaurs that fed on the plant-eaters starved, too.

However, in February 2013, a modified theory surfaced. Some scientists now think that although an asteroid may have delivered the final death blow, dinosaurs had been dying off for years due to climate changes from volcanic eruptions. The newer research pinpointed the date of extinction to slightly over 66 million years ago.

T. Rex, Meat the Competition

CHECK IT OUT!

Tyrannosaurus rex ruled as king of the carnivores 67 million years ago, but millions of years earlier another dinosaur was on top. In 2013 paleontologists dug up bones of a massive meat-eater in eastern Utah. They determined the creature lived 98 million years ago and named it Siats (SEE-atch) after a ferocious human-eating monster from Ute tribal legends.

Scientists say a Siats would have been so big that a tyrannosaur of the time would have been more of a pest than a serious rival. So how did *T. rex* survive to become king of the meat-eaters millions of years later? Siats might have gone extinct, or tyrannosaurs may have outcompeted it for food or other resources.

Insects

Insects come in an amazing number of shapes and colors, but all you have to do is count to three to tell them apart from other creatures. All insects have three pairs of legs and three body parts: the head, the thorax, and the abdomen. Scorpions, ticks, centipedes, and many other creatures that look like insects are not the real thing.

Insects come in an amazing number of species, too. There are about four times as many insects as every other kind of animal, combined. Why so many? Insects have adapted to survive.

They can live in the hottest, coldest, wettest, and driest places. Their small size lets them survive in tiny spaces with practically no food. Some insects can lay many thousands of eggs a day, so there are plenty of young to keep a species alive. Most have wings to fly away from danger.

Bugs may bug us, but only about 1 percent of insects are harmful. On the other hand, bees, wasps, and butterflies help keep us supplied with fruits and vegetables and help keep our world beautiful by pollinating plants and flowers.

Top 10 Most Common Insects

Animal	Approximate number of known species
Beetles	350,000
Butterflies and moths	150,000
True flies	120,000
Ants, bees, and wasps	50,000
True bugs	40,000
Grasshoppers, crickets, and locusts	20,000
Caddis flies	7,000
Lacewings	4,000
Lice	2,900
Dragonflies and damselflies	2,500

To hide from predators, walking sticks can blend into the twigs and branches on which they live. The largest kinds of walking sticks live in Asia and can grow to be more than 22 inches (56 cm) with their legs fully extended.

Insect eyes can have up to 30,000 lenses. Each lens lets in a separate piece of the scene, and then the parts combine to form a whole picture.

Grasshoppers have about 900 muscles—over 200 more muscles than humans. Many insects can lift or pull objects 20 times their weight.

Scientists say the dragonfly is the fastest-flying insect, capable of reaching 38 miles per hour (61 kph).

Fruit farmers love ladybugs because they eat the aphids that destroy crops. Predators hate their gross taste, which comes from a liquid produced from joints in their legs when threatened.

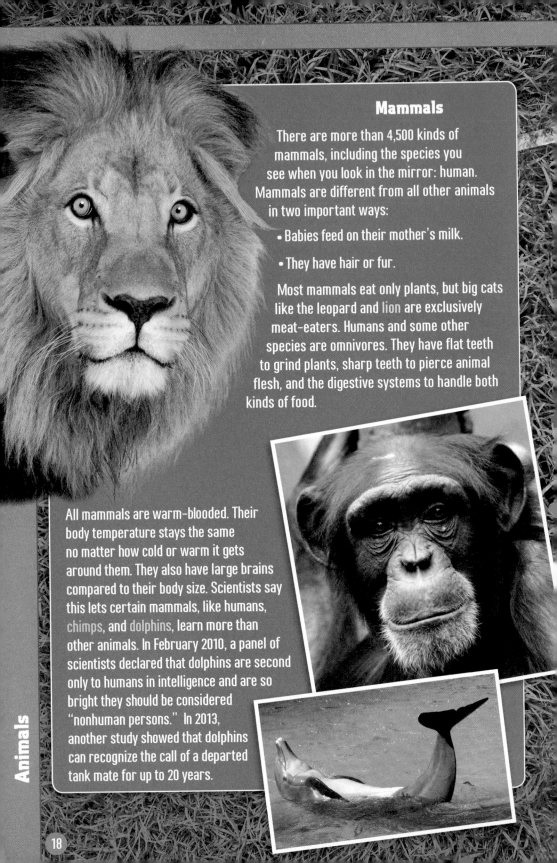

Mammals

There are more than 4,500 kinds of mammals, including the species you see when you look in the mirror: human. Mammals are different from all other animals in two important ways:

- Babies feed on their mother's milk.

- They have hair or fur.

Most mammals eat only plants, but big cats like the leopard and lion are exclusively meat-eaters. Humans and some other species are omnivores. They have flat teeth to grind plants, sharp teeth to pierce animal flesh, and the digestive systems to handle both kinds of food.

All mammals are warm-blooded. Their body temperature stays the same no matter how cold or warm it gets around them. They also have large brains compared to their body size. Scientists say this lets certain mammals, like humans, chimps, and dolphins, learn more than other animals. In February 2010, a panel of scientists declared that dolphins are second only to humans in intelligence and are so bright they should be considered "nonhuman persons." In 2013, another study showed that dolphins can recognize the call of a departed tank mate for up to 20 years.

Unlike kangaroos, koalas, and other marsupials, the opossum does not have a pouch.

Flying squirrels don't really fly. They stretch out a fold of skin between their forelimbs and hind limbs and glide from tree to tree.

What do an armadillo's bony shell and a rhinoceros's thick hide have in common? They both protect against sharp-clawed predators.

The echidna and the platypus are the only mammals that don't give birth to live young. They're *monotremes* that lay eggs with leathery shells.

Many scientists say that a bear's winter sleep isn't true *hibernation* because the animal's body temperature falls only slightly. Other mammals, such as chipmunks and woodchucks, undergo a sharp temperature drop when they take their seasonal snooze.

Heaviest Land Mammals

Mammal	Weight
African elephant	15,000 lb. (6,804 kg)
Hippopotamus	9,920 lb. (4,500 kg)
White rhinoceros	5,000 lb. (2,268 kg)
Giraffe	3,000 lb. (1,361 kg)
Asian water buffalo	2,600 lb. (1,179 kg)
Arabian camel (dromedary)	1,520 lb. (689 kg)
Grizzly bear	1,500 lb. (680 kg)
Gorilla	500 lb. (227 kg)
Siberian tiger	400 lb. (181 kg)

Heaviest Marine Mammals

Mammal	Weight
Blue whale	150 tons
Fin whale	80 tons
Right whale	70 tons
Sperm whale	60 tons
Humpback whale	40 tons
Sei whale	40 tons
Gray whale	15 tons
Baird's beaked whale	14 tons
Orca	10 tons

Animals

Smallest Mammals

Mammal	Weight
Kitti's hog-nosed bat	1.2 in. (3.2 cm)
Pipistrelle bat	1.4 in. (3.6 cm)
Masked shrew	1.8 in. (4.6 cm)
Common (Eurasian) shrew	2.0 in. (5.1 cm)
Harvest mouse	2.0 in. (5.1 cm)
Southern blossom bat	2.0 in. (5.1 cm)
House mouse	2.5 in. (6.4 cm)

Fastest Mammals

Mammal	Maximum speed
Cheetah	70 mph (113 kph)
Pronghorn antelope	61 mph (98 kph)
Springbok	55 mph (89 kph)
Blue wildebeest	50 mph (80 kph)
Lion	50 mph (80 kph)
Brown hare	48 mph (77 kph)
Red fox	30 mph (48 kph)

Birds

If you see an animal with feathers, you can be sure it's a bird. Only birds have them, and they have lots! Scientists say birds have between about 1,000 and 25,000 feathers, which they shed once a year as new ones grow in. Feathers keep birds warm, help them fly, and give them their remarkable variety of colors and markings.

Like mammals, birds are warm-blooded vertebrates. A bird's skeleton is strong because many of the bones are fused together. In humans and other animals, they're separate. At the same time, bird skeletons are lightweight because many of the bones are hollow.

Scientists believe that birds evolved from ancient reptiles—specifically, meat-eating dinosaurs such as *Tyrannosaurus rex* and the *velociraptor*. They say at one time these ferocious dinosaurs may have had feathers!

The feathers of this mallard and of all birds are made of keratin, the same substance that covers a rhinoceros's bony horn and makes up human hair and nails.

Hummingbirds are the only birds that can fly backward. A hummingbird's heart beats 1,000 times a minute.

Parrots have a large cerebrum, the part of the brain that controls learning. Scientists say that may be why they can learn to talk.

Do you have eyes like a hawk? Not a chance! Hawks can see about eight times as well as humans.

Arctic terns migrate the farthest of any bird. Every year they travel about 22,000 miles (35,400 km) from the Arctic to their Antarctic winter home and back again.

All birds have wings, but not all birds can fly. Ostriches, the largest living birds, walk or run. Penguins swim, using their wings as flippers.

When a woodpecker digs for insects in the bark of a tree, it makes a loud hammering sound. It makes the same sound when trying to attract a mate or to claim territory from other birds. Some woodpeckers can make holes large enough to damage trees or even break them in half.

Fish and Other Marine Life

Not every animal that spends its life in the water is a fish—even if its name is *fish*! Jellyfish and starfish are not true fish. Clams, crabs, and scallops are called shellfish, but they're not really fish, either. Why not? None of these animals has a backbone. True fish are vertebrates. In fact, they were the first animals on Earth to have a backbone.

Fish are cold-blooded, which means their body temperature changes to match the temperature of their surroundings. Fish breathe through gills, which filter oxygen out of the water. Almost all fish have fins, which they use for swimming.

Most fish have skeletons made of bone, and most of these bony fish have an inflatable sac called a swim bladder below their backbone. The bladder gives them the buoyancy they need to stay afloat without moving. Sharks, rays and some other fish have skeletons made of cartilage. These types of fish don't have a swim bladder. When they stop swimming, they sink.

There are more than 24,000 species of fish, with scientists discovering more all the time.

Most fish swim horizontally, but the sea horse swims vertically.

Barracudas and piranhas have razor-sharp teeth that can strip the flesh from a large mammal in minutes.

The whale shark is the largest fish. It grows to more than 50 feet (15.2 m) in length and may weigh several tons. The smallest fish—as well as the smallest vertebrate—is the paedocypris, which is less than one-third of an inch (7.9 mm) long.

Sharks have excellent eyesight, especially in the darkness. Bright colors such as yellow and orange seem to attract them. Based on documented attacks, the three most dangerous species of shark are the great white shark, the bull shark, and the tiger shark.

Clown fish stay safe from predators by hiding inside the poisonous stinging tentacles of certain sea anemones. Why aren't the clown fish stung? Scientists say they may be protected by a layer of slime on their skin.

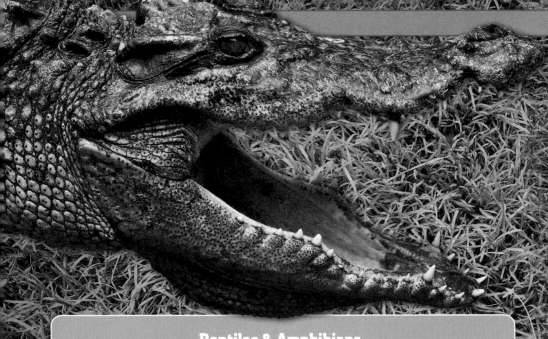

Reptiles & Amphibians

Reptiles and amphibians have a lot in common. They're both vertebrates. They're both cold-blooded, and they've both been around for millions of years. However, there are important differences. Most amphibians hatch from eggs laid in water and then spend their adult lives on land. Reptiles are primarily land animals, although some, like sea turtles and sea snakes, spend their whole life in the water.

Another difference is their skin. A reptile's skin is dry and scaly. Most amphibians have moist skin, which is often kept that way by a slimy coating of mucus.

Lizards and snakes are the most common reptiles—there are thousands of different kinds. Alligators, crocodiles, and turtles are also reptiles. Frogs, toads, and salamanders are the most common amphibians.

Since about the 1980s, the population of some frog species has been declining. Scientists don't fully understand why. However, because frogs and all amphibians absorb gases and other chemicals directly through their skin, there is some worry that disappearing frogs could be an indication of serious environmental problems.

The Gila monster has a poisonous bite, but most reptiles are harmless to humans.

The gray tree frog can freeze solid without harming itself. A substance in its blood works like antifreeze to protect its organs and tissues.

One way to tell a frog from a toad is to look at its skin. A frog's skin is smooth and moist. A toad's is bumpy and dry.

For many years, scientists thought a chameleon changed colors to blend into its surroundings for protection from predators. Now some scientists think that chameleons change colors to stand out to other chameleons. Brighter colors are used to show dominance and attract mates, while drab colors signal surrender.

Animals in Trouble

According to the World Wildlife Fund (WWF), the Amur leopard of the eastern mountains of Russia is one of the most critically endangered animals in the world. Fewer than 40 of these beautiful rare cats are said to exist. In 2012, to try to save the species, the government of Russia created the 650,000-acre Land of the Leopard National Park, protecting the leopard's breeding areas and more than half its remaining habitat.

The 14 animals below are also on the WWF's Critically Endangered list, identified as the species at the highest risk for extinction. Visit worldwildlife.org to read more about these species and learn what you can do to help.

Black rhino	South China tiger
Cross River gorilla	Sumatran elephant
Hawksbill turtle	Sumatran orangutan
Javan rhino	Sumatran rhino
Leatherback turtle	Sumatran tiger
Mountain gorilla	Vaquita
Saola (SOW-la)	Western Lowland gorilla

Habitat loss, environmental changes, poaching, and hunting are some critical threats to these animals' survival.

Names of Male, Female, and Young Animals

Animal	Male	Female	Young
Bear	Boar	Sow	Cub
Cat	Tom	Queen	Kitten
Cow	Bull	Cow	Calf
Chicken	Rooster	Hen	Chick
Deer	Buck	Doe	Fawn
Dog	Dog	Bitch	Pup
Donkey	Jack	Jenny	Foal
Duck	Drake	Duck	Duckling
Elephant	Bull	Cow	Calf
Fox	Dog	Vixen	Kit
Goose	Gander	Goose	Gosling
Horse	Stallion	Mare	Foal
Lion	Lion	Lioness	Cub
Rabbit	Buck	Doe	Bunny
Sheep	Ram	Ewe	Lamb
Swan	Cob	Pen	Cygnet
Swine	Boar	Sow	Piglet
Tiger	Tiger	Tigress	Cub
Whale	Bull	Cow	Calf
Wolf	Dog	Bitch	Pup

Animals

Animal Multiples

ants: colony

bears: sleuth, sloth

bees: grist, hive, swarm

birds: flight, volery

cats: clutter, clowder

chicks: brood, clutch

clams: bed

cows: drove

cranes: sedge, seige

crows: murder

doves: dule

ducks: brace, team

elephants: herd

elks: gang

finches: charm

fish: school, shoal, drought

foxes: leash, skulk

geese: flock, gaggle, skein

gnats: cloud, horde

goats: trip

gorillas: band

hares: down, husk

hawks: cast

hens: brood

hogs: drift

horses: pair, team

hounds: cry, mute, pack

kangaroos: troop

kittens: kindle, litter

larks: exaltation

lions: pride

locusts: plague

magpies: tidings

mules: span

nightingales: watch

oxen: yoke

oysters: bed

parrots: company

partridges: covey

peacocks: muster, ostentation

pheasants: nest, bouquet

pigs: litter

ponies: string

quail: bevy, covey

rabbits: nest

seals: pod

sheep: drove, flock

sparrows: host

storks: mustering

swans: bevy, wedge

swine: sounder

toads: knot

turkeys: rafter

turtles: bale

vipers: nest

whales: gam, pod

wolves: pack, route

woodcocks: fall

Popular Pets in the United States

The American Pet Products Association (APPA) reported in its 2013–2014 survey that 82.5 million (68%) of American households own a pet.

Animal	Millions of households owning
Any pet	82.5
Dog	56.7
Cat	45.3
Freshwater fish	14.3
Bird	6.9
Small animal	6.9
Reptile	5.6
Horse	2.8
Saltwater fish	1.8

Top 10 Registered US Dog Breeds

Labrador retriever

German shepherd

Golden retriever

Beagle

Bulldog

Yorkshire terrier

Boxer

Poodle

Rottweiler

Dachshund

Top 10 Registered US Cat Breeds

Persian

Exotic

Maine coon

Ragdoll

British shorthair

Abyssinian

American shorthair

Sphynx

Siamese

Devon Rex

BIRTHDAYS

Happy Barkday to You!

Want to do something nice for the top dog in your life? Why not plan a party to celebrate his or her birthday or date of adoption? Birthday parties for pets, especially dogs, have become more and more popular.

Animal Planet's Dog Birthday Party Guide, available at animalplanet.com, has ideas for invitations, games, themes, and refreshments. Animal Planet also suggests following these guidelines:

▶ Invite other dogs and their owners or just human friends of the party pooch. If you invite other dogs, they should already know each other.

▶ Have lots of water bowls around, and keep them full.

▶ Have Frisbees, balls, and other toys and games handy.

▶ Make sure each dog has its own bowl for doggie treats or birthday cake.

▶ You can make a birthday cake or buy one from a pet bakery. If you make a cake, avoid chocolate and artificial sweeteners, which can be poisonous to dogs. Carob is a good substitute. Peanut butter, cream cheese, yogurt, and cottage cheese are all good choices for frosting.

YOUR TURN

How old is your dog, anyway? A popular belief is that one human year equals seven dog years, but it's more complicated than that. Go to pets.webmd.com/dogs/how-to-calculate-your-dogs-age.

Which person's birthday only happens once every four years? (See pp. 34-37)

Shaun White

Mark Foster

Lupita Nyong'o

LeBron James

January

1 Paul Revere, American patriot, 1735
2 Kate Bosworth, actor, 1983
3 J. R. R. Tolkien, author, 1892
4 Doris Kearns Goodwin, historian, 1943
5 Bradley Cooper, actor, 1975
6 Joan of Arc, military leader and saint, around 1412
7 Blue Ivy Carter, daughter of Beyoncé and Jay-Z, 2012
8 Stephen Hawking, physicist, 1942
9 Kate Middleton, Duchess of Cambridge, wife of William, Prince of Wales, 1982
10 George Foreman, boxer, 1949
11 Alice Paul, suffragist, 1885
12 Zayn Malik, musician (One Direction), 1993
13 Orlando Bloom, actor, 1977
14 Albert Schweitzer, scientist and humanitarian, 1875
15 Drew Brees, football player, 1979
16 Kate Moss, model, 1974
17 Michelle Obama, US First Lady, 1964
18 Kevin Costner, actor, 1955
19 Edgar Allan Poe, author, 1809
20 Edwin "Buzz" Aldrin, astronaut, 1930
21 Plácido Domingo, operatic tenor, 1941
22 Sir Francis Bacon, explorer, 1561
23 Edouard Manet, painter, 1832
24 Maria Tallchief, ballerina, 1925
25 Alicia Keys, musician, 1981
26 Ellen DeGeneres, TV personality, 1958
27 Wolfgang Amadeus Mozart, composer, 1756
28 Jackson Pollock, artist, 1912
29 Oprah Winfrey, media personality, 1954
30 Christian Bale, actor, 1974
31 Justin Timberlake, entertainer, 1981

February

1 Harry Styles, musician (One Direction), 1994
2 Christie Brinkley, model, 1954
3 Norman Rockwell, painter, 1894
4 Rosa Parks, civil rights activist, 1913
5 Cristiano Ronaldo, soccer player, 1985
6 Babe Ruth, baseball player, 1895
7 Ashton Kutcher, actor, 1978
8 Jules Verne, author, 1828
9 Alice Walker, author, 1944
10 George Stephanopoulos, TV journalist and former political advisor, 1961
11 Thomas Edison, inventor, 1847
12 Judy Blume, author, 1938
13 Chuck Yeager, test pilot, 1923
14 Jack Benny, radio and TV entertainer, 1894
15 Susan B. Anthony, suffragist and civil rights leader, 1820
16 Ice-T, rap musician and actor, 1958
17 Michael Jordan, basketball player, 1963
18 John Travolta, actor, 1954
19 Jeff Kinney, author of Diary of a Wimpy Kid series, 1971
20 Gloria Vanderbilt, fashion designer, 1924
21 W. H. Auden, poet, 1907
22 Edward Kennedy, US senator, 1932
23 Dakota Fanning, actor, 1994
24 Steve Jobs, cofounder of Apple Computers, 1955
25 Sean Astin, actor, 1971
26 Johnny Cash, singer and songwriter, 1932
27 Chelsea Clinton, US presidential daughter, 1980
28 Daniel Handler (Lemony Snicket), author, 1970
29 Mark Foster, musician, 1984

March

1 Lupita Nyong'o, actor, 1983
2 Theodor Geisel (Dr. Seuss), author, 1904
3 Julie Bowen, actor, 1970
4 Knute Rockne, football star, 1888
5 Eva Mendes, actor, 1974
6 Michelangelo, painter, 1475
7 Rachel Weisz, actor, 1970
8 Freddie Prinze Jr., actor, 1976
9 Juliette Binoche, actor, 1964
10 Shannon Miller, gymnast, 1977
11 Terrence Howard, actor, 1969
12 Amelia Earhart, aviator, 1897
13 Abigail Fillmore, US First Lady, 1798
14 Billy Crystal, actor, 1948
15 Ruth Bader Ginsburg, US Supreme Court justice, 1933
16 Jerry Lewis, entertainer, 1926
17 Mia Hamm, soccer player, 1972
18 Queen Latifah, entertainer, 1970
19 Wyatt Earp, US western lawman, 1848
20 Spike Lee, director, 1957
21 Matthew Broderick, actor, 1962
22 Bob Costas, sportscaster, 1952
23 Wernher von Braun, rocket scientist, 1912
24 Peyton Manning, football player, 1976
25 Danica Patrick, race car driver, 1982
26 Sandra Day O'Connor, US Supreme Court justice, 1930
27 Fergie, singer, 1975
28 Lady Gaga, singer, 1986
29 Jessica Chastain, actor, 1981
30 Vincent van Gogh, painter, 1853
31 René Descartes, philosopher, 1596

Birthdays

April

1 Lon Chaney, Sr., horror movie star, 1883
2 Dana Carvey, entertainer, 1955
3 Jane Goodall, primatologist and conservationist, 1934
4 Austin Mahone, singer, 1996
5 Pharrell Williams, singer, 1973
6 Zach Braff, actor, 1975
7 Jackie Chan, actor, 1954
8 Kofi Atta Annan, UN secretary-general, 1938
9 Elle Fanning, actor, 1998
10 Frances Perkins, first female member of US presidential cabinet (secretary of labor), 1880
11 Viola Liuzzo, US civil rights activist, 1925
12 Tom Clancy, author, 1947
13 Samuel Beckett, playwright, 1906
14 Adrien Brody, actor, 1973
15 Emma Watson, actor, 1990
16 Wilbur Wright, aviator, 1867
17 John Pierpoint Morgan, industrialist, 1837
18 Conan O'Brien, TV personality, 1963
19 Kate Hudson, actor, 1979
20 Don Mattingly, baseball player, 1961
21 John Muir, conservationist, 1838
22 Jack Nicholson, actor, 1937
23 William Shakespeare, poet and playwright, 1564
24 Kelly Clarkson, singer, 1982
25 Renée Zellweger, actor, 1969
26 John James Audubon, naturalist, 1785
27 Samuel Morse, inventor, 1791
28 Jay Leno, TV personality, 1950
29 Duke Ellington, jazz musician, 1899
30 Kirsten Dunst, actor, 1982

May

1 Tim McGraw, country singer, 1967
2 David Beckham, soccer player, 1975
3 James Brown, singer and songwriter, 1933
4 Will Arnett, actor, 1970
5 Adele, singer and songwriter, 1988
6 George Clooney, actor, 1961
7 Tim Russert, TV news personality, 1950
8 Adrian Gonzalez, baseball player, 1982
9 Howard Carter, archaeologist, 1873
10 Fred Astaire, actor, 1899
11 Salvador Dalí, painter, 1904
12 Yogi Berra, baseball player, 1925
13 Robert Pattinson, actor, 1986
14 Mark Zuckerberg, Facebook founder, 1984
15 Madeleine Albright, US secretary of state, 1937
16 Adrienne Rich, poet, 1929
17 Craig Ferguson, TV personality, 1962
18 Tina Fey, actor and writer, 1975
19 Nora Ephron, author and director, 1941
20 Bono, musician, 1960
21 Al Franken, entertainer and US senator, 1951
22 Apolo Anton Ohno, speed skater, 1982
23 Jewel, singer and songwriter, 1974
24 Bob Dylan, musician, 1941
25 Mike Myers, actor, 1963
26 Sally Ride, astronaut, 1951
27 Henry Kissinger, US diplomat, 1923
28 Kylie Minogue, singer, 1968
29 Carmelo Anthony, basketball player, 1984
30 Wynonna Judd, country singer and songwriter, 1964
31 Clint Eastwood, actor and director, 1930

June

1 Heidi Klum, model and TV host, 1973
2 Martha Washington, first US First Lady, 1731
3 Rafael Nadal, tennis player, 1986
4 Pal, "Lassie" in *Lassie Come Home*, 1940
5 Mark Wahlberg, actor, 1971
6 Alexander Pushkin, author, 1799
7 Dean Martin, singer and actor, 1917
8 Johnny Depp, actor, 1963
9 Natalie Portman, actor, 1981
10 Maurice Sendak, author, 1928
11 Shia LaBeouf, actor, 1986
12 Anne Frank, Holocaust diarist, 1929
13 Ashley and Mary-Kate Olsen, actors, 1986
14 Donald Trump, businessman, 1946
15 Courteney Cox, actor, 1971
16 Joyce Carol Oates, author, 1938
17 Venus Williams, tennis player, 1981
18 Paul McCartney, musician, 1942
19 Guy Lombardo, band leader, 1902
20 Shefali Chowdhury, actor, 1988
21 Prince William of Wales, British royal, 1982
22 John Dillinger, bank robber, 1903
23 Randy Jackson, TV personality, 1956
24 Mick Fleetwood, musician, 1942
25 Sonia Sotomayor, US Supreme Court justice, 1954
26 Babe Didrikson Zaharias, athlete, 1911
27 Helen Keller, deaf-blind author and activist, 1880
28 John Cusack, actor, 1966
29 George Washington Goethals, chief engineer of the Panama Canal, 1858
30 Michael Phelps, swimmer, 1985

July

1 Benjamin Oliver Davis, first African American general in the US Army, 1877
2 Lindsay Lohan, actor, 1986
3 Tom Cruise, actor, 1962
4 George Steinbrenner, New York Yankees owner, 1930
5 P. T. Barnum, showman and entertainer, 1810
6 50 Cent, rap musician, 1976
7 Michelle Kwan, ice skater, 1980
8 Anna Quindlen, author, 1952
9 Tom Hanks, actor, 1956
10 Jessica Simpson, actor and singer, 1980
11 Sela Ward, actor, 1956
12 Henry David Thoreau, author and philosopher, 1817
13 Harrison Ford, actor, 1942
14 Crown Princess Victoria, Swedish monarch, 1977
15 Rembrandt, painter, 1606
16 Will Ferrell, actor, 1967
17 Erle Stanley Gardner, mystery writer, 1889
18 Nelson Mandela, South African political leader, 1918
19 Edgar Degas, painter, 1834
20 Gisele Bündchen, model, 1980
21 Brandi Chastain, soccer player, 1968
22 Prince George Louis Alexander of Cambridge, British royal, 2013
23 Daniel Radcliffe, actor, 1989
24 Jennifer Lopez, actor and singer, 1969
25 Matt LeBlanc, actor, 1967
26 Sandra Bullock, actor, 1964
27 Alex Rodriguez, baseball player, 1975
28 Beatrix Potter, author, 1866
29 Martina McBride, country singer, 1966
30 Emily Brontë, author, 1818
31 J. K. Rowling, author, 1965

August

1 Francis Scott Key, writer of "The Star-Spangled Banner," 1779
2 James Baldwin, author, 1924
3 Martha Stewart, lifestyle spokesperson and TV personality, 1941
4 Meg Whitman, founder of eBay, 1956
5 Neil Armstrong, astronaut, 1930
6 Lucille Ball, actor, 1911
7 Ralph Bunche, Nobel Peace Prize winner, 1903
8 Roger Federer, tennis player, 1981
9 John Dryden, poet, 1631
10 Betsey Johnson, fashion designer, 1942
11 Suzanne Collins, author of *The Hunger Games*, 1962
12 Pete Sampras, tennis player, 1971
13 Annie Oakley, Wild West entertainer, 1860
14 Tim Tebow, football player, 1987
15 Jennifer Lawrence, actor, 1990
16 Steve Carell, actor, 1962
17 Davy Crockett, frontiersman, 1786
18 Roberto Clemente, baseball player, 1934
19 Veronica Roth, author of the Divergent trilogy, 1988
20 Amy Adams, actor, 1974
21 Wilt Chamberlain, basketball player, 1936
22 Tori Amos, musician, 1963
23 Kobe Bryant, basketball player, 1978
24 Anna Lee Fisher, chemist and astronaut, 1949
25 Leonard Bernstein, conductor and composer, 1918
26 Liam Payne, musician (One Direction), 1993
27 Mother Teresa, nun and humanitarian, 1910
28 Shania Twain, country singer, 1965
29 Michael Jackson, entertainer, 1958
30 Mary Shelley, author of *Frankenstein*, 1797
31 Richard Gere, actor, 1949

September

1 Gloria Estefan, singer, 1957
2 Keanu Reeves, actor, 1964
3 Shaun White, snowboarder, 1986
4 Beyoncé, singer and actress, 1981
5 John Cage, composer, 1912
6 Jane Addams, Nobel Peace Prize winner, 1860
7 Michael DeBakey, pioneer heart surgeon, 1908
8 Pink, singer, 1979
9 Adam Sandler, actor, 1966
10 Colin Firth, actor, 1960
11 William Sydney Porter (O. Henry), short story writer, 1862
12 Yao Ming, basketball player, 1980
13 Milton Hershey, chocolate magnate, 1857
14 Amy Winehouse, singer and songwriter, 1983
15 Prince Henry ("Harry") of Wales, British royal, 1984
16 David Copperfield, magician, 1956
17 William Carlos Williams, poet, 1883
18 Agnes De Mille, choreographer, 1905
19 Trisha Yearwood, country singer, 1964
20 Sophia Loren, actor, 1934
21 Stephen King, author, 1947
22 Joan Jett, singer, 1960
23 Bruce Springsteen, musician, 1949
24 Jim Henson, creator of the Muppets, 1936
25 Will Smith, actor, 1968
26 Serena Williams, tennis player, 1981
27 Avril Lavigne, singer, 1984
28 Caravaggio, painter, 1571
29 Enrico Fermi, physicist and atom bomb developer, 1901
30 Elie Wiesel, author and Holocaust survivor, 1928

Birthdays

October

1 Vladimir Horowitz, pianist, 1904
2 Groucho Marx, comedian, 1890
3 Gwen Stefani, singer, 1969
4 Alicia Silverstone, actor, 1976
5 Maya Lin, architect, 1959
6 George Westinghouse, inventor, 1846
7 Yo-Yo Ma, cellist, 1955
8 Bruno Mars, musician, 1985
9 John Lennon, singer and songwriter, 1940
10 Brett Favre, football player, 1969
11 Eleanor Roosevelt, US First Lady and diplomat, 1884
12 Hugh Jackman, actor, 1968
13 Margaret Thatcher, British prime minister, 1925
14 Usher, rap singer, 1979
15 Emeril Lagasse, chef, 1959
16 John Mayer, singer, 1977
17 Mae Jemison, first African American female astronaut, 1956
18 Lindsey Vonn, skier, 1984
19 Peter Max, artist, 1937
20 Bela Lugosi, actor who played Dracula, 1882
21 Alfred Nobel, scientist, 1883
22 Deepak Chopra, self-help writer, 1946
23 Pelé, soccer player, 1940
24 Kevin Kline, actor, 1947
25 Katy Perry, singer, 1984
26 Hillary Rodham Clinton, US First Lady, US senator, and secretary of state, 1947
27 Captain James Cook, explorer, 1728
28 Bill Gates, founder of Microsoft, 1955
29 Gabrielle Union, actor, 1972
30 Nastia Liukin, gymnast, 1989
31 Chiang Kai-Shek, Nationalist Chinese leader, 1887

November

1 Toni Collette, actor, 1972
2 Daniel Boone, frontiersman, 1734
3 Vincenzo Bellini, composer, 1801
4 Sean Combs, musician, 1969
5 Roy Rogers, TV cowboy, 1911
6 Ethan Hawke, actor, 1970
7 Lorde, musician, 1996
8 Margaret Mitchell, author, 1900
9 Carl Sagan, scientist, 1934
10 Miranda Lambert, singer and songwriter, 1983
11 Leonardo DiCaprio, actor, 1974
12 Elizabeth Cady Stanton, suffragist, 1815
13 Louis Brandeis, US Supreme Court justice, 1856
14 Claude Monet, painter, 1840
15 Shailene Woodley, actor, 1991
16 Shigeru Miyamoto, video game designer, 1952
17 Danny DeVito, actor, 1944
18 Terry, "Toto" in *The Wizard of Oz*, 1933
19 Calvin Klein, fashion designer, 1942
20 Edwin Hubble, scientist, 1889
21 Ken Griffey Jr., boxer, 1969
22 Mark Ruffalo, actor, 1967
23 Miley Cyrus, singer and actor, 1992
24 Scott Joplin, composer, 1868
25 Andrew Carnegie, industrialist, 1883
26 Charles Schulz, cartoonist, 1922
27 Anders Celsius, scientist, 1701
28 Jon Stewart, TV personality, 1965
29 Russell Wilson, football player, 1988
30 Samuel Clemens (Mark Twain), author, 1835

December

1 Woody Allen, actor and director, 1935
2 Britney Spears, singer, 1981
3 Ozzy Osbourne, musician and performer, 1948
4 Jay-Z, rap singer and songwriter, 1969
5 Walt Disney, producer and animator, 1901
6 Ira Gershwin, lyricist, 1896
7 Willa Cather, author, 1873
8 Noelle Pikus-Pace, Olympic skeleton medalist, 1982
9 Clarence Birdseye, frozen food pioneer, 1886
10 Emily Dickinson, poet, 1830
11 Mo'Nique, actor, 1967
12 Frank Sinatra, singer and actor, 1915
13 Taylor Swift, singer, 1989
14 Vanessa Hudgens, actor, 1988
15 Gustave Eiffel, designer of the Eiffel Tower, 1832
16 Jane Austen, author, 1775
17 Milla Jovovich, actor, 1975
18 Christina Aguilera, musician, 1980
19 Edith Piaf, singer, 1915
20 Harvey Samuel Firestone, tire manufacturer, 1868
21 Kiefer Sutherland, actor, 1966
22 Diane Sawyer, TV news personality, 1945
23 Madame C. J. Walker, inventor and businesswoman, 1867
24 Louis Tomlinson, musician (One Direction), 1991
25 Clara Barton, founder, American Red Cross, 1821
26 Chris Daughtry, musician, 1979
27 Louis Pasteur, chemist, 1822
28 Denzel Washington, actor, 1954
29 Charles Goodyear, inventor, 1800
30 LeBron James, basketball player, 1984
31 Henri Matisse, painter, 1869

BOOKS & LITERATURE

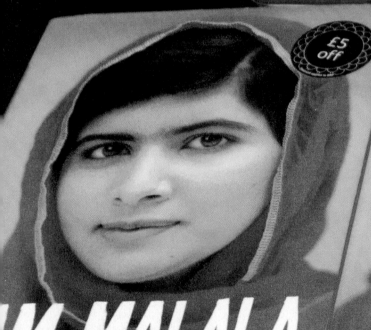

£5 off

I AM MALALA

The Girl Who Stood Up for Education
and was Shot by the Taliban

Malala Yousafzai
with Christina Lamb

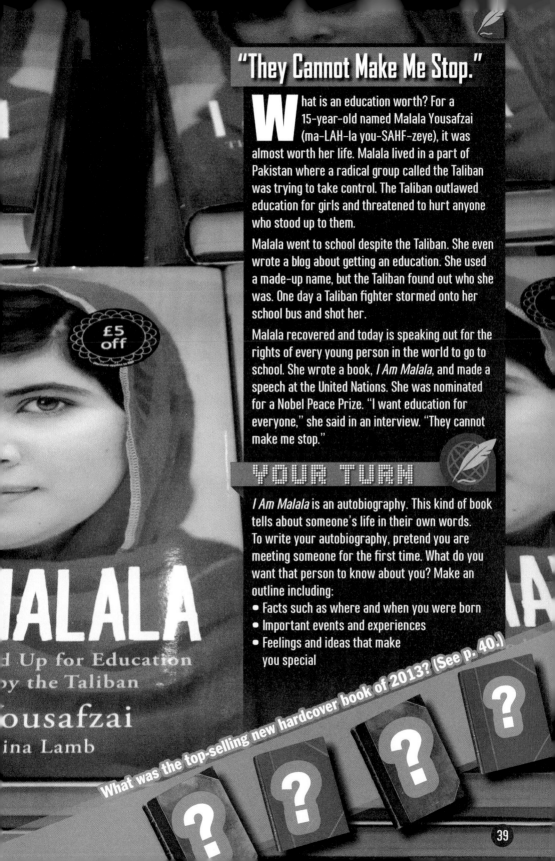

"They Cannot Make Me Stop."

What is an education worth? For a 15-year-old named Malala Yousafzai (ma-LAH-la you-SAHF-zeye), it was almost worth her life. Malala lived in a part of Pakistan where a radical group called the Taliban was trying to take control. The Taliban outlawed education for girls and threatened to hurt anyone who stood up to them.

Malala went to school despite the Taliban. She even wrote a blog about getting an education. She used a made-up name, but the Taliban found out who she was. One day a Taliban fighter stormed onto her school bus and shot her.

Malala recovered and today is speaking out for the rights of every young person in the world to go to school. She wrote a book, *I Am Malala*, and made a speech at the United Nations. She was nominated for a Nobel Peace Prize. "I want education for everyone," she said in an interview. "They cannot make me stop."

YOUR TURN

I Am Malala is an autobiography. This kind of book tells about someone's life in their own words. To write your autobiography, pretend you are meeting someone for the first time. What do you want that person to know about you? Make an outline including:

- Facts such as where and when you were born
- Important events and experiences
- Feelings and ideas that make you special

What was the top-selling new hardcover book of 2013? (See p. 40.)

10 Top-Selling New Young Adult Books of 2013 (Hardcover)

Title	Author
Hard Luck (Diary of a Wimpy Kid #8)	Jeff Kinney
Allegiant (Divergent #3)	Veronica Roth
The House of Hades (Heroes of Olympus #4)	Rick Riordan
Rush Revere and the Brave Pilgrims	Rush Limbaugh
Tales from a Not-So-Happy Heartbreaker (Dork Diaries #6)	Rachel Renée Russell
OMG! All About Me Diary (Dork Diaries)	Rachel Renée Russell
Clockwork Princess (The Infernal Devices)	Cassandra Clare
Big Nate Flips Out	Lincoln Peirce
How I Survived Bullies, Broccoli, and Snake Hill (Middle School #4)	James Patterson and Chris Tebbetts
Revealed	P.C. and Kristin Cast

Top-Selling Young Adult Series of 2013

Title	Author
Divergent	Veronica Roth
Diary of a Wimpy Kid	Jeff Kinney
Percy Jackson & the Olympians; Heroes of Olympus	Rick Riordan
Hunger Games	Suzanne Collins
Dork Diaries	Rachel Rénee Russell
Maximum Ride and other series	James Patterson
Mortal Instruments	Cassandra Clare

10 Top-Selling Ebooks of 2013

Title	Author
Divergent	Veronica Roth
The Fault in Our Stars	John Green
The Book Thief	Markus Zusak
Catching Fire (Hunger Games #2)	Suzanne Collins
Mockingjay (Hunger Games #3)	Suzanne Collins
Insurgent (Divergent #2)	Veronica Roth
Allegiant (Divergent #3	Veronica Roth
Beautiful Creatures	Kami Garcia and Margaret Stohl
The Hunger Games	Suzanne Collins
City of Bones (The Mortal Instruments #1)	Cassandra Clare

2014 Children's Book Award Winners

Caldecott Medal: : *Locomotive*, Brian Floca

Newbery Medal: *Flora & Ulysses: The Illuminated Adventures*, Kate DiCamillo

National Book Award, Young People's Literature:
The Thing About Luck, Cynthia Kadohata *

Printz Award: *Midwinterblood* , Marcus Sedgwick

Coretta Scott King Book Award (Author):
P.S. Be Eleven, Rita Williams-Garcia

Coretta Scott King Book Award (Illustrator):
Knock Knock: My Dad's Dream for Me, Bryan Collier

Scott O'Dell Award for Historical Fiction:
Bo at Ballard Creek, Kirkpatrick Hill

Teen Choice Book of the Year: *The Fault in Our Stars*, John Green

*2013 winner

2014 Nickelodeon Kids' Choice Awards Book Winner

Favorite Book: Wimpy Kid series

Buildings & Landmarks

Willis Tower Stats

- 1,450 feet high (443 m)
- 110 stories
- 25 miles of plumbing, 1,500 miles of electric wiring, 80 miles of elevator cable, and 145,000 light fixtures
- Approximately 16,100 windows
- 104 elevators

In-Spired to New Heights

Since 1973, the Willis Tower, formerly the Sears Tower, in Chicago has been the tallest building in America. However, on November 12, 2013, the new One World Trade Center skyscraper in New York City claimed that crown. Its spire lifted its total height above the Chicago landmark.

The new building was carefully planned to symbolize America's recovery from the September 11, 2001, attacks that destroyed the original World Trade Center. Without the spire it is exactly as tall as the original World Trade Center towers. See the stats at left and below to know more about both these amazing buildings.

One World Trade Center Stats

- 1,368 feet (417 m) without spire
- 1,776 feet tall (541 m) with spire
- 104 stories
- Sustainable design, including reuse of rainwater and recycled construction materials
- Safety features such as a center core surrounded by concrete containing stairs, elevators, gas and water lines, and emergency equipment

Where would you go to see the art and artifact below? (See pp. 50-51.)

Milestones in Modern Architecture Timeline

First modern metal-frame skyscraper, Chicago's ten-story Home Insurance Company Building, is designed by US architect William Jenney (1832–1907). It features a metal skeleton of cast-iron columns and nonsupporting curtain walls, which become characteristic of modern design.

US architect Frank Lloyd Wright (1867–1959) becomes famous for designing houses in the Prairie style, characterized by low, horizontal lines and use of natural earth colors. Wright believes buildings should complement settings.

Walter Gropius (1883–1969) founds Bauhaus, a German school of design, to combine art and architecture with modern industrial technology. Bauhaus styles are notable for geometric lines and the use of steel, glass, and concrete.

Noted American architect R. Buckminster Fuller (1895–1983) designs a self-contained "4-D" prefabricated house. Fuller becomes known for his "Dymaxion" principle of trying to get the most from the least amount of material and energy.

Ludwig Mies van der Rohe (1886–1969) emigrates to the United States and becomes a leader in glass-and-steel architecture. He pioneers rectangular lines in design, including cubelike brick structures, uncovered steel columns, and large areas of tinted glass.

Petronas Twin Towers in Kuala Lumpur, Malaysia, are built and become the world's tallest buildings at a height of 1,483 feet (452 m). In 2003, the towers lose their title to the Taipei 101 Tower in Taiwan. Taipei 101 measures 1,667 feet (508 m) tall.

Finnish-born American architect Eero Saarinen (1910–1961) becomes known for innovative designs for various buildings in the United States. His sweeping style features soaring rooflines, extensive use of glass, and curved lines.

1884
1900
1919
1928
1937
1948
1996
2009

Taipei 101's title falls to Burj Khalifa in Dubai, United Arab Emirates, 2,717 feet (828 m) tall.

Buildings & Landmarks

Construction of Important Earthworks, Dams, and Canals Timeline

Elaborate system of earthen levees is built along the Mississippi River at New Orleans, Lousiana, to control floodwaters.

1718

United States opens New York's Erie Canal, linking the Great Lakes with New York City by way of the Hudson River. The canal leads to increased development of western New York State.

1825

Suez Canal, 101 miles (163 km) long, is completed, built by French engineer Ferdinand de Lesseps (1805–1894) to connect the Mediterranean and Red seas. It is enlarged in 1980 to enable passage of supertankers.

1869

Aswan Dam is built on the Nile River in Egypt. Considered one of the finest dams of all time, it has a record-setting length of 6,400 feet (1,951 m).

1902

Panama Canal, dug across the Isthmus of Panama, connects the Atlantic and Pacific oceans. It is built by US military engineers on land leased from the Republic of Panama. The Canal Zone is returned to Panama beginning in 1979.

1904–1914

Grand Coulee Dam, built for electric generation and irrigation, is completed on the Columbia River in Washington State. At 550 feet (168 m) high and 5,223 feet (1,592 m) long, it is the world's largest concrete structure.

1942

World's longest tunnel, Delaware Aqueduct, is completed. It is 105 miles (169 km) long and supplies water to New York City.

1944

United States and Canada complete construction of the St. Lawrence Seaway. It provides access to Lake Ontario for oceangoing traffic by way of the St. Lawrence River.

1959

Aswan High Dam, on the Nile River in Egypt, is completed. The dam is 364 feet (111 m) high and 12,562 feet (3,829 m) long.

1970

Construction on the world's longest railroad tunnel is completed in Japan. Almost 33.4 miles (54 km) long, the Seikan Tunnel connects the islands of Hokkaido and Honshu.

1988

2000

NEWSworthy

Construction on the 2,749 ft. (838 m) Sky City in Changsha, China, has been delayed. The building, which will be the tallest skyscraper in the world, was originally scheduled for completion by March 2014. Estimates now put the completion date as 2015 at the earliest.

Laerdal-Aurland Tunnel, the world's longest road tunnel, opens in Norway. This 15.2-mile (24.5 km) tunnel connects Oslo to the port of Bergen.

The Seven Wonders of the Modern World

<u>Wonder/Location</u>

<u>Description</u>

Channel Tunnel
England and France

The 31-mile (50-km) Channel Tunnel (Chunnel) is actually three concrete tubes, each 5 feet (2 m) thick, which burrow under the English Channel. They enter the earth at Coquelles, France, and reemerge at Folkstone, England, behind the white cliffs of Dover.

CN Tower
Toronto

The world's third-tallest freestanding tower soars 1,815 feet (553 m) above Toronto, Canada. The CN Tower was designed to withstand 260-mph (418-kph) gusts.

Empire State Building
New York City

At 1,434 feet (437 m), the Empire State Building is the best-known skyscraper in the world. For more than 40 years it was the tallest building in the world. Construction took only one year and 45 days.

Netherlands North Sea Protection Works
Netherlands

This is not just one structure but a complex system of dams, floodgates, storm surge barriers, and other engineered works that protect the country against destructive floods.

Golden Gate Bridge
San Francisco

Once the world's tallest suspension bridge, the Golden Gate Bridge hangs from two 746-foot (227-m) towers and is supported by enough cable to circle Earth three times.

Itaipu Dam
Brazil and Paraguay

Five miles (8 km) wide and as high as a 65-story building, the main dam is made of concrete while the flanking wings are earth and rock fill. The dam generates enough energy to power most of California.

Panama Canal
Panama

To build the Panama Canal, 42,000 workers dredged, blasted, and excavated from Colón to Balboa. They moved enough earth and rubble to bury the island of Manhattan to a depth of 12 feet (4 m)—or enough to open a 16-foot (5-m) wide tunnel to Earth's center.

Buildings & Landmarks

The Seven Wonders of the Ancient World

Wonder/Location	Description
Colossus of Rhodes Harbor of Rhodes, in Aegean Sea, off coast of Turkey	This huge bronze statue of the sun god, Helios, took 12 years to build and stood about 105 feet (32 m) tall. It was destroyed by an earthquake in 225 BCE.
Hanging Gardens of Babylon Ancient city of Babylon (now near Baghdad, Iraq)	The hanging gardens were a series of landscaped terraces along the banks of the Euphrates River, planted with trees, flowers, and shrubs. The gardens were probably built by King Nebuchadnezzar II for his wife.
Pharos (lighthouse) Pharos Island, off coast of Alexandria, Egypt	Built around 270 BCE, this was the world's first important lighthouse. It stood in the harbor for 1,000 years until it was destroyed by an earthquake. It served as a prototype for all other lighthouses built by the Roman Empire.
Mausoleum of Halicarnassus Ancient city of Halicarnassus, now Turkish town of Bodrum	This monumental marble tomb was built by the widow of Mausolus, king of Anatolia, in 353 BCE. 
Statue of Zeus Olympia, Greece	This huge, ornate statue of the god on his throne was almost 60 feet (18 m) tall.
Pyramids of Egypt Giza, Egypt	The oldest pyramid was built with more than two million limestone blocks and stands more than 480 feet (146 m) high. This is the only one of the ancient wonders still in existence.
Temple of Artemis Ancient Greek city of Ephesus, now in Turkey near Selçuk	Built in the sixth century BCE to honor the goddess Artemis, this was one of the largest Greek temples ever built. It was famous for the artistic decoration and use of marble.

World's 10 Tallest Dams

Name	Country	Height above lowest formation
*Rogun	Tajikistan	1,099 ft. (335 m)
*Bakhtiari	Iran	1,033 ft. (315 m)
Jinping	China	1,001 ft. (305 m)
Nurek	Tajikistan	984 ft. (300 m)
Xiaowan	China	958 ft. (292 m)
Grande Dixence	Switzerland	935 ft. (285 m)
Xiluodu	China	912 ft. (278 m)
Inguri	Georgia	892 ft. (272 m)
Vajont	Italy	859 ft. (262 m)
Manuel M. Torres (also known as Chicoasén)	Mexico	856 ft. (261 m)

*Planned or under construction as of mid-2013

Top 10 Longest Suspension Bridges in North America

Name/Location	Completed	Length of main span
Verrazano-Narrows Lower New York Bay, NY	1964	4,260 ft. (1,298 m)
Golden Gate San Francisco Bay, CA	1937	4,200 ft. (1,280 m)
Mackinac Lakes Michigan and Huron, MI	1957	3,800 ft. (1,158 m)
George Washington Hudson River at New York City, NY	1931	3,500 ft. (1,067 m)
Tacoma Narrows II Puget Sound at Tacoma, WA	1950,2007	2,800 ft. (853 m)
Carquinez (Alfred Zampa Memorial) Carquinez Strait, CA	2003	2,388 ft. (728 m)
San Francisco-Oakland Bay San Francisco Bay, CA	1936	2,310 ft. (704 m)
Bronx-Whitestone East River, New York City, NY	1939	2,300 ft. (701 m)
Pierre Laporte Saint Lawrence River at Quebec City, QC	1970	2,190 ft. (668 m)
Delaware Memorial (twin) Delaware River near Wilmington, DE	1951, 1968	2,150 ft. (655 m)

Top 10 Longest Road Tunnels in the World

Name/Location	Completed	Tunnel length
Laerdal-Aurland Norway	2000	15.2 mi. (24.5 km)
Zhongnanshan China	2007	11.2 mi. (18.0 km)
St. Gotthard Switerland	1980	10.5 mi. (16.9 km)
Arlberg Austria	1978	8.7 mi. (14.0 km)
Fréjus France/Italy	1980	8.0 mi. 12.9 km)
Hsuehshan Taiwan	2007	8.0 mi. 12.9 km)
Maijishan China	2009	7.6 mi. (12.3 km)
Mont Blanc France/Italy	1991	7.3 mi. (11.7 km)
Gudvanga Norway	2001	7.1 mi. (11.4 km)
Folgefonn (tie) Norway	1991	7.0 mi. (11.2 km)
Baojishan (tie) China	2009	7.0 mi. (11.2 km)

Buildings & Landmarks

Top 10 Cities with the Tallest Buildings in the World*

City	Number of Towers over 1,000 feet (304.8m)
Dubai, United Arab Emirates	17
New York, New York, United States	6
Hong Kong, China	6
Guangzhou, China	5
Chicago, Illinois, United States	5
Shanghai, China	3
Kuala Lumpur, Malaysia	3
Shenzen, China	3
Los Angeles, California, United States	1
Houston, Texas, United States	1

*Includes buildings that are completed or "topped out"

Top 10 Tallest Completed Buildings in the World

Name/Location	Height
Burj Khalifa Dubai, United Arab Emirates	2,717 ft. (828 m)
Makkah Clock Royal Tower Hotel Mecca, Saudi Arabia	1,971 ft. (601 m)
One World Trade Center New York, New York, United States	1,776 ft. (541 m)
Taipei 101 Taipei, Taiwan	1,667 ft. (508 m)
Shanghai World Financial Center Shanghai, China	1,614 ft. (492 m)
International Commerce Centre Hong Kong, China	1,585 ft. (483 m)
Petronas Tower 1 Kuala Lumpur, Malaysia	1,483 ft. (452 m)
Petronas Tower 2 Kuala Lumpur, Malaysia	1,483 ft. (452 m)
Zifeng Tower Nanjing, China	1,476 ft. (450 m)
Willis (formerly Sears) Tower Chicago, Illinois, United States	1,451 ft. (442 m)

Exploring Museums

Museums are buildings that preserve and display important pieces of history, culture, and human knowledge. They let us explore everything from Renaissance paintings to baseball cards, from mummies to lightning. Read about these famous museums and learn a little of what's inside each one. Visit them online if you can't get there in person.

British Museum

Location: London, England

What's Inside: This London landmark holds seven million objects representing civilizations and cultures from prehistory to modern times. World-famous exhibits include the Rosetta Stone, an ancient (196 BCE) Egyptian tablet that helped us understand Egyptian hieroglyphics.

Website: britishmuseum.org

The Exploratorium

Location: San Francisco, California, United States

What's Inside: "Don't touch" is definitely NOT the rule here. This hands-on museum has hundreds and hundreds of interactive exhibits to let visitors explore sound, light, motion, electricity, perception, the weather, and so much more up close.

Website: exploratorium.edu

Guggenheim Museum Bilbao

Location: Bilbao, Spain

What's Inside: This museum has an impressive collection of art from all over the world, mostly from the last half of the twentieth century. However, equally impressive is the spectacular titanium and glass building itself, designed by famous architect Frank Gehry.

Website: guggenheim.org/bilbao

The Louvre

Location: Paris, France

What's Inside: The most-visited museum in the world, the Louvre is home to 35,000 art objects dating from ancient times to the 19th century. Visitors flock to da Vinci's *Mona Lisa* and the famous sculptures *Winged Victory* and *Venus de Milo*.

Website: louvre.fr

Buildings & Landmarks

Metropolitan Museum of Art

Location: New York, New York, United States

What's Inside: "The Met" is so gigantic that its Egyptian art section contains an entire temple, which was shipped to America as a gift. The massive museum contains art from every period in history and every part of the world. In the Newbery Award—winning novel *From the Mixed-up Files of Mrs. Basil E. Frankweiler*, two kids hide out at the Met for days after running away from home.

Website: metmuseum.org

Museum of Modern Art

Location: New York, New York, United States

What's Inside: This New York City landmark holds one of the world's best collections of modern art, including van Gogh's *Starry Night*, Monet's *Water Lilies*, and Warhol's *Campbell's Soup Cans*.

Website: moma.org

National Baseball Hall of Fame and Museum

Location: Cooperstown, New York, United States

What's Inside: This popular upstate New York attraction is the center of the world of baseball, past and present. There are thousands of clippings, photos, and baseball cards and special displays dedicated to Babe Ruth, Jackie Robinson, and women's baseball. Thirty glass-enclosed lockers, one for each Major League team, contain team jerseys and other items.

Website: baseballhall.org

Smithsonian Institution

Location: Washington, DC, United States

What's Inside: The Smithsonian is the largest museum complex in the world, composed of 19 different museums and the National Zoo. Within the complex you can check out Dorothy's red slippers from *The Wizard of Oz*, the lunar landing "dune buggy" from the Apollo moon missions—and millions of other items and displays.

Website: si.edu

NEWSworthy

On February 22, 2012, the Smithsonian broke ground for the National Museum of African American History and Culture (nmaahc.si.edu), planned as the largest cultural showcase of the African American experience in the country. Exhibits, programs, and thousands of items, including Harriet Tubman's hymnbook and a Spirit of Tuskegee World War II biplane, will help visitors have a closer look at the struggles and accomplishments of black people throughout history. The museum is scheduled to open in 2015.

CALENDARS & HOLIDAYS

THE DAY OF THE DEAD

The tradition of setting aside special days to honor loved ones who have died goes back thousands of years. In Latin America, this special time was called the Day of the Dead, or *Dia de los muertos*.

The Day of the Dead may sound like a sad occasion, but it was really a party. People welcomed spirits back to the living world with bright yellow and orange marigolds, food, music, and dances. They set out candles, bread, and pitchers of water to guide and nourish the spirits on their way back to the afterlife.

In Mexico, the Day of the Dead is November 2, All Souls' Day. Today's modern celebrations include traditional elements, such as sugar skulls. The sugar represents the sweetness of life while the skull symbolizes death.

The holiday has become more and more popular with Latinos in the United States, as a way to celebrate their culture and honor their deceased loved ones.

YOUR TURN

Around the Day of the Dead each year, people in Central Mexico usually welcome the monarch butterfly on its winter migration path. For the past two years, though, the number of butterflies has dramatically decreased. Experts think loss of habitat is one possible reason. Ask your parents or teachers about planting milkweed, the monarch's favorite food, at home or around school. Visit the World Wildlife Fund at wwf.org for other ideas about helping this wonderful creature.

Which day did President Lincoln declare a national holiday? (See p. 61.)

Periods of Time

annual	yearly
biannual	twice a year
bicentennial	marking a period of 200 years
biennial	marking a period of 2 years
bimonthly	every 2 months; twice a month
biweekly	every 2 weeks; twice a week
centennial	marking a period of 100 years
decennial	marking a period of 10 years
diurnal	daily; of a day
duodecennial	marking a period of 12 years
millennial	marking a period of 1,000 years
novennial	marking a period of 9 years
octennial	marking a period of 8 years
perennial	occurring year after year
quadrennial	marking a period of 4 years
quadricentennial	marking a period of 400 years
quincentennial	marking a period of 500 years
quindecennial	marking a period of 15 years
quinquennial	marking a period of 5 years
semiannual	twice a year
semicentennial	marking a period of 50 years
semidiurnal	twice a day
semiweekly	twice a week
septennial	marking a period of 7 years
sesquicentennial	marking a period of 150 years
sexennial	marking a period of 6 years
thrice weekly	3 times a week
tricennial	marking a period of 30 years
triennial	marking a period of 3 years
trimonthly	every 3 months
triweekly	every 3 weeks; 3 times a week
undecennial	marking a period of 11 years
vicennial	marking a period of 20 years

Months of the Year in Different Calendars

Gregorian	Jewish	Hindu	Muslim
January	Shevat	Magha	Muharram
February	Adar	Phalgun	Safar
March	Nisan	Cait	Rabi I
April	Iyar	Baisakh	Rabi II
May	Sivan	Jyeshtha	Jumada I
June	Tammuz	Asarh	Jumada II
July	Av	Sravan	Rajab
August	Elul	Bhadon	Sha'ban
September	Tishrei	Asvin	Ramadan
October	Cheshvan	Kartik	Shawwal
November	Kislev	Margasira	Dhu'l-Qa'dah
December	Tevet	Pus	Dhu'l-Hijja

Wedding Anniversary Gift Chart

Anniversary	Traditional	Modern
1st	paper	clocks
2nd	cotton	china
3rd	leather	crystal
4th	fruit/flowers	linen/silk
5th	wood	silverware
6th	iron	wood
7th	wool	desk sets
8th	bronze	linen
9th	pottery	leather
10th	tin	diamond jewelry
11th	steel	fashion jewelry
12th	silk/linen	pearls
13th	lace	textiles
14th	ivory	gold jewelry
15th	crystal	watches
20th	china	platinum
25th	silver	silver
30th	pearls	diamonds
35th	coral	jade
40th	rubies	rubies
45th	sapphires	sapphires
50th	gold	gold
55th	emeralds	emeralds
60th	diamonds	diamonds

Chinese Years, 1900–2019

Rat	Ox	Tiger	Hare (Rabbit)	Dragon	Snake
1900	1901	1902	1903	1904	1905
1912	1913	1914	1915	1916	1917
1924	1925	1926	1927	1928	1929
1936	1937	1938	1939	1940	1941
1948	1949	1950	1951	1952	1953
1960	1961	1962	1963	1964	1965
1972	1973	1974	1975	1976	1977
1984	1985	1986	1987	1988	1989
1996	1997	1998	1999	2000	2001
2008	2009	2010	2011	2012	2013

Horse	Sheep (Goat)	Monkey	Rooster	Dog	Pig
1906	1907	1908	1909	1910	1911
1918	1919	1920	1921	1922	1923
1930	1931	1932	1933	1934	1935
1942	1943	1944	1945	1946	1947
1954	1955	1956	1957	1958	1959
1966	1967	1968	1969	1970	1971
1978	1979	1980	1981	1982	1983
1990	1991	1992	1993	1994	1995
2002	2003	2004	2005	2006	2007
2014	2015	2016	2017	2018	2019

Perpetual Calendar, 1775–2050

A perpetual calendar lets you find the day of the week for any date in any year. The number next to each year below corresponds to one of the 14 calendars that follow.

Year	No.	Year	No.	Year	No.	Year	No.	Year	No.	Year	No.
1775	1	1821	2	1867	3	1913	4	1959	5	2005	7
1776	9	1822	3	1868	11	1914	5	1960	13	2006	1
1777	4	1823	4	1869	6	1915	6	1961	1	2007	2
1778	5	1824	12	1870	7	1916	14	1962	2	2008	10
1779	6	1825	7	1871	1	1917	2	1963	3	2009	5
1780	14	1826	1	1872	9	1918	3	1964	11	2010	6
1781	2	1827	2	1873	4	1919	4	1965	6	2011	7
1782	3	1828	10	1874	5	1920	12	1966	7	2012	8
1783	4	1829	5	1875	6	1921	7	1967	1	2013	3
1784	12	1830	6	1876	14	1922	1	1968	9	2014	4
1785	7	1831	7	1877	2	1923	2	1969	4	2015	5
1786	1	1832	8	1878	3	1924	10	1970	5	2016	13
1787	2	1833	3	1879	4	1925	5	1971	6	2017	1
1788	10	1834	4	1880	12	1926	6	1972	14	2018	2
1789	5	1835	5	1881	7	1927	7	1973	2	2019	3
1790	6	1836	13	1882	1	1928	8	1974	3	2020	11
1791	7	1837	1	1883	2	1929	3	1975	4	2021	6
1792	8	1838	2	1884	10	1930	4	1976	12	2022	7
1793	3	1839	3	1885	5	1931	5	1977	7	2023	1
1794	4	1840	11	1886	6	1932	13	1978	1	2024	9
1795	5	1841	6	1887	7	1933	1	1979	2	2025	4
1796	13	1842	7	1888	8	1934	2	1980	10	2026	5
1797	1	1843	1	1889	3	1935	3	1981	5	2027	6
1798	2	1844	9	1890	4	1936	11	1982	6	2028	14
1799	3	1845	4	1891	5	1937	6	1983	7	2029	2
1800	4	1846	5	1892	13	1938	7	1984	8	2030	3
1801	5	1847	6	1893	1	1939	1	1985	3	2031	4
1802	6	1848	14	1894	2	1940	9	1986	4	2032	12
1803	7	1849	2	1895	3	1941	4	1987	5	2033	7
1804	8	1850	3	1896	11	1942	5	1988	13	2034	1
1805	3	1851	4	1897	6	1943	6	1989	1	2035	2
1806	4	1852	12	1898	7	1944	14	1990	2	2036	10
1807	5	1853	7	1899	1	1945	2	1991	3	2037	5
1808	13	1854	1	1900	2	1946	3	1992	11	2038	6
1809	1	1855	2	1901	3	1947	4	1993	6	2039	7
1810	2	1856	10	1902	4	1948	12	1994	7	2040	8
1811	3	1857	5	1903	5	1949	7	1995	1	2041	3
1812	11	1858	6	1904	13	1950	1	1996	9	2042	4
1813	6	1859	7	1905	1	1951	2	1997	4	2043	5
1814	7	1860	8	1906	2	1952	10	1998	5	2044	13
1815	1	1861	3	1907	3	1953	5	1999	6	2045	1
1816	9	1862	4	1908	11	1954	6	2000	14	2046	2
1817	4	1863	5	1909	6	1955	7	2001	2	2047	3
1818	5	1864	13	1910	7	1956	8	2002	3	2048	11
1819	6	1865	1	1911	1	1957	3	2003	4	2049	6
1820	14	1866	2	1912	9	1958	4	2004	12	2050	7

3

JANUARY	FEBRUARY	MARCH
APRIL	MAY	JUNE
JULY	AUGUST	SEPTEMBER
OCTOBER	NOVEMBER	DECEMBER

4

JANUARY	FEBRUARY	MARCH
APRIL	MAY	JUNE
JULY	AUGUST	SEPTEMBER
OCTOBER	NOVEMBER	DECEMBER

5

JANUARY	FEBRUARY	MARCH
APRIL	MAY	JUNE
JULY	AUGUST	SEPTEMBER
OCTOBER	NOVEMBER	DECEMBER

6

JANUARY	FEBRUARY	MARCH
APRIL	MAY	JUNE
JULY	AUGUST	SEPTEMBER
OCTOBER	NOVEMBER	DECEMBER

7

JANUARY	FEBRUARY	MARCH
APRIL	MAY	JUNE
JULY	AUGUST	SEPTEMBER
OCTOBER	NOVEMBER	DECEMBER

8

JANUARY	FEBRUARY	MARCH
APRIL	MAY	JUNE
JULY	AUGUST	SEPTEMBER
OCTOBER	NOVEMBER	DECEMBER

Calendars & Holidays

9

JANUARY S M T W T F S
FEBRUARY S M T W T F S
MARCH S M T W T F S
APRIL S M T W T F S
MAY S M T W T F S
JUNE S M T W T F S
JULY S M T W T F S
AUGUST S M T W T F S
SEPTEMBER S M T W T F S
OCTOBER S M T W T F S
NOVEMBER S M T W T F S
DECEMBER S M T W T F S

10

JANUARY S M T W T F S
FEBRUARY S M T W T F S
MARCH S M T W T F S
APRIL S M T W T F S
MAY S M T W T F S
JUNE S M T W T F S
JULY S M T W T F S
AUGUST S M T W T F S
SEPTEMBER S M T W T F S
OCTOBER S M T W T F S
NOVEMBER S M T W T F S
DECEMBER S M T W T F S

11

JANUARY S M T W T F S
FEBRUARY S M T W T F S
MARCH S M T W T F S
APRIL S M T W T F S
MAY S M T W T F S
JUNE S M T W T F S
JULY S M T W T F S
AUGUST S M T W T F S
SEPTEMBER S M T W T F S
OCTOBER S M T W T F S
NOVEMBER S M T W T F S
DECEMBER S M T W T F S

12

JANUARY S M T W T F S
FEBRUARY S M T W T F S
MARCH S M T W T F S
APRIL S M T W T F S
MAY S M T W T F S
JUNE S M T W T F S
JULY S M T W T F S
AUGUST S M T W T F S
SEPTEMBER S M T W T F S
OCTOBER S M T W T F S
NOVEMBER S M T W T F S
DECEMBER S M T W T F S

13

JANUARY S M T W T F S
FEBRUARY S M T W T F S
MARCH S M T W T F S
APRIL S M T W T F S
MAY S M T W T F S
JUNE S M T W T F S
JULY S M T W T F S
AUGUST S M T W T F S
SEPTEMBER S M T W T F S
OCTOBER S M T W T F S
NOVEMBER S M T W T F S
DECEMBER S M T W T F S

14

JANUARY S M T W T F S
FEBRUARY S M T W T F S
MARCH S M T W T F S
APRIL S M T W T F S
MAY S M T W T F S
JUNE S M T W T F S
JULY S M T W T F S
AUGUST S M T W T F S
SEPTEMBER S M T W T F S
OCTOBER S M T W T F S
NOVEMBER S M T W T F S
DECEMBER S M T W T F S

Fixed Dates

These events are celebrated on the same date every year, regardless of where the date falls in the week.

Event	Date
New Year's Day[1]	January 1
Groundhog Day	February 2
Abraham Lincoln's Birthday	February 12
Valentine's Day	February 14
Susan B. Anthony Day	February 15
George Washington's Birthday	February 22
St. Patrick's Day	March 17
April Fools' Day	April 1
Earth Day	April 22
National Maritime Day	May 22
Flag Day	June 14
Canada Day[2]	July 1
Independence Day[1]	July 4
Citizenship Day	September 17
United Nations Day	October 24
Halloween	October 31
Veterans Day[1,3]	November 11
Remembrance Day[2]	November 11
Christmas	December 25
Boxing Day[2]	December 26
New Year's Eve	December 31

Changing Dates

These events are celebrated on different dates every year, but are always on a certain day of a certain week of a certain month.

Event	Day
Martin Luther King Jr. Day[1]	third Monday in January
Presidents' Day[1]	third Monday in February
Daylight saving time begins	second Sunday in March
Arbor Day	last Friday in April
National Teacher Day	Tuesday of the first full week in May
Mother's Day	second Sunday in May
Armed Forces Day	third Saturday in May
Victoria Day[2]	Monday on or before May 24
Memorial Day[1]	last Monday in May
Father's Day	third Sunday in June
Labor Day[1,2]	first Monday in September
Columbus Day[1]	second Monday in October
Thanksgiving Day (Canada)[2]	second Monday in October
Daylight saving time ends	first Sunday in November
Thanksgiving Day (United States)[1]	fourth Thursday in November

1. Federal holiday in United States   2. Federal holiday in Canada   3. Also known as Armistice Day

Calendars & Holidays

Why we celebrate . . .

New Year's Day	Martin Luther King Jr. Day	Groundhog Day	Lincoln's Birthday
The first record of a new year festival is from about 2,000 BCE in Mesopotamia. The festival took place not in January but in mid-March, with the new moon after the spring equinox.	This holiday honors the birthday of the slain civil rights leader who preached nonviolence and led the March on Washington in 1963. Dr. King's most famous speech is entitled "I Have a Dream."	According to legend, if a groundhog in Punxsutawney, Pennsylvania, peeks his head out of his burrow and sees his shadow, he'll return to his hole and there will be six more weeks of winter.	This holiday honors the 16th president of the United States, who led the nation through the Civil War (1861—1865) and was then assassinated. It was first formally observed in Washington, DC, in 1866, when both houses of Congress gathered to pay tribute to the slain president.

Valentine's Day	Presidents' Day	Washington's Birthday	St. Patrick's Day
This holiday of love originated as a festival for several martyrs from the third century, all named St. Valentine. The holiday's association with romance may have come from an ancient belief that birds mate on this day.	This official government holiday was created in observance of both Washington's and Lincoln's birthdays.	This holiday honors the first president of the United States, known as the Father of Our Country. It was first officially observed in America in 1879.	This holiday honors the patron saint of Ireland. Most often celebrated in the United States with parties and special dinners, the most famous event is the annual St. Patrick's Day parade on Fifth Avenue in New York City.

Mother's Day	Memorial Day	Flag Day	Father's Day
First proposed by Anna Jarvis of Philadelphia in 1907, this holiday has become a national time for family gatherings and showing appreciation for mothers.	Also known as Decoration Day, this legal holiday was created in 1868 by order of General John A. Logan as a day on which the graves of Civil War soldiers would be decorated. Since that time, the day has been set aside to honor all American soldiers who have given their lives for their country.	This holiday was set aside to commemorate the adoption of the Stars and Stripes by the Continental Congress on June 14, 1777. It is a legal holiday only in Pennsylvania but is generally acknowledged and observed in many states each year.	This holiday honors the role of the father in the American family, as Mother's Day honors the role of the mother.

Independence Day	Labor Day	Columbus Day	United Nations Day
This holiday celebrates the signing of the Declaration of Independence, on July 4, 1776. It has been celebrated nationwide since 1777, the first anniversary of the signing.	First proposed by Peter J. McGuire in New York in 1882, this holiday was created to honor the labor unions and workers who built the nation.	This holiday commemorates the discovery of the New World by Italian explorer Christopher Columbus in 1492. Even though the land was already populated by Native Americans when Columbus arrived, this discovery marks the beginning of European influence in America.	This holiday marks the founding of the United Nations, which began in its present capacity in 1945 but had already been in operation as the League of Nations.

Halloween	Election Day	Veterans Day	Thanksgiving
Also known as All Hallows' Eve, this holiday has its origins in ancient Celtic rituals that marked the beginning of winter with bonfires, masquerades, and dressing in costume to frighten away spirits.	Since Congress declared it an official holiday in 1845, this has been the day for presidential elections every four years. Most statewide elections are also held on this day, but election years vary according to state.	Originally called Armistice Day, this holiday was created to celebrate the end of World War I in 1918. In June 1954, Congress changed the name of the holiday to Veterans Day and declared that the day would honor all men and women who have served in America's armed forces.	President Lincoln proclaimed Thanksgiving a national holiday in 1863. Most people believe the tradition of reserving a day of thanks began with a 1621 order by Governor Bradford of Plymouth Colony.

Major World Holidays

January 1 New Year's Day throughout the Western world and in India, Indonesia, Japan, Korea, the Philippines, Singapore, Taiwan, and Thailand; Founding Day of Republic of China (Taiwan)

January 2 Berchtoldstag in Switzerland

January 3 Genshi-Sai (First Beginning) in Japan

January 5 Twelfth Night (Wassail Eve or Eve of Epiphany) in England

January 6 Epiphany, observed by Catholics throughout Europe and Latin America

Mid-January Martin Luther King Jr.'s Birthday on the third Monday in the Virgin Islands

January 15 Adults' Day in Japan

January 20 St. Agnes Eve in Great Britain

January 26 Republic Day in India; Australia Day in Australia

January–February Chinese New Year and Vietnamese New Year (Tet)

February 3 Setsubun (Bean-throwing Festival) in Japan

February 5 Promulgation of the Constitution Day in Mexico

February 11 National Foundation Day in Japan

February 27 Independence Day in the Dominican Republic

March 1 Independence Movement Day in Korea

March 8 International Women's Day in China, Russia, Great Britain, and the United States

March 17 St. Patrick's Day in Ireland and Northern Ireland

March 19 St. Joseph's Day in Colombia, Costa Rica, Italy, and Spain

March 21 Benito Juarez's Birthday in Mexico

March 22 Arab League Day in Arab League countries

March 23 Pakistan Day in Pakistan

March 25 Independence Day in Greece; Lady Day (Quarter Day) in Great Britain

March 26 Fiesta del Arbol (Arbor Day) in Spain

March 29 Youth and Martyr's Day in Taiwan

March 30 Muslim New Year in Indonesia

March–April Carnival/Lent/Easter: The pre-Lenten celebration of Carnival (Mardi Gras) and the post-Lenten celebration of Easter are movable feasts widely observed in Christian countries

April 1 April Fools' Day (All Fools' Day) in Great Britain and the United States

April 5 Arbor Day in Korea

April 7 World Health Day in UN member nations

April 8 Buddha's Birthday in Korea and Japan; Hana Matsuri (Flower Festival) in Japan

April 14 Pan American Day in the Americas

April 19 Declaration of Independence Day in Venezuela

April 22 Queen Isabella Day in Spain

April 23 St. George's Day in England

April 25 Liberation Day in Italy; ANZAC Day in Australia and New Zealand

April 30 Queen's Birthday in the Netherlands; Walpurgis Night in Germany and Scandinavia

May 3 Constitution Day in Japan

May 1 May Day (Labor Day) in Russia and most of Europe and Latin America

May 5 Children's Day in Japan and Korea; Cinco de Mayo in Mexico; Liberation Day in the Netherlands

May 8 V-E Day in Europe

May 9 Victory over Fascism Day in Russia

Late May Victoria Day on Monday before May 25 in Canada

June 2 Founding of the Republic Day in Italy

June 5 Constitution Day in Denmark

June 6 Memorial Day in Korea; Flag Day in Sweden

June 10 Portugal Day in Portugal

June 12 Independence Day in the Philippines

Mid-June Queen's Official Birthday on second Saturday in Great Britain

June 16 Soweto Day in UN member nations

June 20 Flag Day in Argentina

June 24 Midsummer's Day in Great Britain

June 29 Feasts of Saints Peter and Paul in Chile, Colombia, Italy, Peru, Spain, and Venezuela

July 1 Canada Day in Canada; Half-year Holiday in Hong Kong; Bank Holiday in Taiwan

July 5 Independence Day in Venezuela

July 9 Independence Day in Argentina

July 12 Orangemen's Day in Northern Ireland

July 14 Bastille Day in France

Mid-July Feria de San Fermin during second week in Spain

July 17 Constitution Day in Korea

July 20 Independence Day in Colombia

July 21 National Holiday in Belgium

July 22 National Liberation Day in Poland

July 24 Simón Bolivar's Birthday in Ecuador and Venezuela

July 25 St. James Day in Spain

Calendars & Holidays

JAN 20

MAY 9

JUNE 20

July 28 Independence Day in Peru

August Holiday on first Monday in Grenada, Guyana, and Ireland

August 1 Lammas Day in England; National Day in Switzerland

August 6 Independence Day in Jamaica

August 9 National Day in Singapore

August 10 Independence Day in Ecuador

August 12 Queen's Birthday in Thailand

August 14 Independence Day in Pakistan

August 15 Independence Day in India and Korea; Assumption Day in Catholic countries

August 16 National Restoration Day in the Dominican Republic

August 17 Independence Day in Indonesia

August 31 Independence Day in Trinidad and Tobago

September Respect for the Aged Day in Japan on third Monday

September 7 Independence Day in Brazil

September 9 Choxo-no-Sekku (Chrysanthemum Day) in Japan

September 14 Battle of San Jacinto Day in Nicaragua

Mid-September Sherry Wine Harvest in Spain

September 15 Independence Day in Costa Rica, Guatemala, and Nicaragua

September 16 Independence Day in Mexico and Papua New Guinea

September 18–19 Independence Day in Chile; St. Gennaro Day in Italy

September 28 Confucius's Birthday in Taiwan

October 1 National Day in People's Republic of China; Armed Forces Day in Korea; National Holiday in Nigeria

October 2 Mahatma Gandhi's Birthday in India

October 3 National Foundation Day in Korea; Day of German Unity in Germany

October 5 Proclamation of the Portuguese Republic Day in Portugal

October 9 Korean Alphabet Day in Korea

October 10 Kruger Day in South Africa; Founding Day of the Republic of China in Taiwan

October 12 Columbus Day in Spain and widely throughout Mexico, and Central and South America

October 20 Revolution Day in Guatemala; Kenyatta Day in Kenya

October 24 United Nations Day in UN member nations

October 26 National Holiday in Austria

October 28 Greek National Day in Greece

November 1 All Saints' Day, observed by Catholics in most countries

November 2 All Souls' Day in Ecuador, El Salvador, Luxembourg, Macao, Mexico (Day of the Dead), San Marino, Uruguay, and Vatican City

November 4 National Unity Day in Italy

November 5 Guy Fawkes Day in Great Britain

November 7–8 October Revolution Day in Russia

November 11 Armistice Day in Belgium, France, French Guiana, and Tahiti; Remembrance Day in Canada

November 12 Sun Yat-sen's Birthday in Taiwan

November 15 Proclamation of the Republic Day in Brazil

November 17 Day of Penance in Federal Republic of Germany

November 19 National Holiday in Monaco

November 20 Anniversary of the Revolution in Mexico

November 23 Kinro-Kansha-no-Hi (Labor Thanksgiving Day) in Japan

November 30 Bonifacio Day in the Philippines

December 5 Discovery by Columbus Day in Haiti; Constitution Day in Russia

December 6 Independence Day in Finland

December 8 Feast of the Immaculate Conception, widely observed in Catholic countries

December 10 Constitution Day in Thailand; Human Rights Day in UN member nations

December 12 Jamhuri Day in Kenya; Guadalupe Day in Mexico

Mid-December Nine Days of Posada during third week in Mexico

December 25 Christmas Day, widely observed in all Christian countries

December 26 St. Stephen's Day in Christian countries; Boxing Day in Canada, Australia, and Great Britain

December 26–January 1 Kwanzaa in the United States

December 31 New Year's Eve throughout the world; Omisoka (Grand Last Day) in Japan; Hogmanay Day in Scotland

NOV
5

DEC
5

WHAT'S YOUR SIGN?

The original zodiac signs are thought to have originated in Mesopotamia as far back as 2000 BCE. The Greeks later picked up some of the symbols from the Babylonians and then passed them on to other ancient cultures. Some other societies that developed their own zodiac charts based on these early ideas include the Egyptians, the Chinese, and the Aztecs.

The positions of celestial objects such as the Sun, Moon, and planets in the zodiac on the day you are born determine your astrological sign. **What's yours?**

Aries, the Ram

March 21–April 19

Planet: Mars
Element: Fire
Personality Traits: Independent, enthusiastic, bold, impulsive, confident

Taurus, the Bull

April 20–May 20

Planet: Venus
Element: Earth
Personality Traits: Decisive, determined, stubborn, stable

Gemini, the Twins

May 21–June 21

Planet: Mercury
Element: Air
Personality Traits: Curious, sociable, ambitious, alert, intelligent, temperamental

Cancer, the Crab

June 22–July 22

Planet (Celestial Object): Moon
Element: Water
Personality Traits: Organized, busy, moody, sensitive, supportive

Leo, the Lion

July 23–August 22

Planet (Celestial Object): Sun
Element: Fire
Personality Traits: Born leader, bold, noble, generous, enthusiastic, sympathetic

Virgo, the Virgin

August 23–September 22

Planet: Mercury
Element: Earth
Personality Traits: Analytical, critical, intellectual, clever

Libra, the Scales

September 23–October 23

Planet: Venus
Element: Air
Personality Traits: Affectionate, thoughtful, sympathetic, orderly, persuasive

Scorpio, the Scorpion

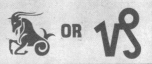

October 24–November 21

Planet (Celestial Object): Pluto
Element: Water
Personality Traits: Intense, fearless, loyal, willful

Sagittarius, the Archer

November 22–December 21

Planet: Jupiter
Element: Fire
Personality Traits: Energetic, good-natured, practical, clever

Capricorn, the Goat

December 22–January 19

Planet: Saturn
Element: Earth
Personality Traits: Serious, domineering, ambitious, blunt, loyal, persistent

Aquarius, the Water Bearer

January 20–February 18

Planet: Uranus
Element: Air
Personality Traits: Independent, unselfish, generous, idealistic

Pisces, the Fishes

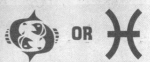

February 19–March 20

Planet: Neptune
Element: Water
Personality Traits: Compassionate, sympathetic, sensitive, timid, creative

CRIME

A BIG New Breakthrough in DNA Testing

DNA testing of evidence has freed more than 300 wrongfully convicted prisoners in the United States. These prisoners spent an average of 13 years in jail. That's more than 4,000 years altogether. Eighteen prisoners were saved from a death sentence by DNA results.

Now there is another crime-fighting use for DNA: tracking elephant poachers. Poaching is increasing in Africa because of a high demand for ivory, which comes from elephant tusks. In 2012, 96 elephants on average were killed every day.

Experts have created a map based on elephants' DNA, showing where certain herds live. They can compare DNA results from poachers' blood-stained clothing or recovered ivory to figure out which herds are being targeted. The efforts are already starting to pay off.

YOUR TURN

DNA is in every cell of every living thing. You can see for yourself with this cool experiment using strawberries: invention. smithsonian.org/centerpieces/ sparklab/spark-experiments- dna.html.

What do all of these have to do with a famous unsolved case? (See p. 68.)

Cases Not Yet Cracked

Not every crime can be solved. In these famous cases, the criminals were either never caught or never identified.

Jack the Ripper

The real identity of the serial killer who terrorized parts of London, England, in 1888 has never been proved. There have been many suspects—including Prince Albert Victor, the grandson of Queen Victoria. The name "Jack the Ripper" came from letters to the police claiming to be from the killer.

D. B. Cooper

In 1971, after hijacking a plane and receiving $200,000 in ransom money, Cooper boarded another plane and parachuted out a rear door somewhere between Seattle, WA, and Portland, OR. He had 20 pounds of cash strapped to his body. Some of the money was later found, and a parachute turned up in 2008, but there has been no trace of Cooper.

Jimmy Hoffa

Jimmy Hoffa, former president of the Teamsters Union, disappeared from a Detroit, MI, restaurant in July 1975 and was never seen again. He was officially declared dead in 1982, but his body has never been found. It is thought that he was murdered. Hoffa's ruthless way of doing business made him a lot of enemies, leading to many theories about what happened, who did it, and where Hoffa is buried.

Tylenol Poisoning

In 1982, seven people died after swallowing Tylenol pain-relieving pills that someone had laced with cyanide, a deadly poison. The criminal was never caught, but the incident led to the institution of tamper-proof seals on medicines.

Innocent Until Proven Guilty

Even if you are suspected of committing a crime, as a citizen of the United States you have rights. You're protected by the 14th Amendment of the US Constitution:

"Nor shall any state deprive any person of life, liberty, or property, without due process of law."

In other words, anyone accused of committing a crime is considered legally innocent until proven guilty. In certain other countries, it's the other way around: You're presumed guilty and have to prove your innocence.

Crime

How Due Process Works

Criminal cases are heard in a state or federal court of law, where both sides are represented.

The **defendant** is the person accused of the crime.

The **defense attorney** represents the defendant and presents his or her side of the case.

The **prosecutor** represents the state or federal government in trying to prove the defendant's guilt.

The **judge** presides over the courtroom and determines the sentence.

All the information and evidence is presented to a **jury**, citizens chosen to decide whether or not the defendant has been proven guilty. Their decision is called the **verdict**.

Miranda Rights

The Miranda rights are named for Ernesto Miranda, whose 1963 conviction on kidnapping and assault charges was reversed by the US Supreme Court because his confession was obtained without providing him access to a lawyer. Since that court decision, police officers are required to give some form of the following warning to any person being arrested:

"You have the right to remain silent. Anything you say can and will be used against you in a court of law. You have the right to an attorney. If you cannot afford an attorney, one will be appointed to you. Do you understand these rights as they have been read to you?"

DISASTERS

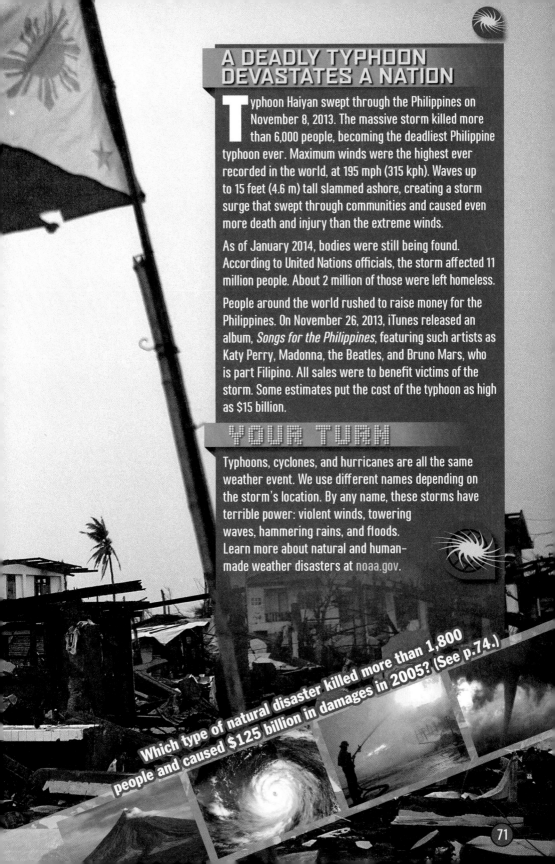

A DEADLY TYPHOON DEVASTATES A NATION

Typhoon Haiyan swept through the Philippines on November 8, 2013. The massive storm killed more than 6,000 people, becoming the deadliest Philippine typhoon ever. Maximum winds were the highest ever recorded in the world, at 195 mph (315 kph). Waves up to 15 feet (4.6 m) tall slammed ashore, creating a storm surge that swept through communities and caused even more death and injury than the extreme winds.

As of January 2014, bodies were still being found. According to United Nations officials, the storm affected 11 million people. About 2 million of those were left homeless.

People around the world rushed to raise money for the Philippines. On November 26, 2013, iTunes released an album, *Songs for the Philippines*, featuring such artists as Katy Perry, Madonna, the Beatles, and Bruno Mars, who is part Filipino. All sales were to benefit victims of the storm. Some estimates put the cost of the typhoon as high as $15 billion.

YOUR TURN

Typhoons, cyclones, and hurricanes are all the same weather event. We use different names depending on the storm's location. By any name, these storms have terrible power: violent winds, towering waves, hammering rains, and floods. Learn more about natural and human-made weather disasters at noaa.gov.

Which type of natural disaster killed more than 1,800 people and caused $125 billion in damages in 2005? (See p.74.)

What Makes an Earthquake?

At certain places, there are breaks in the rocks that make up Earth's surface. These places are called faults. An earthquake is a shock wave that occurs when the tectonic plates beneath a fault rub or crash together. The US Geological Survey estimates that there are several million earthquakes a year. Most are too small to be detected.

10 Deadliest Earthquakes

Date	Place	Number of Deaths
Jan. 24, 1556	Shaanxi, China	830,000
Jan. 12, 2010	near Port-au-Prince, Haiti	316,000
Oct. 11, 1737	Calcutta, India	300,000
May 20, 526 CE	Antioch, Syria	250,000
July 28, 1976	Tangshan, China	242,769
Aug. 9, 1138	Aleppo, Syria	230,000
Dec. 26, 2004	near Sumatra, Indonesia	227,898
Dec. 22, 856 CE	Damghan, Iran	200,000
Dec. 16, 1920	Gansu, China	200,000
March 23, 893 CE	Ardabil, Iran	150,000

NEWSworthy

The California-based Search Dog Foundation (SDF) trains dogs to help humans after disasters. SDF has sent dogs to more than 80 emergencies and disasters, including Hurricane Katrina, the 2010 Haiti earthquake, and the Japan earthquake and tsunami of 2011. In Haiti, canine search teams helped bring 12 people to safety. SDF recruits dogs from shelters and rescue groups, looking for young dogs with drive, energy, and focus. The dogs are mostly Labrador retrievers, golden retrievers, border collies, and mixes. SDF hopes to begin building the first national training center for search and rescue dogs in the United States in 2014. Visit searchdogfoundation.org to learn more.

What Makes a Volcano?

A volcano is an opening in Earth's surface that allows hot melted rock, called magma, to escape from below the surface. Scientists say there are about 550 historically active volcanoes.

Gently curved shield volcanoes build up over thousands of years. Mauna Loa is a shield volcano on the island of Hawaii. It rises about 56,000 feet (17 km) above the ocean floor.

Some of the most famous volcanoes in the world are stratovolcanoes, including Mt. Vesuvius, Krakatau, and Mt. Mayon, the most active volcano in the Philippines.

10 Deadliest Volcanic Eruptions

Date	Volcano	Number of Deaths
April 10–12, 1815	Mt. Tambora, Indonesia	92,000
Aug. 26–28, 1883	Krakatau, Indonesia	36,000
May 8, 1902	Mt. Pelee, Martinique	28,000
Nov. 13, 1985	Nevado del Ruiz, Colombia	23,000
Aug. 24, 79 CE	Mt. Vesuvius, Italy	16,000
May 21, 1792	Mt. Unzen, Japan	14,500
1586 (month and day unknown)	Kelut, Indonesia	10,000
June 8, 1783	Laki, Iceland	9,350
May 19, 1919	Mt. Kelut, Indonesia	5,000
Dec. 15, 1631	Mt. Vesuvius, Italy	4,000

What Makes a Tsunami?

A tsunami is a wave that is often caused by an underwater earthquake. The wave travels across the ocean at speeds up to 600 miles per hour (970 kph), then crashes on shore with devastating power. A massive tsunami triggered by an earthquake in the Indian Ocean struck parts of Asia and Africa in December 2004, causing about 225,000 people to lose their lives.

Wild Windstorms

Hurricanes

Hurricanes are huge storms with winds over 74 mph (119 kph) blowing around a center, or eye. Most hurricanes form over the mild waters of the southern Atlantic Ocean, the Caribbean Sea, or the Gulf of Mexico. Equally powerful storms that form over the western Pacific Ocean are called typhoons. If they form over the Indian Ocean, they're called cyclones.

Hurricane Katrina, which hit the Gulf Coast in 2005, was the costliest natural disaster in US history and the third-deadliest hurricane, causing $125 billion in damages and 1,836 deaths.

Tornadoes

Tornadoes are powerful storms with funnels of furious wind spinning from 40 mph (64 kph) to more than 300 mph (482.8 kph). The funnels touch down and rip paths of destruction on land. About 1,500 tornadoes hit the United States every year.

A group of tornadoes is called an outbreak. On April 3, 1974, a group of 148 tornadoes swept through 13 states and parts of Canada in the 1974 Super Outbreak. The storm's path on the ground covered almost 2,500 miles (4,023 km).

Disasters

Major US Natural Disasters

Earthquake **When**: April 18, 1906
Where: San Francisco, California
An earthquake accompanied by a fire
destroyed more than 4 square miles (10 sq km)
and left at least 3,000 dead or missing.

Hurricane **When**: August 27–September 15, 1900
Where: Galveston, Texas
More than 6,000 died from the devastating
combination of high winds and tidal waves.

Tornado **When**: March 18, 1925
Where: Missouri, Illinois, and Indiana
Called the Great Tri-State Tornado, this twister
caused 747 deaths and ripped along a path of
219 miles (352 km) after touching down
near Ellington, Missouri.

Blizzard **When**: March 11–14, 1888
Where: East Coast
Four hundred people died, and 40–50 inches
(101.6–127 cm) of snow fell in the Blizzard of '88.
Damage was estimated at $20 million.

Major US Disasters Caused by Humans

Aircraft **When**: September 11, 2001
Where: New York, New York; Arlington, Virginia; Shanksville, Pennsylvania
Hijacked planes crashed into the World Trade Center, the Pentagon, and a
field in Pennsylvania, causing nearly 3,000 deaths.

Fire **When**: March 25, 1911
Where: New York, New York
The Triangle Shirtwaist Factory caught fire,
trapping workers inside and causing 146 deaths.

Passenger **When**: July 9, 1918
Train **Where**: Nashville, Tennessee
An inbound and an outbound train collided in a crash
that witnesses heard miles away and took more
than 100 lives. The crash was caused by errors and
misunderstandings by both train crews.

Environmental **When**: April 20, 2010
Where: Gulf of Mexico, 42 miles off the Louisiana coast
The Deepwater Horizon oil rig exploded, killing 11 workers and letting loose
an underwater gush of about 4.9 million barrels of oil over 86 days. The spill
was called the worst environmental disaster in US history. However, after a
massive offshore and onshore cleanup effort, by 2011 Gulf fish, shrimp, and
oysters were deemed safe to eat and most Gulf beaches were open.

Pedal Power Gets the Ball Rolling— Well, Dropping

At one minute before midnight every December 31, a glowing crystal ball begins a slow drop down a flagpole in New York City's Times Square. It's a powerful event, in more ways than one. It has the power to attract crowds in New York and TV viewers all over the world. And it takes a lot of electrical power to light up the glittering ball and flagpole.

In 2013, the New Year's celebration got a little boost from another kind of power—pedal power. Officials from Citibank, which runs a bike share program in New York, set up seven stationary bikes hooked up to batteries on the sidewalk in Times Square. Over three days, 2,194 people passing by jumped on the bikes and pedaled away, charging the batteries. When the batteries were fully charged, they were connected to the power grid that lights up the ball.

The bikers made enough energy to light the ball's one-minute countdown, with enough left over for two more minutes. Ten, nine, eight . . . Happy New, Green, Year!

YOUR TURN

In 2015, Earth Hour will be Saturday, March 28, between 8:30 and 9:30 p.m., your local time. During this hour, thousands of cities will turn off lights and other devices in homes, buildings, and landmarks such as the Sydney Opera House and the Empire State Building. Visit earthhour.org to see what's going on near you.

Which item can last 500 years in a landfill? (See p. 83.)

What's in Our Trash?

According to the Environmental Protection Agency (EPA), in 2012 Americans produced about 251 million tons of municipal solid waste (MSW), or 4.38 pounds (2.0 kg) per person per day. The chart shows types of MSW and how much of each type we generated in 2012.

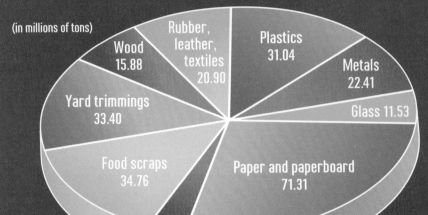

(in millions of tons)

Wood 15.88

Rubber, leather, textiles 20.90

Plastics 31.04

Metals 22.41

Glass 11.53

Yard trimmings 33.40

Food scraps 34.76

Paper and paperboard 71.31

Other 4.79

How Much Do We Recycle?

In 2012, we recycled 34.5 percent of the total amount of trash we generated. We recycle more of some materials than others.

Material	Percentage recycled in 2012
Paper and paperboard	64.6
Yard trimmings	57.7
Metals	34.0
Rubber, leather, textiles	33.6
Glass	27.7
Wood	15.2
Plastics	8.8
Food	4.8

Paper Power

In 2012, we recycled 51.1 million tons of paper. This was 1.7 million tons less than in 2011 and about the same as 2010.

Paper Products Recycling Rates

Product category	Percent recycled in 2012
Corrugated boxes	90.1
Newsprint	70.4
Paper and paperboard	65.1
Printing and writing papers	54.5

More than 5,000 different products can be made from recycled paper, including lampshades, money, and bandages.

CHECK IT OUT !

79

Rising Carbon Dioxide Levels

The amount of the main greenhouse gas in the atmosphere, carbon dioxide (CO_2), has been steadily rising for more than a century. Experts say the increase comes mostly from the burning of fossil fuels for energy.

Carbon Dioxide in the Atmosphere, 1903–2014

Year	CO_2 (parts per million)
1903	295
1915	301
1927	306
1943	308
1960	317
1970	326
1980	339
1990	354
2000	367
2005	377
2006	379
2007	381
2008	383
2009	385
2013	395
2014 (preliminary data)	398

10 Worst Carbon Dioxide-Producing Countries

Country	Millions of Metric Tons Produced Annually
China	8,715.3
United States	5490.6
Russia	1,788.1
India	1,725.8
Japan	1,180.6
Germany	748.5
Iran	624.9
South Korea	611.0
Canada	552.6
Saudi Arabia	513.5

Environment

Something's in the Air

There are six common air pollutants: ground-level ozone, carbon monoxide, sulfur and nitrogen oxides, lead, and particulate matter such as soot and smoke. The charts on this page show the urban areas with the lowest and highest year-round levels of particle pollution. Find out more at lung.org.

Most Polluted US Cities/Urban Areas
(by year-round particle pollution)

Rank	City
1	Bakersfield-Delano, CA*
1	Merced, CA*
3	Fresno-Madera, CA
4	Hanford-Corcoran, CA*
4	Los Angeles-Long Beach-Riverside, CA*
6	Modesto, CA
7	Visalia-Porterville, CA
8	Pittsburgh-New Castle, CA
9	El Centro, CA
10	Cincinnati-Middletown-Wilmington, OH-KY-IN

*Tie

Cleanest US Cities/Urban Areas
(by year-round particle pollution)

Rank	City
1	Cheyenne, WY
2	St. George, UT*
2	Santa Fe-Espanola, NM*
4	Prescott, AZ
5	Farmington, NM
6	Pocatello, ID
7	Redding, CA
8	Tucson, AZ
9	Flagstaff, AZ**
9	Rapid City, SD**
9	Colorado Springs, CO**
9	Albuquerque, NM**

*Tie   ** Four-way tie

Going G-R-R-R-E-E-N!

You won't find *green* spelled that way in any dictionary, but if we all remember the environmental 3 Rs—Reduce, Reuse, Recycle—we can improve the health and life of our planet. Here are simple things everyone can do.

REDUCE

5 Reducing Tips

1. Buy less. Try to purchase only what you need.

2. Use less. For instance, instead of buying two notepads and using only one side of the paper, buy one and use both sides.

3. Buy with minimum packaging in mind. Suggest that your family buy large sizes of cereal, toothpaste, and other things you use all the time to eliminate multiple boxes.

4. Buy longer-lasting products. Compact fluorescent lightbulbs make the same amount of light and use only one-fourth the amount of electricity that incandescent ones use.

5. Make things last longer. Fix your old bike rather than asking for a new one.

What a Waste!

Municipal solid waste (MSW) is trash—the stuff that we dump in landfills by millions of tons every year. What's the best way to reduce waste? Don't make it in the first place!

REUSE

Second Chance

You may be surprised at how many things can be reused. Think before tossing!

5 Reusing Tips

1. Pack your lunch in reusable containers instead of plastic or paper bags. If 25 percent of American homes used 10 fewer plastic bags a month, it would keep 2.5 billion bags out of landfills every year.

2. Use washable cups, travel mugs, and reusable sports bottles for beverages on the go. If you have to use plastic cups or plates, wash and reuse them a few times.

3. Use a sponge to wipe up spills instead of reaching for paper towels.

4. Save wrapping paper and ribbon from gifts and reuse them.

5. Use rechargeable batteries whenever you can. Americans use approximately 2 billion unrechargeable batteries, which can release harmful metals into landfills, every year.

Environment

RECYCLE

Around We Go

In the United States, we recycle about 34 percent of our MSW. More than 30 percent of the raw material used in glass production comes from recycled glass. That's good news, but we can do better. Even recycling a tiny amount makes a huge difference:

5 Recycling Stats

1. Recycling one glass bottle saves enough energy to light a 100-watt lightbulb for four hours.

2. If every American household recycled the Sunday newspaper, more than half a million trees would be saved—every week!

3. Recycling one aluminum can saves enough energy to run a TV for three hours.

4. Manufacturing one ton of recycled paper takes about 60 percent of the energy to make a ton of paper from raw pulp.

5. In 2010, Americans recycled about 53 billion aluminum cans. That's more than 100,000 every minute. If they were lined up end to end on the ground, the cans could circle the earth 169 times.

Always Recycle These Items

Acid batteries	Electronic equipment	Newspaper	Steel cans
Aluminum cans	Glass (particularly bottles and jars)	Oil	Tires
Appliances		Paint	Wood
Building materials	Lead	Paper	Writing/copy paper
Cardboard	Magazines	Plastic bags	Yard waste
Chemicals	Metal	Plastic bottles	

Some of these items have special rules for handling or disposal. Look online for your local recycling office. Check out the Environmental Protection Agency (EPA) website at epa.gov for a state-by-state list of locations and other helpful information.

CHECK IT OUT!

Styrofoam cups and food containers are useful, but discarded foam breaks into pieces that can stay in the environment at least 500 years. In December 2013, New York lawmakers voted to ban foam food containers and foam "peanuts" used in packing. The law is set to take effect July 1, 2015. San Francisco, Seattle, and Portland, OR, already have bans against foam.

Tips to Save Energy and Natural Resources

Close It Up
Close fireplace dampers when there's no fire burning. An open fireplace damper can let 8 percent of the heat from your furnace escape. Close the refrigerator door to keep the cold air inside.

Turn It Up
When it's warm outside, set your home thermostat at 78°F (25.5°C). When no one's home, set it at 85°F (29.4°C). (Check with an adult first.)

Turn It Down
When it's cold, set the thermostat at 68°F (20°C) or lower during the day. Turn it down to 55°F (12.7°C) or turn it off at night. (Again, check with an adult before changing household routines.)

Turn It Off
Save up to 20,000 gallons of water a year by not leaving the faucet running when brushing teeth, washing dishes, or washing the car. Turn off lights, the TV, your computer, radios, and stereos if the room is going to be empty for more than five minutes.

Trees, please! If every American family planted just one tree, more than a billion pounds of greenhouse gases would be removed from the atmosphere every year.

CHECK IT OUT !

Bike It or Hike It!

Every time you travel, you have choices about how you impact the environment. When you go, go green!

Skateboard, walk, or ride your bike whenever safety and weather permit. These are the greenest ways to travel, and they're great for your health.

Take the bus. A bus carrying 40 passengers takes one-sixth the energy of one car carrying each passenger, while replacing six city blocks' worth of cars.

Suggest that the adults in your family drive less or carpool. Driving 25 fewer miles (40 km) every week can eliminate 1,500 pounds (680 km) of carbon dioxide from the air. Riding with two or more people two days a week can eliminate 1,590 pounds (721 kg) from the air.

CHECK IT OUT !

Shrink Your Carbon Footprint

You can't control the size of your sneakers, but you can control the size of your carbon footprint. Go to cooltheworld.com/kidscarboncalculator.php to measure your impact on the environment and learn ways to shrink it.

COUNTRIES OF THE WORLD

PRETTY NICE ICE!

Every winter, the northeastern Chinese city of Harbin turns into a glittering landscape straight out of a fairy tale. The annual Harbin International Ice and Snow Sculpture Festival brings 7,000 sculptors and artists together from around the world to carve castles, pagodas, skyscrapers, waterfalls, tigers, dragons, and more out of snow and ice. Colored LED lights embedded inside these sculptures, called ice lanterns, make a gorgeous glow visible for miles.

Early ice lanterns date back to the Quing (CHING) Dynasty, 1644-1911. Fishermen left water to freeze in a bucket and warmed it just enough to pull out the bucket-shaped ice block that formed. Then they cut a hole in the top and stuck a candle inside. The result: a lantern that worked like a windproof candle.

In 2014 the Harbin International Ice and Snow Sculpture Festival celebrated its 30th anniversary. Next year's festival opens on January 5, 2015.

YOUR TURN

See photos and read more about Chinese history and the Harbin festival at harbinice.com. Learn facts and stats about China, where one-fifth of the world's population lives, on page 95.

The flags below include the two most common colors in national flags. What are they? What is the third most common color? (See Answers, p. 350.)

Countries of the World

ARCTIC OCEAN

75°N

GREENLAND
(Denmark)

Arctic Circle

ICELAND

Prime Meridian

CANADA

45°N

IRELAND | UNITED
KINGDOM | NET
BELGIUM
LUX.
FRANCE
ANDORRA
PORTUGAL | SPAIN
AZORES
(Portugal)
MOROCCO

UNITED STATES

ATLANTIC OCEAN

30°N

CANARY ISLANDS
(Spain) | ALGERIA
WESTERN
SAHARA
Tropic of Cancer

MEXICO

BAHAMAS

CUBA
DOMINICAN
REPUBLIC
HAITI
JAMAICA

CAPE VERDE | MAURITANIA | MALI

SENEGAL
GAMBIA
GUINEA-BISSAU | GUINEA | BURKINA
FASO
BENIN

15°N

BELIZE
HONDURAS
GUATEMALA
NICARAGUA
EL SALVADOR
COSTA RICA
PANAMA

SIERRA LEONE | CÔTE
D'IVOIRE | GHANA
LIBERIA

PACIFIC OCEAN

VENEZUELA
SURINAME
GUYANA
FRENCH
GUIANA
(France)

TOGO
EQ. GUI.

COLOMBIA

SÃO TOMÉ & PRÍNC
GA

0°

Equator

ECUADOR

°Equator

FRENCH POLYNESIA
(France)

PERU

BRAZIL

15°S

BOLIVIA

Tropic of Capricorn

PARAGUAY

0   1,000   2,000 Miles

0   1,000   2,000 Kilometers

30°S

URUGUAY

CHILE

ARGENTINA

ATLANTIC OCEAN

Prime Meridian

45°S

FALKLAND ISLANDS
(U.K.)

SOUTH GEORGIA
(U.K.)

60°S

165°W | 150°W | 135°W | 120°W | 105°W | 90°W | 75°W | 60°W | 45°W | 30°W | 15°W | 0°

Antarctic Circle

Countries of the World

ARCTIC OCEAN

ARCTIC OCEAN

SWEDEN
FINLAND

RUSSIA

ESTONIA
LATVIA
LITHUANIA
RUS.
BELARUS

MANY
POLAND

CZECH REP.
SLOVAKIA
AUSTRIA HUNGARY
SLOVENIA
CROATIA SERBIA
BOSNIA &
MONT. KOS. BULGARIA
ALBANIA MAC.

KAZAKHSTAN

MONGOLIA

ITALY

GREECE
TURKEY

GEORGIA
ARMENIA AZERBAIJAN
UZBEKISTAN
KYRGYZSTAN
TURKMENISTAN
TAJIKISTAN

NORTH
KOREA
SOUTH
KOREA
JAPAN

PACIFIC OCEAN

MALTA
CYPRUS
LEBANON
ISRAEL
SYRIA
JORDAN
IRAQ
IRAN
AFGHANISTAN

CHINA

LIBYA
EGYPT

KUWAIT
BAHRAIN
QATAR
U.A.E.
SAUDI ARABIA
OMAN

PAKISTAN

NEPAL
BHUTAN

INDIA
BURMA

Tropic of Cancer

GER
CHAD
SUDAN

ERITREA
DJIBOUTI

YEMEN

BANGLADESH

LAOS
THAILAND
VIETNAM
CAMBODIA

NORTHERN
MARIANA ISLANDS
(U.S.)

PHILIPPINES

CENTRAL
AFRICAN REP
SOUTH
SUDAN
ETHIOPIA
SOMALIA

SRI
LANKA

BRUNEI
MALAYSIA
SINGAPORE

PALAU

FEDERATED STATES
OF MICRONESIA

MARSHALL
ISLANDS

CAMEROON
REP.
OF
THE
CONGO
DEMOCRATIC
REPUBLIC OF
THE CONGO
UGANDA
RWANDA
BURUNDI
KENYA
TANZANIA

MALDIVES

Equator

INDONESIA

KIRIBATI

PAPUA
NEW GUINEA
SOLOMON
ISLANDS

TUVALU

TIMOR-LESTE

ANGOLA
ZAMBIA
MALAWI
COMOROS

SAMOA

NEW CALEDONIA
(France)

VANUATU
FIJI

NAMIBIA
ZIMBABWE
BOTSWANA
MOZAMBIQUE
MADAGASCAR

INDIAN OCEAN

Tropic of Capricorn

AUSTRALIA

TONGA

SOUTH
AFRICA
SWAZILAND
LESOTHO

NEW
ZEALAND

N
W E
S

15°E   30°E   45°E   60°E   75°E   90°E   105°E   120°E   135°E   150°E   165°E   180°

ANTARCTICA

AFGHANISTAN

Capital: Kabul
Population: 32,564,342
Area: 250,001 sq. mi. (647,500 sq km)
Language: Dari (Afghan Persian), Pashto
Money: Afghani
Government: Islamic republic

CHECK IT OUT

Kite running is a popular sport in Afghanistan. Kids fly kites, cut them loose, and then race to recover them.

ALBANIA

Capital: Tirana
Population: 3,029,278
Area: 11,100 sq. mi. (28,748 sq km)
Language: Albanian, Greek
Money: Lek
Government: Republic

CHECK IT OUT

The Adriatic and Ionian Seas border the western coast of Albania.

ALGERIA

Capital: Algiers
Population: 39,542,166
Area: 919,595 sq. mi.
(2,381,740 sq km)
Language: Arabic, Berber, French
Money: Dinar
Government: Republic

CHECK IT OUT

Algeria is the second-largest country in Africa.

ANDORRA

Capital: Andorra la Vella
Population: 85,580
Area: 180 sq. mi. (468 sq km)
Language: Catalan, French, Castillan, Portuguese
Money: Euro
Government: Parliamentary democracy

CHECK IT OUT

Andorra is about half the size of New York City. For 700 years, until 1993, this little country had two rulers: France and Spain.

ANGOLA

Capital: Luanda
Population: 19,625,353
Area: 481,400 sq. mi. (1,246,700 sq km)
Language: Portuguese, Bantu, others
Money: Kwanza
Government: Republic

CHECK IT OUT

Eighty-five percent of the country's revenue (GDP) comes from oil production.

ANTIGUA AND BARBUDA

Capital: St. John's
Population: 92,436
Area: 171 sq. mi. (443 sq km)
Language: English
Money: Dollar
Government: Parliamentary democracy; independent sovereign state within the Commonwealth

CHECK IT OUT

Thousands of frigate birds live in a sanctuary on Barbuda. A frigate bird's wingspan can reach nearly eight feet (2.4 m).

Countries of the World

ARGENTINA

Capital: Buenos Aires
Population: 43,431,886
Area: 1,068,302 sq. mi.
(2,766,890 sq km)
Language: Spanish, Italian,
English, German, French
Money: Peso
Government: Republic

CHECK IT OUT

The Andes mountains run along
the western edge of Argentina,
on the border with Chile.

ARMENIA

Capital: Yerevan
Population: 3,056,871
Area: 11,484 sq. mi. (29,743 sq km)
Language: Armenian, Yezidi,
Russian
Money: Dram
Government: Republic

CHECK IT OUT

Armenia was the first nation to
formally adopt Christianity (in the
early fourth century).

AUSTRALIA

Capital: Canberra
Population: 22,751,014
Area: 2,967,909 sq. mi.
(7,686,850 sq km)
Language: English, Chinese,
Italian, aboriginal languages
Money: Dollar
Government: Constitutional
monarchy; democratic, federal-
state system recognizing British
monarchy as sovereign

CHECK IT OUT

The Great Barrier Reef, off the
coast of Australia, is larger than
the Great Wall of China.

AUSTRIA

Capital: Vienna
Population: 8,224,038
Area: 32,382 sq. mi. (83,870 sq km)
Language: German
Money: Euro
Government: Federal
parliamentary democracy

CHECK IT OUT

The Habsburg family ruled
Austria for nearly 750 years,
until the Treaty of St. Germain
in 1919 established the Republic
of Austria.

AZERBAIJAN

Capital: Baku
Population: 9,780,780
Area: 33,436 sq. mi. (86,600 sq km)
Language: Azerbaijani, Russian,
Armenian, others
Money: Manat
Government: Republic

CHECK IT OUT

The country's name is thought to
come from the ancient Persian
phrase that means "Land of Fire."

THE BAHAMAS

Capital: Nassau
Population: 324,597
Area: 5,382 sq. mi. (13,940 sq km)
Language: English, Creole
Money: Dollar
Government: Constitutional
parliamentary democracy

CHECK IT OUT

More than eight out of ten
Bahamians are of African
heritage.

BAHRAIN

Capital: Manama
Population: 1,346,613
Area: 257 sq. mi. (665 sq km)
Language: Arabic, English,
Farsi, Urdu
Money: Dinar
Government: Constitutional
monarchy

CHECK IT OUT

The land area of Bahrain is only three and a half times the size of Washington, DC.

BANGLADESH

Capital: Dhaka
Population: 168,957,745
Area: 55,599 sq. mi. (144,000 sq km)
Language: Bengali, Chakma, Bagh
Money: Taka
Government: Parliamentary
democracy

CHECK IT OUT

The Bengal tiger is the national animal of Bangladesh.

BARBADOS

Capital: Bridgetown
Population: 290,604
Area: 166 sq. mi. (431 sq km)
Language: English
Money: Dollar
Government: Parliamentary
democracy

CHECK IT OUT

The British settled Barbados in 1627. When they arrived, there was no one living there.

BELARUS

Capital: Minsk
Population: 9,589,689
Area: 80,155 sq. mi.
(207,600 sq km)
Language: Belarusian, Russian
Money: Ruble
Government: Republic

CHECK IT OUT

The name of this Eastern European country means "White Russia."

BELGIUM

Capital: Brussels
Population: 10,453,761
Area: 11,787 sq. mi. (30,528 sq km)
Language: Dutch, French,
German
Money: Euro
Government: Parliamentary
democracy under a constitutional
monarchy

CHECK IT OUT

Many people call Belgium the chocolate capital of the world. Hundreds of thousands of tons of the sweet stuff are produced here yearly.

BELIZE

Capital: Belmopan
Population: 347,369
Area: 8,867 sq. mi. (22,966 sq km)
Language: English, Creole,
Spanish, Mayan dialects
Money: Dollar
Government: Parliamentary
democracy

CHECK IT OUT

The mahogany industry was central to Belize's economy hundreds of years ago. That's why a mahogany tree is pictured on the country's flag.

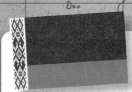

Countries of the World

BENIN

Capital: Porto-Novo
Population: 10,448,647
Area: 43,483 sq. mi.
(112,620 sq km)
Language: French, Fon, Yoruba
in the south; Nagot, Bariba, Dendi
in the north
Money: CFA franc
Government: Republic under
multiparty democratic rule

CHECK IT OUT

Benin is only 215 miles across
(about 325 km) at its widest point.
It's eight times smaller than
Nigeria, its neighbor.

BHUTAN

Capital: Thimphu
Population: 741,919
Area: 18,147 sq. mi. (47,000 sq km)
Language: Dzongkha, Nepali,
Tibetan
Money: Ngultrum
Government: Constitutional
monarchy

CHECK IT OUT

The Great Himalaya Range, the
highest mountain system in the
world, runs through northern
Bhutan.

BOLIVIA

Capital: La Paz
Population: 10,800,882
Area: 424,164 sq. mi.
(1,098,580 sq km)
Language: Spanish, Quecha,
Aymara, Guarani
Money: Boliviano
Government: Republic

CHECK IT OUT

Bolivia is named after
independence fighter Simón
Bolívar.

BOSNIA AND HERZEGOVINA

Capital: Sarajevo
Population: 3,867,055
Area: 19,772 sq. mi. (51,209 sq km)
Language: Bosnian, Serbian,
Croatian
Money: Convertible marka
Government: Federal
democratic republic

CHECK IT OUT

Sarajevo, the country's capital,
hosted the 1984 Winter Olympics.

BOTSWANA

Capital: Gaborone
Population: 2,182,719
Area: 231,804 sq. mi.
(600,370 sq km)
Language: English, Setswana,
Kalanga
Money: Pula
Government: Parliamentary
republic

CHECK IT OUT

Botswana has one of the healthiest
economies in Africa. About 70—80
percent of its export revenues
come from diamond mining.

BRAZIL

Capital: Brasilia
Population: 204,259,812
Area: 3,286,488 sq. mi.
(8,511,965 sq km)
Language: Portuguese
Money: Real
Government: Federative
republic

CHECK IT OUT

Brazil has the largest population
in Latin America and the fifth-
largest in the world.

BRUNEI

Capital: Bandar Seri Begawan
Population: 429,646
Area: 2,228 sq. mi. (5,770 sq km)
Language: Malay, English, Chinese
Money: Dollar
Government: Constitutional sultanate

! CHECK IT OUT

For more than six centuries, the same royal family has ruled Brunei.

BULGARIA

Capital: Sofia
Population: 6,867,134
Area: 42,823 sq. mi. (110,910 sq km)
Language: Bulgarian, Turkish, Roma
Money: Lev
Government: Parliamentary democracy

! CHECK IT OUT

One of Bulgaria's sweetest exports is rose oil, which is used throughout the world to make perfume.

BURKINA FASO

Capital: Ouagadougou
Population: 18,931,686
Area: 105,869 sq. mi. (274,200 sq km)
Language: French
Money: CFA franc
Government: Republic

! CHECK IT OUT

Burkina Faso has western Africa's largest elephant population.

BURMA

Capital: Yangon (Rangoon)
Population: 56,320,206
Area: 261,970 sq. mi. (678,500 sq km)
Language: Burmese, many ethnic languages
Money: Kyat
Government: Military junta

! CHECK IT OUT

The military junta ruling the nation changed Burma's name to Myanmar in 1989, but several countries, including the United States, refused to acknowledge the change. Others recognize Myanmar as the official name.

BURUNDI

Capital: Bujumbura
Population: 10,742,276
Area: 10,745 sq. mi. (27,830 sq km)
Language: Kirundi, French, Swahili
Money: Franc
Government: Republic

! CHECK IT OUT

Burundi is on the shoreline of Lake Tanganyika, the second-deepest lake in the world.

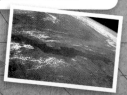

CAMBODIA

Capital: Phnom Penh
Population: 15,708,756
Area: 69,900 sq. mi. (181,040 sq km)
Language: Khmer, French, English
Money: Riel
Government: Multiparty democracy under a constitutional monarchy

! CHECK IT OUT

The Mekong River system, which runs through Cambodia, is the home of the giant catfish. These fish can reach 10 feet (3 m) in length and weigh up to 650 pounds (295 kg).

CAMEROON

Capital: Yaoundé
Population: 23,739,218
Area: 183,568 sq. mi. (475,440 sq km)
Language: French, English, 24 major African language groups
Money: CFA franc
Government: Republic

! CHECK IT OUT

Mount Cameroon, the highest mountain in sub-Saharan west Africa, is an active volcano that last erupted in 2000.

CANADA

Capital: Ottawa
Population: 35,099,836
Area: 3,855,103 sq. mi.
(9,984,670 sq km)
Language: English, French
Money: Dollar
Government: Confederation
with parliamentary democracy
and constitutional monarchy

CHECK IT OUT

In land area, Canada is the second-largest country in the world. In population, it ranks only 37.

CAPE VERDE

Capital: Praia
Population: 538,535*
Area: 1,557 sq. mi. (4,033 sq km)
Language: Portuguese, Crioulo
Money: Escudo
Government: Republic

CHECK IT OUT

The group of islands that make up Cape Verde was uninhabited until the Portuguese discovered it in 1460.

*2014 estimate, *CIA World Factbook*

CENTRAL AFRICAN REPUBLIC

Capital: Bangui
Population: 5,391,539
Area: 240,535 sq. mi.
(622,984 sq km)
Language: Sangho, French, tribal languages
Money: CFA franc
Government: Republic

CHECK IT OUT

There are more than 80 ethnic groups in the Central African Republic. Each group speaks its own language.

CHAD

Capital: N'Djaména
Population: 11,631,456
Area: 495,755 sq. mi.
(1,284,000 sq km)
Language: French, Arabic, more than 120 others
Money: CFA franc
Government: Republic

CHECK IT OUT

Chad is about three times the size of California.

CHILE

Capital: Santiago
Population: 17,508,260
Area: 292,260 sq. mi.
(756,950 sq km)
Language: Spanish
Money: Peso
Government: Republic

CHECK IT OUT

The blue in Chile's flag stands for the sky and the white for the snow of the Andes mountains on its eastern border.

CHINA

Capital: Beijing
Population: 1,361,512,535
Area: 3,705,407 sq. mi.
(9,596,960 sq km)
Language: Mandarin, Yue, Wu, Minhel, Minnan, Xiang, Gan, Hakka dialects, others
Money: Yuan
Government: Communist Party—led state

CHECK IT OUT

The name *China* comes from the Qin (or Ch'in) Dynasty, under which China was unified in 221 BCE.

COLOMBIA

Capital: Bogotá
Population: 46,736,728
Area: 439,736 sq. mi.
(1,138,910 sq km)
Language: Spanish
Money: Peso
Government: Republic

! CHECK IT OUT

Historically Colombia has been the world's top producer of emeralds.

COMOROS

Capital: Moroni
Population: 780,971
Area: 838 sq. mi. (2,170 sq km)
Language: Arabic, French, Shikomoro
Money: Franc
Government: Republic

! CHECK IT OUT

The three islands that make up Comoros are sometimes called the Perfume Islands. The country is the world's leading producer of essence of ylang-ylang, a flower oil used to make perfumes and soaps.

CONGO, Democratic Republic of the

Capital: Kinshasa
Population: 79,375,136
Area: 905,588 sq. mi.
(2,345,410 sq km)
Language: French, Lingala, Swahili, Kikongo, Tshiluba
Money: CFA franc
Government: Republic

! CHECK IT OUT

This country's enormous land area is equal to the United States east of the Mississippi River, or all of western Europe.

CONGO, Republic of the

Capital: Brazzaville
Population: 4,755,097
Area: 132,047 sq. mi. (342,000 sq km)
Language: French, Lingala, Monokutuba, Kikongo
Money: CFA franc
Government: Republic

! CHECK IT OUT

Oil is the country's largest revenue-generating industry.

COSTA RICA

Capital: San José
Population: 4,814,144
Area: 19,730 sq. mi. (51,100 sq km)
Language: Spanish, English
Money: Colón
Government: Democratic republic

! CHECK IT OUT

For a bird's-eye view of the rain forest, tourists in Costa Rica swing through the canopy on pulleys attached to treetops.

CÔTE d'IVOIRE (Ivory Coast)

Capital: Yamoussoukro
Population: 22,848,945*
Area: 124,503 sq. mi.
(322,460 sq km)
Language: French, Dioula, 59 other native dialects
Money: CFA franc
Government: Republic with multiparty presidential regime

! CHECK IT OUT

Côte d'Ivoire is home to more than 60 ethnic groups.

*2014 estimate, *CIA World Factbook*

CROATIA

Capital: Zagreb
Population: 4,464,844
Area: 21,831 sq. mi. (56,542 sq km)
Language: Croatian, Serbian
Money: Kuna
Government: Parliamentary democracy

CHECK IT OUT

Civil war ended in Croatia in 1998. Now tourists flock to its beautiful islands and national parks.

CUBA

Capital: Havana
Population: 11,031,433
Area: 42,803 sq. mi. (110,860 sq km)
Language: Spanish
Money: Peso
Government: Communist state

CHECK IT OUT

Cuba was controlled by the same leader, Fidel Castro, for nearly 50 years.

CYPRUS

Capital: Nicosia
Population: 1,189,197
Area: 3,571 sq. mi. (9,250 sq km)
Language: Greek, Turkish, English
Money: Euro
Government: Republic

CHECK IT OUT

Mythology says the goddess Aphrodite arose from the waves at a rock formation in Cyprus called *Petra tou Romiou.*

CZECH REPUBLIC

Capital: Prague
Population: 10,644,842
Area: 30,450 sq. mi. (78,866 sq km)
Language: Czech, Slovak
Money: Koruna
Government: Parliamentary democracy

CHECK IT OUT

In the country's capital is Prague Castle, the world's largest medieval castle.

DENMARK

Capital: Copenhagen
Population: 5,581,503
Area: 16,639 sq. mi. (43,094 sq km)
Language: Danish, Faroese, Greenlandic, English
Money: Krone
Government: Constitutional monarchy

CHECK IT OUT

LEGO blocks were invented in Denmark. The name comes from the Danish words *leg* and *godt*, which mean "play well."

DJIBOUTI

Capital: Djibouti
Population: 828,324
Area: 8,880 sq. mi. (23,000 sq km)
Language: French, Arabic, Afar, Somali
Money: Franc
Government: Republic

CHECK IT OUT

The Djibouti countryside features dramatic limestone chimneys created by deposits of calcium carbonate from hot springs.

DOMINICA

Capital: Roseau
Population: 73,607
Area: 291 sq. mi. (754 sq km)
Language: English, French patois
Money: Dollar
Government: Parliamentary democracy

! CHECK IT OUT

Parts of Dominica can receive as much as 300 inches (762 cm) of rain every year.

DOMINICAN REPUBLIC

Capital: Santo Domingo
Population: 10,478,756
Area: 18,815 sq. mi. (48,730 sq km)
Language: Spanish
Money: Peso
Government: Democratic republic

! CHECK IT OUT

The Dominican Republic is the second-largest country in the West Indies.

ECUADOR

Capital: Quito
Population: 15,868,396
Area: 109,483 sq. mi. (283,560 sq km)
Language: Spanish, Quechua, Jivaroan
Money: Dollar
Government: Republic

! CHECK IT OUT

The Galápagos Islands, off Ecuador's coast, are home to the Galápagos tortoise. These ancient creatures can weigh up to 475 pounds (215 kg) and live more than 100 years.

EGYPT

Capital: Cairo
Population: 88,487,396
Area: 386,662 sq. mi. (1,001,450 sq km)
Language: Arabic, English, French
Money: Pound
Government: Republic

! CHECK IT OUT

The Great Pyramid of Khufu (Cheops) is 480 feet (146 m) high—about the height of a 48-story building.

EL SALVADOR

Capital: San Salvador
Population: 6,141,350
Area: 8,124 sq. mi. (21,040 sq km)
Language: Spanish, Nahua
Money: Colón
Government: Republic

! CHECK IT OUT

El Salvador is the smallest and most densely populated country in Central America.

EQUATORIAL GUINEA

Capital: Malabo
Population: 740,743
Area: 10,831 sq. mi. (28,051 sq km)
Language: Spanish, French, Fang, Bubi
Money: CFA franc
Government: Republic

! CHECK IT OUT

Scientists come to Bioko Island, where this country's capital is located, to study unique species of plants and animals, including a rare monkey called a drill.

ERITREA

Capital: Asmara
Population: 6,527,689
Area: 46,842 sq. mi. (121,320 sq km)
Language: Afar, Arabic, Tigre, Kunama
Money: Nakfa
Government: In transition

CHECK IT OUT

Many Eritreans wear a traditional shawl known as a *gabbi*.

ESTONIA

Capital: Tallinn
Population: 1,249,312
Area: 17,462 sq. mi. (45,226 sq km)
Language: Estonian, Russian, Latvian
Money: Kroon
Government: Parliamentary republic

CHECK IT OUT

Estonia is home to Old Town Tallinn, one of Europe's best-preserved medieval communities. It has 26 watchtowers and cobblestone streets.

ETHIOPIA

Capital: Addis Ababa
Population: 99,465,819
Area: 435,186 sq. mi. (1,127,127 sq km)
Language: Amarigna, Oromigna, Tigrigna, Somaligna, English
Money: Birr
Government: Federal republic

CHECK IT OUT

The Blue Nile river runs for more than 500 miles (800 km) through Ethiopia and carries the runoff from the highlands to the desert.

FIJI

Capital: Suva
Population: 909,389
Area: 7,054 sq. mi. (18,270 sq km)
Language: English, Fijian, Hindustani
Money: Dollar
Government: Republic

CHECK IT OUT

Fiji is composed of 333 different islands in the South Pacific, but most people live on the largest one—Viti Levu.

FINLAND

Capital: Helsinki
Population: 5,270,966
Area: 130,559 sq. mi. (338,145 sq km)
Language: Finnish, Swedish
Money: Euro
Government: Constitutional republic

CHECK IT OUT

One-fourth of Finland is north of the Arctic Circle, making winters there long and very cold.

FRANCE

Capital: Paris
Population: 66,553,766
Area: 248,429 sq. mi. (643,427 sq km)
Language: French
Money: Euro
Government: Republic

CHECK IT OUT

The TGV train, France's high-speed rail service, runs at speeds of up to 200 miles per hour (322 kph).

GABON

Capital: Libreville
Population: 1,705,336
Area: 103,347 sq. mi.
(267,667 sq km)
Language: French, Fang, others
Money: CFA franc
Government: Republic

CHECK IT OUT

The Kongou Falls, located in Gabon's Invindo National Park, is 2 miles (3.2 km) wide.

THE GAMBIA

Capital: Banjul
Population: 1,967,709
Area: 4,363 sq. mi. (11,300 sq km)
Language: English, Mandinka, Wolof, Fula, others
Money: Dalasi
Government: Republic

CHECK IT OUT

The Gambia is the smallest country on the African continent.

GEORGIA

Capital: Tbilisi
Population: 4,931,226
Area: 26,911 sq. mi. (69,700 sq km)
Language: Georgian, Russian, Abkhaz
Money: Lari
Government: Republic

CHECK IT OUT

Krubera Cave, in Georgia's Caucasus Mountains, is said to be the deepest cave in the world. It has been explored to depths of 7,185 feet (2,190 m).

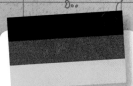

GERMANY

Capital: Berlin
Population: 80,854,408
Area: 137,847 sq. mi.
(357,021 sq km)
Language: German
Money: Euro
Government: Federal republic

CHECK IT OUT

The spires of the Cologne Cathedral are an amazing 515 feet (157 m) high—taller than a 50-story building.

GHANA

Capital: Accra
Population: 26,327,649
Area: 92,456 sq. mi. (239,460 sq km)
Language: English, Asante, Ewe, Fante
Money: Cedi
Government: Constitutional democracy

CHECK IT OUT

Until 1957 Ghana was known as the Gold Coast because of the vast amounts of gold Portuguese explorers found there.

GREECE

Capital: Athens
Population: 10,775,643
Area: 50,942 sq. mi. (131,940 sq km)
Language: Greek, Turkish, English
Money: Euro
Government: Parliamentary republic

CHECK IT OUT

The Parthenon, in Athens, is one of the oldest and most famous buildings in the world. The ancient temple was built to honor the Greek goddess Athena almost 2,500 years ago.

GRENADA

Capital: St. George's
Population: 111,000
Area: 133 sq. mi. (344 sq km)
Language: English, French patois
Money: Dollar
Government: Parliamentary democracy

CHECK IT OUT
Grenada is known as the Spice of the Caribbean. The country produces one-third of the world's nutmeg.

GUATEMALA

Capital: Guatemala City
Population: 14,918,999
Area: 42,043 sq. mi. (108,890 sq km)
Language: Spanish, 23 Amerindian dialects
Money: Quetzal
Government: Constitutional democratic republic

CHECK IT OUT
More than one-half of Guatemalans are descended from the Mayas. The Mayan Indian civilization developed a calendar with a 365-day year, among many other achievements.

GUINEA

Capital: Conakry
Population: 11,780,162
Area: 94,926 sq. mi. (245,857 sq km)
Language: French, Peul, Malinke, Soussou
Money: Franc
Government: Republic

CHECK IT OUT
Despite its name, the guinea pig does not come from Guinea. It is native to South America. (And it's not a pig!)

GUINEA-BISSAU

Capital: Bissau
Population: 1,726,170
Area: 13,946 sq. mi. (36,120 sq km)
Language: Portuguese, Creole, French, others
Money: CFA franc
Government: Republic

CHECK IT OUT
Guinea-Bissau's main export crop is cashew nuts.

GUYANA

Capital: Georgetown
Population: 735,222
Area: 83,000 sq. mi. (214,970 sq km)
Language: English, Guyanese, Creole
Money: Dollar
Government: Republic

CHECK IT OUT
Guyana's Kaieteur Falls is five times as tall as Niagara Falls.

HAITI

Capital: Port-au-Prince
Population: 10,110,019
Area: 10,714 sq. mi. (27,750 sq km)
Language: French, Creole
Money: Gourde
Government: Republic

CHECK IT OUT
On January 12, 2010, a devastating earthquake struck Haiti, killing or injuring hundreds of thousands in the Port-au-Prince area.

THE HOLY SEE
(VATICAN CITY)

Capital: Vatican City
Population: 842*
Area: 0.17 sq. mi. (0.44 sq km)
Language: Italian, Latin, French, various others
Money: Euro
Government: Ecclesiastical

CHECK IT OUT

Vatican City, the seat of the Roman Catholic Church, is the world's smallest independent nation.

*2014 estimate, *CIA World Factbook*

HONDURAS

Capital: Tegucigalpa
Population: 8,746,673
Area: 43,278 sq. mi. (112,090 sq km)
Language: Spanish, Amerindian dialects
Money: Lempira
Government: Democratic constitutional republic

CHECK IT OUT

The word *honduras* means "depths" in Spanish. Christopher Columbus named the area after the deep water off its coast when he landed there in 1502.

HUNGARY

Capital: Budapest
Population: 9,897,541
Area: 35,919 sq. mi. (93,030 sq km)
Language: Hungarian
Money: Forint
Government: Parliamentary democracy

CHECK IT OUT

The Danube River splits the capital city into two sides: Buda and Pest.

ICELAND

Capital: Reykjavik
Population: 319,395
Area: 39,769 sq. mi. (103,000 sq km)
Language: Icelandic
Money: Krona
Government: Constitutional republic

CHECK IT OUT

Iceland's glaciers, geysers, and warm, mineral-rich pools attract more than a quarter of a million tourists every year.

INDIA

Capital: New Delhi
Population: 1,251,695,584
Area: 1,269,346 sq. mi. (3,287,590 sq km)
Language: Hindi, English, 21 others
Money: Rupee
Government: Federal republic

CHECK IT OUT

India's Taj Mahal is one of the wonders of the world. It was built in the 1600s by Shah Jahan for his wife, Mumtaz Mahal.

INDONESIA

Capital: Jakarta
Population: 255,993,674
Area: 741,100 sq. mi. (1,919,440 sq km)
Language: Bahasa Indonesia, English, Dutch, Javanese
Money: Rupiah
Government: Republic

CHECK IT OUT

The largest volcanic eruption in history happened on the Indonesian island of Sumbawa in 1815. Scientists say that the eruption of Mount Tambora sent a massive cloud of ash 30 miles (43 km) into the atmosphere—much higher than a plane can fly—and killed 100,000 people.

IRAN

Capital: Tehran
Population: 81,824,270
Area: 636,296 sq. mi. (1,648,000 sq km)
Language: Persian, Turkic, Kurdish, Arabic, others
Money: Rial
Government: Islamic republic

CHECK IT OUT

For most of its history, Iran was called Persia.

IRAQ

Capital: Baghdad
Population: 33,309,836
Area: 168,754 sq. mi.
(437,072 sq km)
Language: Arabic, Kurdish,
Turkoman, Assyrian, Armenian
Money: Dinar
Government: Parliamentary
democracy

CHECK IT OUT

Iraq contains more oil than any
country in the world, except for
Saudi Arabia and Canada.

IRELAND

Capital: Dublin
Population: 4,892,305
Area: 27,135 sq. mi. (70,280 sq km)
Language: English, Gaelic
Money: Euro
Government: Parliamentary
republic

CHECK IT OUT

Ireland is known as the Emerald
Isle because of its beautiful green
fields and hillsides.

ISRAEL

Capital: Jerusalem
Population: 7,935,149
Area: 8,019 sq. mi. (20,770 sq km)
Language: Hebrew, Arabic,
English
Money: New shekel
Government: Republic

CHECK IT OUT

The Western Wall in Jerusalem
is also called the Wailing Wall. It
is one of Judaism's holiest places
and most sacred symbols.

ITALY

Capital: Rome
Population: 61,855,120
Area: 116,306 sq. mi.
(301,230 sq km)
Language: Italian, German,
French, Slovene
Money: Euro
Government: Republic

CHECK IT OUT

Engineers successfully stopped
Italy's famous Leaning Tower of
Pisa from collapsing through a
construction project in 2001.

JAMAICA

Capital: Kingston
Population: 2,950,210
Area: 4,244 sq. mi. (10,991 sq km)
Language: English, English patois
Money: Dollar
Government: Constitutional
monarchy with parliamentary
system

CHECK IT OUT

The pirate known as Blackbeard
(Edward Teach) is said to have
operated out of Jamaica in the
1700s. Some stories say that he
went into battle with lit matches
stuck in his hat to make enemies
think his head was smoking.

JAPAN

Capital: Tokyo
Population: 126,919,659
Area: 145,883 sq. mi.
(337,835 sq km)
Language: Japanese
Money: Yen
Government: Constitutional
monarchy with parliamentary
democracy

CHECK IT OUT

Japan has four major islands—
Honshu, Hokkaido, Kyushu, and
Shikoku—and thousands of
smaller ones.

JORDAN

Capital: Amman
Population: 6,623,279
Area: 35,637 sq. mi. (92,300 sq km)
Language: Arabic, English
Money: Dinar
Government: Constitutional monarchy

☝CHECK IT OUT

The points of the star on Jordan's flag stand for the first seven verses of the Koran, the holy book of Islam.

KAZAKHSTAN

Capital: Astana
Population: 18,157,122
Area: 1,049,155 sq. mi. (2,717,300 sq km)
Language: Kazakh, Russian, German
Money: Tenge
Government: Republic

☝CHECK IT OUT

The Caspian Sea, which borders Kazakhstan, is the largest enclosed body of water on Earth.

KENYA

Capital: Nairobi
Population: 45,925,301
Area: 224,962 sq. mi. (582,650 sq km)
Language: Kiswahili, English, numerous indigenous languages
Money: Shilling
Government: Republic

☝CHECK IT OUT

In Kenya's Lake Turkana area, scientists discovered a fossil known as Kenya Man, thought to be over three million years old.

KIRIBATI

Capital: Tawara
Population: 105,711
Area: 313 sq. mi. (811 sq km)
Language: English, I-Kiribati
Money: Dollar
Government: Republic

☝CHECK IT OUT

Kiribati consists of three groups of islands surrounded by coral reefs, roughly halfway between Australia and Hawaii.

NORTH KOREA

Capital: Pyongyang
Population: 24,983,205
Area: 46,541 sq. mi. (120,540 sq km)
Language: Korean
Money: Won
Government: Communist state

☝CHECK IT OUT

North Korea has the fourth-largest army in the world.

SOUTH KOREA

Capital: Seoul
Population: 49,115,196
Area: 38,023 sq. mi. (98,480 sq km)
Language: Korean, English
Money: Won
Government: Republic

☝CHECK IT OUT

South Korea has about twice as many people as North Korea, but much less land area. It's one of the mostly densely populated countries in the world.

KOSOVO

Capital: Pristina
Population: 1,870,981
Area: 4,203 sq. mi.
(10,887 sq km)
Language: Albanian, Serbian,
Bosnian, Turkish, Roma
Money: Euro
Government: Republic

CHECK IT OUT
Kosovo, a country in southeastern
Europe that is about the size
of Connecticut, declared its
independence from Serbia on
February 17, 2008.

KUWAIT

Capital: Kuwait City
Population: 2,788,534
Area: 6,880 sq. mi. (17,820 sq km)
Language: Arabic, English
Money: Dinar
Government: Constitutional
emirate

CHECK IT OUT
Summers in Kuwait are dry and
extremely hot, averaging
108—115°F (42—46°C).

KYRGYZSTAN

Capital: Bishkek
Population: 5,664,939
Area: 76,641 sq. mi.
(198,500 sq km)
Language: Kyrgyz, Russian, Uzbek
Money: Som
Government: Republic

CHECK IT OUT
Kyrgyzstan is one of 15
countries that became
independent with the collapse
of the Soviet Union in 1991.

LAOS

Capital: Vientiane
Population: 6,911,544
Area: 91,429 sq. mi.
(236,800 sq km)
Language: Lao, French,
English, other ethnic languages
Money: Kip
Government: Communist state

CHECK IT OUT
In 2008, cavers exploring the 6-
mile-long (almost 10 km) Xe Bang
Fai River cave in central Laos
found huge rooms and spiders
as big as dinner plates.

LATVIA

Capital: Riga
Population: 2,151,638
Area: 24,938 sq. mi.
(64,589 sq km)
Language: Latvian,
Lithuanian, Russian
Money: Lat
Government: Parliamentary
democracy

CHECK IT OUT
Latvia has a 100 percent
literacy rate.

LEBANON

Capital: Beirut
Population: 4,151,234
Area: 4,015 sq. mi.
(10,400 sq km)
Language: Arabic, English,
French, Armenian
Money: Pound
Government: Republic

CHECK IT OUT
Beirut is a lively pop music
center, with TV music
channels, yearly festivals,
and talent shows such
as *Star Academy* and
Superstar.

LESOTHO

Capital: Maseru
Population: 1,947,701
Area: 11,720 sq. mi.
(30,355 sq km)
Language: Sesotho,
English, Zulu, Xhosa
Money: Loti
Government:
Parliamentary constitutional
monarchy

CHECK IT OUT
To visualize Lesotho, think
of a doughnut hole—a small
circle of land surrounded
by the much larger nation of
South Africa.

LIBERIA

Capital: Monrovia
Population: 4,195,666
Area: 43,000 sq. mi. (111,370 sq km)
Language: English, about 20 ethnic languages
Money: Dollar
Government: Republic

CHECK IT OUT

Many Liberians are descendants of American slaves who were advised to live there in freedom by a US antislavery group in the 1800s.

LIBYA

Capital: Tripoli
Population: 6,411,776
Area: 679,362 sq. mi. (1,759,540 sq km)
Language: Arabic, Italian, English
Money: Dinar
Government: In transition

CHECK IT OUT

Libya has a young population. About one-third of all Libyans are under 15.

LIECHTENSTEIN

Capital: Vaduz
Population: 37,624
Area: 62 sq. mi. (160 sq km)
Language: German, Alemannic dialect
Money: Swiss franc
Government: Constitutional monarchy

CHECK IT OUT

Tiny Liechtenstein shares some services with neighboring Switzerland. Its residents use Swiss money, and Switzerland runs Liechtenstein's telephone and postal systems.

LITHUANIA

Capital: Vilnius
Population: 3,495,316
Area: 25,212 sq. mi. (65,300 sq km)
Language: Lithuanian, Russian, Polish
Money: Litas
Government: Parliamentary democracy

CHECK IT OUT

Lithuania is the largest of the Baltic states, three countries on the eastern edge of the Baltic Sea. The others are Estonia and Latvia.

LUXEMBOURG

Capital: Luxembourg-Ville
Population: 526,510
Area: 998 sq. mi. (2,586 sq km)
Language: Luxembourgish, German, French
Money: Euro
Government: Constitutional monarchy

CHECK IT OUT

Luxembourg is an industrial country known particularly for two products: steel and computers.

MACEDONIA

Capital: Skopje
Population: 2,096,015
Area: 9,781 sq. mi. (25,333 sq km)
Language: Macedonian, Albanian, Turkish
Money: Denar
Government: Parliamentary democracy

CHECK IT OUT

About 80 percent of Macedonia consists of hills and mountains, but more than half the population lives in cities.

MADAGASCAR

Capital: Antananarivo
Population: 23,812,681
Area: 226,657 sq. mi.
(587,040 sq km)
Language: Malagasy, English,
French
Money: Ariary
Government: Republic

CHECK IT OUT

Madagascar is the world's fourth-largest island, after Greenland, New Guinea, and Borneo. It is home to a huge variety of unique plants and animals that evolved 165 million years ago.

MALAWI

Capital: Lilongwe
Population: 17,715,075
Area: 45,745 sq. mi. (118,480 sq km)
Language: Chichewa, Chinyan'ji,
Chiyao, Chitumbka
Money: Kwacha
Government: Multiparty
democracy

CHECK IT OUT

Lake Malawi is nearly 9,000 square miles (23,310 sq km). It takes up about a fifth of the country's total area.

MALAYSIA

Capital: Kuala Lumpur
Population: 30,513,848
Area: 127,317 sq. mi. (329,750
sq km)
Language: Bahasa Malaysia,
English, Chinese dialects, Panjabi,
Thai
Money: Ringgit
Government: Constitutional
monarchy

CHECK IT OUT

Malaysia's capital is the home of the 1,483-foot (452 m) Petronas Twin Towers. They were the tallest buildings in the world from 1996 to 2003.

MALDIVES

Capital: Male
Population: 393,253
Area: 116 sq. mi. (300 sq km)
Language: Maldivian Dhivehi,
English
Money: Rufiyaa
Government: Republic

CHECK IT OUT

About 1,000 of the 1,190 coral islands that make up Maldives, located south of India in the Indian Ocean, are uninhabited.

MALI

Capital: Bamako
Population: 16,955,536
Area: 478,767 sq. mi.
(1,240,000 sq km)
Language: French, Bambara,
numerous African languages
Money: CFA franc
Government: Republic

CHECK IT OUT

Most of Mali's people make their living farming or fishing around the Niger River.

MALTA

Capital: Valletta
Population: 413,965
Area: 122 sq. mi. (316 sq km)
Language: Maltese, English
Money: Euro
Government: Republic

CHECK IT OUT

This group of islands in the Mediterranean Sea south of Sicily has one of the world's healthiest populations. The average life expectancy is over 79 years.

MARSHALL ISLANDS

Capital: Majuro
Population: 72,191
Area: 70 sq. mi. (181 sq km)
Language: Marshallese, English
Money: US dollar
Government: Constitutional government in free association with the United States

CHECK IT OUT

The first hydrogen bomb was exploded in the Marshall Islands in 1952. Radiation levels in some areas are still high, but improving through environmental cleanup programs.

MAURITANIA

Capital: Nouakchott
Population: 3,596,702
Area: 397,955 sq. mi. (1,030,700 sq km)
Language: Arabic, Pulaar, Soninke, Wolof, French
Money: Ouguiya
Government: Military junta

CHECK IT OUT

This western African nation has it together! It's a major producer of gum arabic, used to make glue.

MAURITIUS

Capital: Port Louis
Population: 1,339,827
Area: 788 sq. mi. (2,040 sq km)
Language: Creole, Bhojpuri, French
Money: Rupee
Government: Parliamentary democracy

CHECK IT OUT

Mauritius has the second-highest per-person income in Africa. Most of the country's money comes from sugarcane.

MEXICO

Capital: Mexico City
Population: 121,736,809
Area: 761,606 sq. mi. (1,972,550 sq km)
Language: Spanish, various Mayan, Nahuati, other regional indigenous dialects
Money: Peso
Government: Federal republic

CHECK IT OUT

Mexico has dozens of bullfighting rings, including one that holds 50,000 people—about the entire population of Biloxi, Mississippi.

MICRONESIA

Capital: Palikir
Population: 105,216
Area: 271 sq. mi. (702 sq km)
Language: English, Chuukese, Kosrean, Pohnpeian, Yapese
Money: US dollar
Government: Constitutional government in free association with the United States

CHECK IT OUT

Micronesia's first settlers have been traced back more than 4,000 years.

MOLDOVA

Capital: Chisinau
Population: 3,546,847
Area: 13,067 sq. mi. (333,843 sq km)
Language: Moldovan, Russian, Gagauz
Money: Leu
Government: Republic

CHECK IT OUT

Moldova was the first former Soviet state to elect a Communist as president.

MONACO

Capital: Monaco
Population: 30,535
Area: 0.75 sq. mi. (1.95 sq km)
Language: French, English, Italian, Monegasque
Money: Euro
Government: Constitutional monarchy

CHECK IT OUT

Mini-sized Monaco covers about as much area as New York City's Central Park.

MONGOLIA

Capital: Ulan Bator
Population: 2,992,908
Area: 603,909 sq. mi. (1,564,116 sq km)
Language: Khalka Mongol, Turkic, Russian
Money: Togrog/Tughrik
Government: Mixed parliamentary/presidential

CHECK IT OUT

Mongolia's average population density is only 5 people per square mile (1.9 per sq km), although many people live in the cities.

MONTENEGRO

Capital: Podgorica
Population: 647,073
Area: 5,415 sq. mi. (14,026 sq km)
Language: Montenegrin, Serbian, Bosnian, Albanian, Croatian
Money: Euro
Government: Republic

CHECK IT OUT

Montenegro's name means "black mountain." The name comes from the dark forests on the mountains that once covered most of the country.

MOROCCO

Capital: Rabat
Population: 33,322,699
Area: 172,414 sq. mi. (446,550 sq km)
Language: Arabic, Berber dialects, French
Money: Dirham
Government: Constitutional monarchy

CHECK IT OUT

Morocco is a North African country about the size of California. Part of it is covered by the Sahara Desert, whose 3,500,000 square miles (9,064,958 sq km) make it the largest desert in the world.

MOZAMBIQUE

Capital: Maputo
Population: 25,303,113
Area: 309,496 sq. mi. (801,590 sq km)
Language: Portuguese, Emakhuwa, Xichangana, Elomwe, Cisena
Money: Metical
Government: Republic

CHECK IT OUT

Portuguese is the official language of Mozambique. However, most residents, who are of African descent, speak a form of Bantu.

NAMIBIA

Capital: Windhoek
Population: 2,212,307
Area: 318,696 sq. mi. (825,418 sq km)
Language: Afrikaans, German, English, other indigenous languages
Money: Dollar, South African rand
Government: Republic

CHECK IT OUT

Namibia's rich diamond deposits have made it one of the world's best sources of high-quality diamonds.

NAURU

Capital: Yaren
Population: 9,540
Area: 8 sq. mi. (21 sq km)
Language: Nauruan, English
Money: Australian dollar
Government: Republic

CHECK IT OUT

Nauru joined the United Nations in 1999 as the world's smallest independent republic.

NEPAL

Capital: Kathmandu
Population: 31,551,305
Area: 56,827 sq. mi. (147,181 sq km)
Language: Nepali, Maithali, English
Money: Rupee
Government: Federal democratic republic

CHECK IT OUT

Eight of the world's ten highest mountain peaks are in Nepal, including Mount Everest, the highest of them all—29,035 feet (8,850 m).

NETHERLANDS

Capital: Amsterdam
Population: 16,947,904
Area: 16,033 sq. mi. (41,526 sq km)
Language: Dutch, Frisian
Money: Euro
Government: Constitutional monarchy

CHECK IT OUT

Most Netherlanders dress in modern clothing, but many farmers say wooden shoes, known as *klompen*, keep feet drier.

NEW ZEALAND

Capital: Wellington
Population: 4,438,393
Area: 103,738 sq. mi. (268,680 sq km)
Language: English, Maori, sign language
Money: Dollar
Government: Parliamentary democracy

CHECK IT OUT

New Zealand was settled by the Polynesian Maori in 800 CE. Today Maori make up about 9.38 percent of the country's population.

NICARAGUA

Capital: Managua
Population: 5,907,881
Area: 49,998 sq. mi. (129,494 sq km)
Language: Spanish, English, indigenous languages on Atlantic coast
Money: Gold cordoba
Government: Republic

CHECK IT OUT

Nicaragua got its name from Nicarao, a tribal chief who lived and reigned here in the 16th century.

NIGER

Capital: Niamey
Population: 18,045,729
Area: 489,191 sq. mi.
(1,267,000 sq km)
Language: French, Hausa, Djerma
Money: CFA franc
Government: Republic

CHECK IT OUT

Niger is known as the Frying Pan of the World. It can get hot enough to make raindrops evaporate before they hit the ground.

NIGERIA

Capital: Abuja
Population: 181,562,056
Area: 356,669 sq. mi.
(923,768 sq km)
Language: English, Hausa, Yoruba, Igbo, Fulani
Money: Naira
Government: Federal republic

CHECK IT OUT

Nigeria is the most heavily populated country in Africa. More than half the continent's people live there.

NORWAY

Capital: Oslo
Population: 5,207,689
Area: 125,021 sq. mi.
(323,802 sq km)
Language: Bokmal Norwegian, Nynorsk Norwegian, Sami
Money: Krone
Government: Constitutional monarchy

CHECK IT OUT

Moving glaciers during the Ice Age left Norway with a jagged coastline marked by long strips of water-filled fjords and thousands of islands.

OMAN

Capital: Muscat
Population: 3,286,936
Area: 82,031 sq. mi.
(212,460 sq km)
Language: Arabic, English, Baluchi, Urdu, Indian dialects
Money: Rial
Government: Monarchy

CHECK IT OUT

Members of the Al Bu Said family have ruled Oman for more than 250 years.

PAKISTAN

Capital: Islamabad
Population: 199,085,847
Area: 310,403 sq. mi.
(803,940 sq km)
Language: English, Urdu, Punjabi, Sindhi, Siraiki, Pashtu
Money: Rupee
Government: Federal republic

CHECK IT OUT

Pakistan is the sixth most heavily populated country in the world. The others, in order, are China, India, the United States, Indonesia, and Brazil.

PALAU

Capital: Melekeok
Population: 21,265
Area: 177 sq. mi. (458 sq km)
Language: English, Palauan, various Asian languages
Money: US dollar
Government: Constitutional government in free association with the United States

CHECK IT OUT

In March 2008, thousands of human bones, some of them ancient and very small, were found by scientists in Palau.

PANAMA

Capital: Panama City
Population: 3,657,024
Area: 30,193 sq. mi. (78,200 sq km)
Language: Spanish, English
Money: Balboa
Government: Constitutional democracy

CHECK IT OUT

Spain was the first country to think of cutting a canal across the Isthmus of Panama. The French started building the 51-mile-long (82 km) canal in 1881 and the United States finished it in 1914.

PAPUA NEW GUINEA

Capital: Port Moresby
Population: 6,672,429
Area: 178,704 sq. mi. (462,840 sq km)
Language: Melanesian Pidgin, English, 820 indigenous languages
Money: Kina
Government: Constitutional parliamentary democracy

CHECK IT OUT

Living in Papua New Guinea means coping with the constant threat of active volcanoes, frequent earthquakes, mud slides, and tsunamis.

PARAGUAY

Capital: Asuncíon
Population: 6,783,272
Area: 157,047 sq. mi. (406,750 sq km)
Language: Spanish, Guarani
Money: Guarani
Government: Constitutional republic

CHECK IT OUT

Paraguay's got the power! Hydroelectric dams, including the largest one in the world, keep the country well supplied with electricity.

PERU

Capital: Lima
Population: 30,444,999
Area: 496,226 sq. mi. (1,285,220 sq km)
Language: Spanish, Quechua, Aymara, numerous minor languages
Money: Nuevo sol
Government: Constitutional republic

CHECK IT OUT

The third-largest country in South America (after Brazil and Argentina), Peru is three times as big as California but has only two-thirds of that state's population.

PHILIPPINES

Capital: Manila
Population: 109,615,913
Area: 115,831 sq. mi. (300,000 sq km)
Language: Filipino, English, 8 major dialects
Money: Peso
Government: Republic

CHECK IT OUT

Almost half of all working Filipinos earn their living by farming, although the farmland itself is owned by a wealthy few.

POLAND

Capital: Warsaw
Population: 38,301,885
Area: 120,726 sq. mi. (312,679 sq km)
Language: Polish
Money: Zloty
Government: Republic

CHECK IT OUT

Physicist Marie Curie and composer Frederic Chopin are just two of the many world-famous people who came from Poland.

Machu Picchu, Peru →

Countries of the World

PORTUGAL

Capital: Lisbon
Population: 10,825,309
Area: 35,672 sq. mi. (92,391 sq km)
Language: Portuguese, Mirandese
Money: Euro
Government: Republic, parliamentary democracy

CHECK IT OUT

The national music of Portugal is called *fado*. The songs are often sad but can also be funny.

QATAR

Capital: Doha
Population: 2,194,817
Area: 4,416 sq. mi. (11,437 sq km)
Language: Arabic, English
Money: Rial
Government: Emirate

CHECK IT OUT

Qatar is only about as big as Los Angeles County, California, but it holds more than 15 percent of the world's gas reserves.

ROMANIA

Capital: Bucharest
Population: 21,666,350
Area: 91,699 sq. mi. (237,500 sq km)
Language: Romanian, Hungarian, Romany (Gypsy)
Money: New leu
Government: Republic

CHECK IT OUT

Cruel 15th-century Romanian prince Vlad Tepes was the model for the horror novel *Dracula*. One of Vlad's homes, Bran Castle, is Romania's most popular tourist attraction.

RUSSIA

Capital: Moscow
Population: 142,423,773
Area: 6,592,772 sq. mi. (17,075,200 sq km)
Language: Russian, many minority languages
Money: Ruble
Government: Federation

CHECK IT OUT

Russia is the largest country in the world and contains the ninth-largest population. It was formerly the center of the Union of Soviet Socialist Republics (USSR), which broke up into 15 separate states in 1991.

RWANDA

Capital: Kigali
Population: 12,661,733
Area: 10,169 sq. mi. (26,338 sq km)
Language: Kinyarwanda, French, English, Swahili
Money: Franc
Government: Republic, presidential-multiparty system

CHECK IT OUT

Rwanda leads the world in terms of female representation in its parliamentary body. Roughly half of its legislators are women.

SAINT KITTS and NEVIS

Capital: Basseterre
Population: 51,936
Area: 101 sq. mi. (261 sq km)
Language: English
Money: Dollar
Government: Parliamentary democracy

CHECK IT OUT

These two Caribbean islands have been a single state since 1983.

SAINT LUCIA

Capital: Castries
Population: 163,922
Area: 238 sq. mi. (616 sq km)
Language: English, French patois
Money: Dollar
Government: Parliamentary democracy

CHECK IT OUT

This small Caribbean island changed hands between France and England 14 times before being given to the United Kingdom in 1814. It became independent in 1979.

SAINT VINCENT and the GRENADINES

Capital: Kingstown
Population: 102,627
Area: 150 sq. mi. (389 sq km)
Language: English, French patois
Money: Dollar
Government: Parliamentary democracy

CHECK IT OUT

These islands are the world's leading suppliers of arrowroot, which is used to thicken fruit pie fillings and sauces.

SAMOA

Capital: Apia
Population: 197,773
Area: 1,137 sq. mi. (2,944 sq km)
Language: Samoan, English
Money: Tala
Government: Parliamentary democracy

CHECK IT OUT

Author Robert Louis Stevenson (*Treasure Island*, *Kidnapped*) lived in Samoa from 1890 until he died in 1894. His Polynesian neighbors called him *Tusitala*, or "Storyteller."

SAN MARINO

Capital: San Marino
Population: 33,020
Area: 24 sq. mi. (61 sq km)
Language: Italian
Money: Euro
Government: Republic

CHECK IT OUT

San Marino, in central Italy, is the third-smallest state in Europe. Some historians say it was founded in 301 CE, making it the world's oldest republic.

SÃO TOMÉ and PRINCIPE

Capital: São Tomé
Population: 194,006
Area: 387 sq. mi. (1,001 sq km)
Language: Portuguese
Money: Dobra
Government: Republic

CHECK IT OUT

São Tomé and Principe are the two largest islands in an African island group in the Gulf of Guinea.

SAUDI ARABIA

Capital: Riyadh
Population: 27,752,316
Area: 830,000 sq. mi. (2,149,690 sq km)
Language: Arabic
Money: Riyal
Government: Monarchy

CHECK IT OUT

Saudi Arabia is known as the birthplace of Islam.

SENEGAL

Capital: Dakar
Population: 13,975,834
Area: 75,749 sq. mi. (196,190 sq km)
Language: French, Wolof, Pulaar, Jola, Mandinka
Money: CFA Franc
Government: Republic

CHECK IT OUT

Senegal's economy depends on peanuts. In recent years the country has produced more than 800,000 tons of them, 95 percent for oil.

SERBIA

Capital: Belgrade
Population: 7,176,794
Area: 29,913 sq. mi. (77,474 sq km)
Language: Serbian, Hungarian
Money: Dinar
Government: Republic

CHECK IT OUT

Favorite foods in Serbia are *cevacici*, a grilled meatball sandwich with raw onions, and *burek*, a pastry layered with cheese, meat, or jam.

SEYCHELLES

Capital: Victoria
Population: 92,430
Area: 176 sq. mi. (455 sq km)
Language: Creole, English
Money: Rupee
Government: Republic

CHECK IT OUT

From the early 1500s to the 1700s, Seychelles was a popular pirate hideout.

SIERRA LEONE

Capital: Freetown
Population: 5,879,098
Area: 27,699 sq. mi. (71,740 sq km)
Language: English, Mende and Temne vernaculars, Krio (English-based Creole)
Money: Leone
Government: Constitutional democracy

CHECK IT OUT

Sierra Leone is one of the wettest places in western Africa. Rainfall can reach 195 inches (495 cm) a year.

SINGAPORE

Capital: Singapore
Population: 5,674,472
Area: 269 sq. mi. (697 sq km)
Language: Mandarin, English, Malay, Hokkien, Cantonese, Teochew
Money: Dollar
Government: Republic

CHECK IT OUT

Singapore is a city-state—an independent state made up of a city and the areas around it. It is an important international business center with one of the busiest harbors in the world.

SLOVAKIA

Capital: Bratislava
Population: 5,495,998
Area: 18,859 sq. mi. (48,845 sq km)
Language: Slovak, Hungarian
Money: Koruna
Government: Parliamentary democracy

CHECK IT OUT

Following World War I, Slovaks and Czechs were joined into a single nation: Czechoslovakia. But in 1993 Czechoslovakia redivided into Slovakia and the Czech Republic.

SLOVENIA

Capital: Ljubljana
Population: 1,983,412
Area: 7,827 sq. mi. (20,273 sq km)
Language: Slovenian, Serbo-Croatian
Money: Euro
Government: Parliamentary democracy

CHECK IT OUT

Big puddles and small lakes can appear and disappear suddenly in Slovenia because of underground caves and channels.

SOLOMON ISLANDS

Capital: Honiara
Population: 622,469
Area: 10,985 sq. mi. (28,450 sq km)
Language: English, Melanesian pidgin, 120 indigenous languages
Money: Dollar
Government: Parliamentary democracy

CHECK IT OUT

On April 1, 2007, a massive underwater earthquake triggered a tsunami that caused widespread destruction in the Solomon Islands.

SOMALIA

Capital: Mogadishu
Population: 10,616,380
Area: 246,201 sq. mi. (637,657 sq km)
Language: English, Arabic, Italian
Money: Shilling
Government: In transition

CHECK IT OUT

Each point of the flag's white star stands for a region of Somalia.

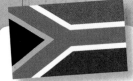

SOUTH AFRICA

Capital: Pretoria (administrative), Cape Town (legislative), Bloemfontein (judicial)
Population: 48,286,277
Area: 471,011 sq. mi. (1,219,912 sq km)
Language: IsiZulu, IsiXhosa, Afrikaans, English, Sepedi, Setswana, Sesotho
Money: Rand
Government: Republic

CHECK IT OUT

South Africa is in a subtropical location—so how come penguins thrive there? The penguins' breeding grounds are cooled by Antarctic Ocean currents on the west coast.

SOUTH SUDAN

Capital: Juba
Population: 12,042,910
Area: 248,777 sq. mi. (644,329 sq km)
Language: English, Arabic, Dinka, Nuer, Bari, Zande, Shilluk
Money: South Sudanese pound
Government: Republic

CHECK IT OUT

South Sudan won its independence from Sudan on July 9, 2011. Its national anthem, "South Sudan Oyee! (Hooray!)," was written by a group of 49 students, poets, and teachers.

SPAIN

Capital: Madrid
Population: 48,146,134
Area: 194,897 sq. mi. (504,782 sq km)
Language: Castilian Spanish, Catalan, Galician, Basque
Money: Euro
Government: Parliamentary monarchy

CHECK IT OUT

Spain's capital city is in almost the exact center of the country.

SRI LANKA

Capital: Colombo
Population: 22,053,488
Area: 25,332 sq. mi. (65,610 sq km)
Language: Sinhala, Tamil, English
Money: Rupee
Government: Republic

! CHECK IT OUT

Once named Ceylon, Sri Lanka was an important port in the ancient world. Arab traders called it Serendip, the origin of the word *serendipity*, which means "a pleasing chance discovery."

SUDAN

Capital: Khartoum
Population: 36,108,853
Area: 718,723 sq. mi. (1,861,484 sq km)
Language: Arabic, Nubian, Ta Bedawie, Nilotic, Nilo-Hamitic, Sudanic dialects, English
Money: Pound
Government: Power sharing, with military dominant (elections in April 2010)

! CHECK IT OUT

Two branches of the Nile River, the White Nile and the Blue Nile, meet in Khartoum to form the main Nile River corridor.

SURINAME

Capital: Paramaribo
Population: 579,633
Area: 63,039 sq. mi. (163,270 sq km)
Language: Dutch, English, Sranang Tongo, Caribbean Hindustani, Javanese
Money: Dollar
Government: Constitutional democracy

! CHECK IT OUT

Suriname is the smallest independent country in South America. It could fit into Brazil, its massive neighbor to the south, 52 times.

SWAZILAND

Capital: Mbabane
Population: 1,435,613
Area: 6,704 sq. mi. (17,363 sq km)
Language: English, siSwati
Money: Lilangeni
Government: Monarchy

! CHECK IT OUT

Other parts of southern Africa suffer from drought, but four major rivers—the Komati, the Umbuluzi, the Ingwavuma, and the Great Usutu—keep Swaziland's water supply healthy.

SWEDEN

Capital: Stockholm
Population: 9,801,616
Area: 173,732 sq. mi. (449,964 sq km)
Language: Swedish, Finnish, Sami
Money: Krona
Government: Constitutional monarchy

! CHECK IT OUT

Sweden has an army, navy, and air force, but its military can only be used in peacekeeping actions, not wars.

SWITZERLAND

Capital: Bern
Population: 8,121,830
Area: 15,942 sq. mi. (41,290 sq km)
Language: German, French, Italian, Romansch
Money: Franc
Government: Federal republic-like confederation

! CHECK IT OUT

Switzerland's famous flag comes in two shapes. A square version is flown on land and a rectangular flag (like the one above) is flown at sea.

SYRIA

Capital: Damascus
Population: 22,878,524
Area: 71,498 sq. mi. (185,180 sq km)
Language: Arabic, Kurdish, Armenian, Aramaic, Circassian
Money: Pound
Government: Republic (under military regime)

! CHECK IT OUT

In 2008, archaeologists excavating in the Syrian desert dug up a camel jawbone they said could be a million years old.

TAIWAN

Capital: Taipei
Population: 23,415,126
Area: 13,892 sq. mi. (35,980 sq km)
Language: Mandarin, Taiwanese, Hakka
Money: Dollar (yuan)
Government: Multiparty democracy

CHECK IT OUT

Taiwan's Palace Museum's collection of Chinese bronze, jade, calligraphy, painting, and porcelain is so big that only 1 percent of it is displayed at any one time.

TAJIKISTAN

Capital: Dushanbe
Population: 8,191,958
Area: 55,251 sq. mi. (143,100 sq km)
Language: Tajik, Russian
Money: Somoni
Government: Republic

CHECK IT OUT

When mountainous Tajikistan became independent after the breakup of the Soviet Union, it inherited a mountain called Communism Peak. The Tajiks quickly changed the name to Imeni Ismail Samani Peak.

TANZANIA

Capital: Dodoma
Population: 51,045,882
Area: 364,900 sq. mi. (945,087 sq km)
Language: Kiswahili, English, Arabic, many local languages
Money: Shilling
Government: Republic

CHECK IT OUT

Africa's highest mountain, 19,340-foot-high (5,895 m) Mount Kilimanjaro, is in Tanzania. Lions, elephants, giraffes, and other animals roam free, protected by the government, in Serengeti Park.

THAILAND

Capital: Bangkok
Population: 67,976,405
Area: 198,457 sq. mi. (514,000 sq km)
Language: Thai, English, other ethnic languages
Money: Baht
Government: Constitutional monarchy

CHECK IT OUT

Formerly Siam, this Southeast Asian country has contributed Thai food, kickboxing, and the musical *The King and I* to world culture—among many other things.

TIMOR-LESTE

Capital: Dili
Population: 1,231,116
Area: 5,794 sq. mi. (15,007 sq km)
Language: Tetum, Portuguese, Indonesian, English
Money: US dollar
Government: Republic

CHECK IT OUT

Timor-Leste is a really young nation. It became independent amid protests in 1999, and in 2007 it held largely peaceful presidential and parliamentary elections for the first time.

TOGO

Capital: Lomé
Population: 7,552,318
Area: 21,925 sq. mi. (56,785 sq km)
Language: French, Ewe, Mina, Kabye, Dagomba
Money: CFA franc
Government: Republic (under transition to multiparty democratic rule)

CHECK IT OUT

Watch your step! Poisonous vipers—cobras, pythons, and green and black mambas—are abundant here. So are scorpions and spiders.

TONGA

Capital: Nuku'alofa
Population: 106,501
Area: 289 sq. mi. (748 sq km)
Language: Tongan, English
Money: Pa'anga
Government: Constitutional monarchy

CHECK IT OUT

Tonga, an archipelago of about 150 islands east of Australia, is the last remaining monarchy in the Pacific.

TRINIDAD and TOBAGO

Capital: Port of Spain
Population: 1,222,363
Area: 1,980 sq. mi. (5,128 sq km)
Language: English, Caribbean Hindustani, French, Spanish, Chinese
Money: Dollar
Government: Parliamentary democracy

CHECK IT OUT

Native animals include the quenck, a kind of wild hog, and the agouti, a rabbitlike rodent. Howler monkeys are also native, but increasing development has made them rare.

TUNISIA

Capital: Tunis
Population: 11,037,225
Area: 63,170 sq. mi. (163,610 sq km)
Language: Arabic, French
Money: Dinar
Government: Republic

CHECK IT OUT

Every Star Wars movie but one was filmed in Tunisia. So was *Indiana Jones: Raiders of the Lost Ark.*

TURKEY

Capital: Ankara
Population: 82,523,053
Area: 301,384 sq. mi. (780,580 sq km)
Language: Turkish, Kurdish, Dimli
Money: New lira
Government: Republican parliamentary democracy

CHECK IT OUT

Turkey gave the world the man who would become Santa Claus: St. Nicholas, a fourth-century bishop.

TURKMENISTAN

Capital: Ashgabat
Population: 5,231,422
Area: 188,456 sq. mi. (488,100 sq km)
Language: Turkmen, Russian, Uzbek
Money: Manat
Government: Republic under authoritarian presidential rule

CHECK IT OUT

Turkmenistan's stunning flag incorporates five traditional carpet designs. Each design is associated with a particular tribe.

TUVALU

Capital: Funafuti
Population: 10,869
Area: 10 sq. mi. (26 sq km)
Language: Tuvaluan, English, Samoan
Money: Australian dollar
Government: Constitutional monarchy with parliamentary democracy

CHECK IT OUT

Tuvalu is made up of nine coral atolls in the South Pacific. Eight are inhabited. The word *tuvalu* means "group of eight."

UGANDA

Capital: Kampala
Population: 37,101,745
Area: 91,136 sq. mi.
(236,040 sq km)
Language: English, Ganda,
Luganda
Money: Shilling
Government: Republic

CHECK IT OUT

Ugandans speak in more than 42 different dialects. In fact, no single language is understood by all Ugandans.

UKRAINE

Capital: Kyiv (Kiev)
Population: 44,008,507
Area: 233,090 sq. mi.
(603,700 sq km)
Language: Ukrainian,
Russian, Romanian, Polish,
Hungarian
Money: Hryvnia
Government: Republic

CHECK IT OUT

Ukraine is the largest country completely landlocked within Europe.

UNITED ARAB EMIRATES

Capital: Abu Dhabi
Population: 5,779,760
Area: 32,278 sq. mi.
(83,600 sq km)
Language: Arabic, Persian,
English, Hindi, Urdu
Money: Dirham
Government: Federation of
emirates

CHECK IT OUT

The United Arab Emirates consists of seven independent Arab states in southwestern Asia. City dwellers live in modern buildings. Country people live in huts, and most wear long robes. Nomadic tribes roam the desert regions with camels, goats, and sheep.

UNITED KINGDOM

Capital: London
Population: 64,088,222
Area: 94,526 sq. mi.
(244,820 sq km)
Language: English, Welsh,
Scottish form of Gaelic
Money: Pound
Government:
Constitutional monarchy

CHECK IT OUT

Today the United Kingdom (UK) consists of England, Scotland, Wales, and Northern Ireland. At one time the British Empire extended to five other continents.

UNITED STATES

Capital: Washington, DC
Population: 321,362,789
Area: 3,794,083 sq. mi.
(9,826,630 sq km)
Language: English, Spanish,
Hawaiian, other minority languages
Money: Dollar
Government: Federal republic
with strong democratic tradition

CHECK IT OUT

What is now the United States was the first European colony to become independent from its motherland (England).

URUGUAY

Capital: Montevideo
Population: 3,341,893
Area: 68,039 sq. mi. (176,220 sq km)
Language: Spanish, Portunol,
Brazilero
Money: Peso
Government: Constitutional
republic

CHECK IT OUT

Uruguay's name comes from a Guarani word meaning "river of painted birds."

UZBEKISTAN

Capital: Tashkent
Population: 29,199,942
Area: 172,742 sq. mi.
(447,400 sq km)
Language: Uzbek, Russian, Tajik
Money: Som
Government: Republic with
authoritarian presidential rule

CHECK IT OUT

The cities of Uzbekistan—Samarkand, Bukhara, and Khiva—were well-traveled centers on the Silk Road, an ancient trade route linking Asia to Europe.

Countries of the World

VANUATU

Capital: Port-Vila
Population: 272,264
Area: 4,710 sq. mi. (12,200 sq km)
Language: Bislama, English, French, 100 local languages
Money: Vatu
Government: Parliamentary republic

CHECK IT OUT
Vanuatu is not just one island but more than 80 volcanic islands in a South Pacific archipelago.

VENEZUELA

Capital: Caracas
Population: 29,275,460
Area: 352,144 sq. mi. (912,050 sq km)
Language: Spanish, indigenous dialects
Money: Bolivar Fuerte
Government: Federal republic

CHECK IT OUT
Venezuela is home to the largest rodents in the world—the capybaras. They measure up to 4.3 feet (1.3 m) long and weigh up to 140 pounds (about 64 kg).

VIETNAM

Capital: Hanoi
Population: 94,348,835
Area: 127,244 sq. mi. (329,560 sq km)
Language: Vietnamese, English, French, Chinese, Khmer
Money: Dong
Government: Communist state

CHECK IT OUT
Vietnam is shaped like a long, skinny 5. It measures 1,031 miles (1,650 km) from north to south, but at its narrowest point is only 31 miles (50 km) across.

YEMEN

Capital: Sanaa
Population: 26,737,317
Area: 203,850 sq. mi. (527,970 sq km)
Language: Arabic
Money: Rial
Government: Republic

CHECK IT OUT
According to legend, coffee was discovered by a goat herder who noticed his goats got livelier after eating berries from a certain plant. The plant was brought to Yemen, where it was developed into a drink.

ZAMBIA

Capital: Lusaka
Population: 15,066,266
Area: 290,586 sq. mi. (752,614 sq km)
Language: English, numerous vernaculars
Money: Kwacha
Government: Republic

CHECK IT OUT
One of the world's highest waterfalls, the Victoria Falls is created by the Zambezi River tumbling over cliffs between Zambia and Zimbabwe. The waterfall is twice as high as Niagara Falls.

ZIMBABWE

Capital: Harare
Population: 14,229,541
Area: 150,804 sq. mi. (390,580 sq km)
Language: English, Shona, Sindebele, minor tribal dialects
Money: Dollar
Government: Parliamentary democracy

CHECK IT OUT
Zimbabwe means "stone house." Ruins of the stone palaces of African kings can be seen in many parts of the country.

FLAGS & FACTS
States OF THE UNITED STATES

In One Way, the United States Is a Monarch-y

The beautiful orange-and-black monarch butterfly* is so beloved in America that seven states have named it either their state insect or butterfly: Alabama, Idaho, Illinois, Minnesota, Texas, Vermont, and West Virginia. The tiger swallowtail is the next most popular. However, the bug with the biggest fan club is the busy honeybee. Seventeen states recognize it as an official state insect.

In this chapter, you will learn which state is called the Last Frontier, and which is nicknamed the Empire State and the Empire State of the South. You'll find out which state was home to the most US presidents and where you will find more mammal species than anywhere else in the country. Check out the fascinating facts about the Fabulous 50!

* Recently there have been signs that the monarch is in trouble, possibly because of loss of habitat. See p. 53 for ways you can help.

YOUR TURN

Did you know that most states have state fossils or dinosaurs? That Texas, Oklahoma, and Virginia have a state bat? Dig deep into even more fun state facts at statesymbolsusa.org.

Which is the state bird in seven states? (See pp.128-145.)

Alaska

Juneau

⊙ Olympia
Washington

⊙ Salem

Oregon

Montana

Helena ⊙

Idaho

⊙ Boise

North Dakota

⊙ Bismarck

South Dakota

Pierre ⊙

Wyoming

Cheyenne ⊙

Sacramento ⊙ Carson City

Nevada

Salt Lake City ⊙

Utah

California

Colorado

Denver ⊙

Nebraska

Lincoln ⊙

Topeka ⊙

Kansas

Arizona

Phoenix ⊙

Santa Fe ⊙

New Mexico

Oklahoma

Oklahoma City ⊙

Texas

Austin ⊙

Honolulu ⊙

Hawaii

US States and Their Capital Cities

New Hampshire

Maine

Vermont

Augusta ⊙

Concord ⊙

Montpelier ⊙

Massachusetts

Albany ⊙

Boston ⊙

nesota

New York

Providence ⊙

St. Paul ⊙

Wisconsin

Michigan

Hartford ⊙

Rhode Island

Madison ⊙

Lansing ⊙

Connecticut

Pennsylvania

Trenton ⊙

Iowa

Harrisburg ⊙

New Jersey

Ohio

Dover ⊙

Des Moines ⊙

Indiana

Columbus ⊙

West Virginia

Delaware

Illinois

★ Annapolis

Springfield ⊙

Indianapolis ⊙

Maryland

Richmond ⊙

Jefferson City ⊙

Charleston ⊙

Washington, DC

Missouri

Frankfort ⊙

Virginia

Kentucky

Raleigh ⊙

Nashville ⊙

North Carolina

Arkansas

Tennessee

Columbia

Little Rock ⊙

Atlanta ⊙

South Carolina

Mississippi

Alabama

Jackson ⊙

Montgomery ⊙

Georgia

Louisiana

Baton Rouge ⊙

Tallahassee ⊙

Florida

State Quarters by Release Date (and Statehood Dates)

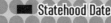 ■ Release Date   ■ Statehood Date

Delaware
January 4, 1999
December 7, 1787

Pennsylvania
March 8, 1999
December 12, 1787

New Jersey
May 17, 1999
December 18, 1787

Georgia
July 19, 1999
January 2, 1788

Connecticut
October 12, 1999
January 9, 1788

Massachusetts
January 3, 2000
February 6, 1788

Maryland
March 13, 2000
April 28, 1788

South Carolina
May 22, 2000
May 23, 1788

New Hampshire
August 7, 2000
June 21, 1788

Virginia
October 16, 2000
June 25, 1788

New York
January 2, 2001
July 26, 1788

North Carolina
March 12, 2001
November 21, 1789

Rhode Island
May 21, 2001
May 29, 1790

Vermont
August 6, 2001
March 4, 1791

Kentucky
October 15, 2001
June 1, 1792

Tennessee
January 2, 2002
June 1, 1796

Ohio
March 11, 2002
March 1, 1803

Louisiana
May 20, 2002
April 30, 1812

Indiana
August 2, 2002
December 11, 1816

Mississippi
October 15, 2002
December 10, 1817

Illinois
January 2, 2003
December 3, 1818

Alabama
March 17, 2003
December 14, 1819

Maine
June 2, 2003
March 15, 1820

Missouri
August 4, 2003
August 10, 1821

Arkansas
October 20, 2003
June 15, 1836

States of the United States

126

■ Release Date   ■ Statehood Date

Michigan
January 26, 2004
January 26, 1837

Florida
March 29, 2004
March 3, 1845

Texas
June 1, 2004
December 29, 1845

Iowa
August 30, 2004
December 28, 1846

Wisconsin
October 25, 2004
May 29, 1848

California
January 31, 2005
September 9, 1850

Minnesota
April 4, 2005
May 11, 1858

Oregon
June 6, 2005
February 14, 1859

Kansas
August 29, 2005
January 29, 1861

West Virginia
October 14, 2005
June 20, 1863

Nevada
January 31, 2006
October 31, 1864

Nebraska
April 3, 2006
March 1, 1867

Colorado
June 14, 2006
August 1, 1876

North Dakota
August 28, 2006
November 2, 1889

South Dakota
November 6, 2006
November 2, 1889

Montana
January 29, 2007
November 8, 1889

Washington
April 2, 2007
November 11, 1889

Idaho
June 4, 2007
July 3, 1890

Wyoming
September 3, 2007
July 10, 1890

Utah
November 5, 2007
January 4, 1896

Oklahoma
January 28, 2008
November 16, 1907

New Mexico
April 7, 2008
January 6, 1912

Arizona
June 2, 2008
February 14, 1912

Alaska
August 25, 2008
January 3, 1959

Hawaii
November 3, 2008
August 21, 1959

ALABAMA

Capital: Montgomery
Postal Code: AL
Nickname: Heart of Dixie
Flower: Camellia
Bird: Yellowhammer
Area: 52,420 sq. mi. (135,768 sq km)
Population: 4,833,722

CHECK IT OUT

Huntsville, Alabama, is the site where the first rocket that took people to the Moon was built.

ALASKA

Capital: Juneau
Postal Code: AK
Nickname: Last Frontier
Flower: Forget-me-not
Bird: Willow ptarmigan
Area: 664,988 sq. mi. (1,722,319 sq km)
Population: 735,132

CHECK IT OUT

Woolly mammoth remains have been found in Alaska's frozen ground.

ARIZONA

Capital: Phoenix
Postal Code: AZ
Nickname: Grand Canyon State
Flower: Saguaro cactus blossom
Bird: Cactus wren
Area: 113,990 sq. mi. (295,235 sq km)
Population: 6,626,624

CHECK IT OUT

There are more species of hummingbirds in Arizona than in any other state.

ARKANSAS

Capital: Little Rock
Postal Code: AR
Nickname: Land of Opportunity
Flower: Apple blossom
Bird: Mockingbird
Area: 53,178 sq. mi. (137,732 sq km)
Population: 2,959,373

CHECK IT OUT

Stuttgart, Arkansas, is home to the annual World's Championship Duck Calling Contest.

CALIFORNIA

Capital: Sacramento
Postal Code: CA
Nickname: Golden State
Flower: Golden poppy
Bird: California quail
Area: 163,694 sq. mi. (423,967 sq km)
Population: 38,332,521

CHECK IT OUT

The highest and lowest points in the continental United States are in California—Mount Whitney (14,494 ft./4,418 m) and Badwater in Death Valley (282 ft./86 m below sea level).

COLORADO

Capital: Denver
Postal Code: CO
Nickname: Centennial State
Flower: Rocky Mountain columbine
Bird: Lark bunting
Area: 104,094 sq. mi. (269,604 sq km)
Population: 5,268,367

CHECK IT OUT

The streets in Victor, Colorado, were actually paved in a low grade of gold back in 1890 to make use of the low-quality ore that couldn't be refined.

DECEMBER 7, 1787

CONNECTICUT

Capital: Hartford
Postal Code: CT
Nickname: Constitution State
Flower: Mountain laurel
Bird: American robin
Area: 5,544 sq. mi. (14,358 sq km)
Population: 3,596,080

CHECK IT OUT

America's first newspaper, the *Hartford Courant*, was printed in 1764 in Connecticut.

DELAWARE

Capital: Dover
Postal Code: DE
Nickname: First State
Flower: Peach blossom
Bird: Blue hen chicken
Area: 2,489 sq. mi. (6,445 sq km)
Population: 925,749

CHECK IT OUT

Delaware was the first state to ratify the US Constitution.

FLORIDA

Capital: Tallahassee
Postal Code: FL
Nickname: Sunshine State
Flower: Orange blossom
Bird: Mockingbird
Area: 65,758 sq. mi. (170,312 sq km)
Population: 19,552,860

CHECK IT OUT

Florida's name comes from the Spanish word for "flowery." Ponce de Leon named it after the beautiful flowers he saw all around when he arrived there in 1513.

Florida wildflowers

States of the United States

GEORGIA

Capital: Atlanta
Postal Code: GA
Nickname: Empire State of the South
Flower: Cherokee rose
Bird: Brown thrasher
Area: 59,425 sq. mi. (153,911 sq km)
Population: 9,992,167

CHECK IT OUT

Georgia's top crops include peaches. The "World's Largest Peach Cobbler," which uses 75 gallons (285 L) of peaches and 150 pounds (68 kg) each of sugar and flour, is the star of the annual Georgia Peach Festival.

HAWAII

Capital: Honolulu
Postal Code: HI
Nickname: Aloha State
Flower: Yellow hibiscus
Bird: Nene, or Hawaiian goose
Area: 10,926 sq. mi. (28,300 sq km)
Population: 1,404,054

CHECK IT OUT

Hawaii is made up of 132 islands. The 8 main ones are Niihau, Kauai, Oahu, Maui, Molokai, Lanai, Kahoolawe, and the Big Island of Hawaii.

IDAHO

Capital: Boise
Postal Code: ID
Nickname: Gem State
Flower: Syringa
Bird: Mountain bluebird
Area: 83,568 sq. mi. (216,442 sq km)
Population: 1,612,136

CHECK IT OUT

The largest freshwater fish ever caught in America was a white sturgeon hauled out of Idaho's Snake River in 1898. It weighed 1,500 pounds (680 kg), about as much as a grown Holstein cow.

ILLINOIS

ILLINOIS

Capital: Springfield
Postal Code: IL
Nickname: Land of Lincoln
Flower: Native violet
Bird: Northern cardinal
Area: 57,916 sq. mi. (150,002 sq km)
Population: 12,882,135

CHECK IT OUT

The second tallest building America is the Willis (formerly Sears) Tower in Chicago, measuring 1,725 feet (526 m) from the ground to the tip of the antenna.

IOWA

INDIANA

Capital: Indianapolis
Postal Code: IN
Nickname: Hoosier State
Flower: Peony
Bird: Northern cardinal
Area: 36,417 sq. mi. (94,321 sq km)
Population: 6,570,902

CHECK IT OUT

Santa Claus, Indiana, receives over half a million letters at Christmastime.

IOWA

Capital: Des Moines
Postal Code: IA
Nickname: Hawkeye State
Flower: Wild prairie rose
Bird: Eastern goldfinch (also called American goldfinch)
Area: 56,273 sq. mi. (145,746 sq km)
Population: 3,090,416

CHECK IT OUT

Iowa is the only state name in America that begins with two vowels.

KANSAS

KANSAS

Capital: Topeka
Postal Code: KS
Nickname: Sunflower State
Flower: Native sunflower
Bird: Western meadowlark
Area: 82,278 sq. mi. (213,101 sq km)
Population: 2,893,957

CHECK IT OUT

In 1905, the element helium was discovered at the University of Kansas.

KENTUCKY

Capital: Frankfort
Postal Code: KY
Nickname: Bluegrass State
Flower: Goldenrod
Bird: Northern cardinal
Area: 40,411 sq. mi. (104,665 sq km)
Population: 4,395,295

CHECK IT OUT

The Kentucky Derby, held the first Saturday in May, is the oldest annual horse race in the United States.

LOUISIANA

Capital: Baton Rouge
Postal Code: LA
Nickname: Pelican State
Flower: Magnolia
Bird: Eastern brown pelican
Area: 51,988 sq. mi. (134,649 sq km)
Population: 4,625,470

CHECK IT OUT

Louisiana is the only state divided into parishes instead of counties.

MAINE

Capital: Augusta
Postal Code: ME
Nickname: Pine Tree State
Flower: White pine cone and tassel
Bird: Black-capped chickadee
Area: 35,384 sq. mi. (91,644 sq km)
Population: 1,328,302

CHECK IT OUT

Eastport, Maine, is the first town in America to see the sunrise because it is the town farthest east.

MARYLAND

Capital: Annapolis
Postal Code: MD
Nickname: Old Line State
Flower: Black-eyed Susan
Bird: Baltimore oriole
Area: 12,406 sq. mi. (32,131 sq km)
Population: 5,928,814

CHECK IT OUT

Maryland is famous for having the first dental school in the United States.

MASSACHUSETTS

Capital: Boston
Postal Code: MA
Nickname: Bay State
Flower: Mayflower
Bird: Black-capped chickadee
Area: 10,554 sq. mi. (27,336 sq km)
Population: 6,692,824

CHECK IT OUT

Volleyball was invented in 1895 in Holyoke, Massachusetts, by gym teacher William Morgan. The game was originally called mintonette. Basketball was invented in nearby Springfield.

MICHIGAN

Capital: Lansing
Postal Code: MI
Nickname: Wolverine State
Flower: Apple blossom
Bird: American robin
Area: 96,713 sq. mi. (250,486 sq km)
Population: 9,895,622

CHECK IT OUT

With over 11,000 inland lakes and over 36,000 miles (57,936 km) of rivers and streams, Michigan has the longest freshwater shoreline in the world.

MINNESOTA

Capital: St. Paul
Postal Code: MN
Nickname: Gopher State
Flower: Pink and white lady's slipper
Bird: Common loon
Area: 86,935 sq. mi. (225,163 sq km)
Population: 5,420,380

CHECK IT OUT

The Mall of America in Bloomington, Minnesota, is 9.5 million square feet (8,825,780 sq m)—about the size of 78 football fields!

MISSISSIPPI

Capital: Jackson
Postal Code: MS
Nickname: Magnolia State
Flower: Magnolia
Bird: Mockingbird
Area: 48,432 sq. mi. (125,438 sq km)
Population: 2,991,207

CHECK IT OUT

Edward Adolf Barq Sr. invented root beer in Biloxi, Mississippi, in 1898.

MISSOURI

Capital: Jefferson City
Postal Code: MO
Nickname: Show Me State
Flower: Hawthorn
Bird: Eastern bluebird
Area: 69,702 sq. mi. (180,529 sq km)
Population: 6,044,171

CHECK IT OUT

The St. Louis World's Fair in 1904 was so hot that Richard Blechyden decided to serve his tea over ice—and invented iced tea.

MONTANA

Capital: Helena
Postal Code: MT
Nickname: Treasure State
Flower: Bitterroot
Bird: Western meadowlark
Area: 147,039 sq. mi. (380,831 sq km)
Population: 1,015,165

CHECK IT OUT

The average square mile (1.6 sq km) of land in Montana contains 1.4 pronghorn antelope, 1.4 elk, and 3.3 deer. Montana has the largest number of mammal species in the United States.

NEBRASKA

Capital: Lincoln
Postal Code: NE
Nickname: Cornhusker State
Flower: Goldenrod
Bird: Western meadowlark
Area: 77,349 sq. mi. (200,334 sq km)
Population: 1,868,516

CHECK IT OUT

About 95 percent of Nebraska's area is taken up by farms and ranches—a higher percentage than any other state. The state's top crop is corn.

NEVADA

Capital: Carson City
Postal Code: NV
Nickname: Silver State
Flower: Sagebrush
Bird: Mountain bluebird
Area: 110,572 sq. mi. (286,382 sq km)
Population: 2,790,136

CHECK IT OUT

The Silver State produces more gold than any other state and is the fourth-largest producer in the world.

NEW HAMPSHIRE

Capital: Concord
Postal Code: NH
Nickname: Granite State
Flower: Purple lilac
Bird: Purple finch
Area: 9,348 sq. mi. (24,210 sq km)
Population: 1,323,459

CHECK IT OUT

The winds on top of New Hampshire's Mount Washington have been recorded at speeds over 231 miles (372 km) an hour—the fastest winds on Earth!

NEW JERSEY

Capital: Trenton
Postal Code: NJ
Nickname: Garden State
Flower: Purple violet
Bird: Eastern goldfinch
Area: 8,723 sq. mi. (22,592 sq km)
Population: 8,899,339

CHECK IT OUT

The street names in the game Monopoly come from real street names in Atlantic City, New Jersey.

NEW MEXICO

Capital: Santa Fe
Postal Code: NM
Nickname: Land of Enchantment
Flower: Yucca flower
Bird: Roadrunner (also called greater roadrunner)
Area: 121,590 sq. mi. (314,919 sq km)
Population: 2,085,287

CHECK IT OUT

There are more than 110 caves in Carlsbad Caverns. One cave is 22 stories high and is home to tens of thousands of bats.

NEW YORK

Capital: Albany
Postal Code: NY
Nickname: Empire State
Flower: Rose
Bird: Eastern bluebird
Area: 54,555 sq. mi. (141,298 sq km)
Population: 19,651,127

CHECK IT OUT

More than 100 million people have visited the top of the Empire State Building in New York City. The building is 1,434 feet (437 m) from the street to the top of the lightning rod.

NORTH CAROLINA

Capital: Raleigh
Postal Code: NC
Nickname: Tar Heel State
Flower: Dogwood
Bird: Northern cardinal
Area: 53,819 sq. mi. (139,391 sq km)
Population: 9,848,060

CHECK IT OUT

On March 7, 1914, in Fayetteville, North Carolina, George Herman "Babe" Ruth hit his first professional home run.

NORTH DAKOTA

Capital: Bismarck
Postal Code: ND
Nickname: Flickertail State
Flower: Wild prairie rose
Bird: Western meadowlark
Area: 70,698 sq. mi. (183,109 sq km)
Population: 723,393

🔎 CHECK IT OUT

Jamestown, North Dakota, is home to the World's Largest Buffalo monument. It stands 26 feet (7.9 m) high and 46 feet (14 m) long, and weighs 60 tons (54,441 kg).

OHIO

Capital: Columbus
Postal Code: OH
Nickname: Buckeye State
Flower: Scarlet carnation
Bird: Northern cardinal
Area: 44,825 sq. mi. (116,097 sq km)
Population: 11,570,808

🔎 CHECK IT OUT

The first traffic light in America began working on August 5, 1914, in Cleveland, Ohio.

OKLAHOMA

OKLAHOMA

Capital: Oklahoma City
Postal Code: OK
Nickname: Sooner State
Flower: Mistletoe
Bird: Scissor-tailed flycatcher
Area: 69,899 sq. mi. (181,038 sq km)
Population: 3,850,568

🔎 CHECK IT OUT

Not every state has a state amphibian, but Oklahoma does—the American bullfrog.

OREGON

Capital: **Salem**
Postal Code: OR
Nickname: Beaver State
Flower: Oregon grape
Bird: Western meadowlark
Area: 98,379 sq. mi. (254,801 sq km)
Population: 3,930,065

CHECK IT OUT

Two pioneers founded Portland, Oregon. One was from Boston, Massachusetts, and the other was from Portland, Maine. They couldn't decide what to name the city, so they flipped a coin. Guess who won!

PENNSYLVANIA

Capital: Harrisburg
Postal Code: PA
Nickname: Keystone State
Flower: Mountain laurel
Bird: Ruffed grouse
Area: 46,055 sq. mi. (119,281 sq km)
Population: 12,773,801

CHECK IT OUT

In 1953, Dr. Jonas Salk created the polio vaccine at the University of Pittsburgh.

RHODE ISLAND

Capital: Providence
Postal Code: RI
Nickname: Ocean State
Flower: Violet
Bird: Rhode Island Red chicken
Area: 1,545 sq. mi. (4,001 sq km)
Population: 1,051,511

CHECK IT OUT

"I'm a Yankee Doodle Dandy" and "You're a Grand Old Flag" were written by George M. Cohan, who was born in Providence, Rhode Island, in 1878.

SOUTH CAROLINA

Capital: Columbia
Postal Code: SC
Nickname: Palmetto State
Flower: Yellow jessamine
Bird: Great Carolina wren
Area: 32,021 sq. mi. (82,934 sq km)
Population: 4,774,839

CHECK IT OUT

The first battle of the Civil War was fought at Fort Sumter, South Carolina.

SOUTH DAKOTA

Capital: Pierre
Postal Code: SD
Nickname: Mount Rushmore State
Flower: Pasqueflower
Bird: Ring-necked pheasant
Area: 77,116 sq. mi. (199,730 sq km)
Population: 844,877

CHECK IT OUT

The faces of George Washington, Thomas Jefferson, Theodore Roosevelt, and Abraham Lincoln are sculpted into Mount Rushmore, the world's greatest mountain carving. The carvings are taller than a four-story building.

TENNESSEE

Capital: Nashville
Postal Code: TN
Nickname: Volunteer State
Flower: Iris
Bird: Mockingbird
Area: 42,144 sq. mi. (109,154 sq km)
Population: 6,495,978

CHECK IT OUT

More than nine million people visit Smoky Mountain National Park in Tennessee every year, making it America's most visited national park. Over 30 species of salamanders and 1,500 black bears live there year-round.

TEXAS

Capital: Austin
Postal Code: TX
Nickname: Lone Star State
Flower: Bluebonnet
Bird: Mockingbird
Area: 268,597 sq. mi. (695,666 sq km)
Population: 26,448,193

CHECK IT OUT

The name *Texas* is actually derived from a misunderstanding of *tejas*, a Caddo Indian word meaning "friend."

UTAH

Capital: Salt Lake City
Postal Code: UT
Nickname: Beehive State
Flower: Sego lily
Bird: California gull
Area: 84,897 sq. mi. (219,883 sq km)
Population: 2,900,872

CHECK IT OUT

Utah's Great Salt Lake is several times saltier than seawater. It's so salty that you'd float on the surface of the water like a cork if you swam there!

VERMONT

Capital: Montpelier
Postal Code: VT
Nickname: Green Mountain State
Flower: Red clover
Bird: Hermit thrush
Area: 9,616 sq. mi. (24,906 sq km)
Population: 626,630

CHECK IT OUT

Vermont is the only New England state that doesn't border the Atlantic Ocean.

VIRGINIA

Capital: Richmond
Postal Code: VA
Nickname: Old Dominion
Flower: American dogwood
Bird: Northern cardinal
Area: 42,775 sq. mi. (110,787 sq km)
Population: 8,260,405

CHECK IT OUT

More US presidents come from Virginia than from any other state—George Washington, Thomas Jefferson, James Madison, James Monroe, William Henry Harrison, John Tyler, Zachary Taylor, and Woodrow Wilson.

WASHINGTON

Capital: Olympia
Postal Code: WA
Nickname: Evergreen State
Flower: Coast rhododendron
Bird: Willow goldfinch (also called American goldfinch)
Area: 71,298 sq. mi. (184,661 sq km)
Population: 6,971,406

CHECK IT OUT

Washington is a hotbed of volcanic activity. Mount Rainier erupted in 1969 and Mount St. Helens erupted in 1980.

WEST VIRGINIA

Capital: Charleston
Postal Code: WV
Nickname: Mountain State
Flower: Big rhododendron
Bird: Cardinal
Area: 24,230 sq. mi. (62,755 sq km)
Population: 1,854,304

CHECK IT OUT

Before the Civil War, West Virginia was part of Virginia. It became a separate state and remained part of the Union when Virginia decided to secede at the dawn of the war.

WISCONSIN

1848

WISCONSIN

Capital: Madison
Postal Code: WI
Nickname: Badger State
Flower: Wood violet
Bird: American robin
Area: 65,496 sq. mi. (169,636 sq km)
Population: 5,742,713

CHECK IT OUT

Wisconsin produces 40 percent of all the cheese and 20 percent of all the butter melted, slathered, spread, and devoured in the United States. No wonder folks from Wisconsin are sometimes called "cheeseheads."

WYOMING

Capital: Cheyenne
Postal Code: WY
Nickname: Equality State
Flower: Indian paintbrush
Bird: Western meadowlark
Area: 97,812 sq. mi. (253,334 sq km)
Population: 582,658

CHECK IT OUT

Devils Tower in northeastern Wyoming was the first national monument. It has been considered a sacred site by Northern Plains tribes for thousands of years.

Washington, DC
Our Nation's Capital

Every state has a capital, the city where all the state's official government business takes place. Our country's capital, Washington, DC, is the center for all national, or federal, business. But our nation's capital isn't located in a state. It's part of a federal district, the District of Columbia. Congress wanted the capital to be in a district, not a state, so as not to favor any one state above the others.

The city is named after our first president, George Washington, who chose its location in 1791. It became the capital in 1800. Before that the center of the federal government was Philadelphia, Pennsylvania.

The United States Capitol

WASHINGTON, DC

Flower: American Beauty rose
Area: 68 sq. mi. (177 sq km)
Population: 646,449
Government: Federal district under the authority of Congress; mayor and city council, elected to four-year terms, run the local government

CHECK IT OUT

The White House, at 1600 Pennsylvania Ave., is the official presidential residence. George Washington is the only US president who never lived there.

PUERTO RICO

Besides the 50 states and the District of Columbia, the United States also includes a number of commonwealths and territories. A commonwealth has its own constitution and has more rights and independence than a territory, but neither one has all the rights of a state.

The largest commonwealth is Puerto Rico, which is made up of one large island and three smaller ones in the Caribbean Sea. Puerto Rico was given to the United States by Spain in 1898 and became a commonwealth in 1952.

PUERTO RICO

Capital: San Juan
Area: 5,325 sq. mi. (13,791 sq km)
Population: 3,615,086
Language: Spanish, English
Money: US dollar
Goverment: US territory with commonwealth status

CHECK IT OUT

Puerto Ricans are American citizens, but they cannot vote in US presidential elections.

Other US Commonwealths and Territories

The Northern Mariana Islands in the North Pacific Ocean are the only other US commonwealth. US territories are:

- American Samoa
- Guam
- The US Virgin Islands

The United States Minor Outlying Islands:

- Midway Islands
- Johnston Atoll
- Navassa Island
- Baker, Howland, and Jarvis Islands
- Wake Island
- Kingman Reef
- Palmyra Atoll

GAMES

lives: 3   score: 150   lev

Are Video Games a Brain Drain or a Brain-Booster?

Who can forget Flappy Bird? Flappy Bird was a super-popular smartphone game where players had to help birds navigate through a series of pipes without touching. It looked easy, but it was really pretty hard. People played it for hours, trying to score. In fact, they played so much that the game's creator, Dong Nguyen, deleted the app. He said people liked to play it too much. The game was taking up too much of their time and energy. They were becoming addicted.

To learn why people become addicted to certain video games, researchers in California are scanning players' brains as they play. The researchers say what they learn could help them create different kinds of games—ones that could treat illnesses like depression and ADD (attention deficit disorder).

YOUR TURN

Video games are fun—everyone knows that. But kids need to be doing lots of other activities too, especially ones that involve exercise, to keep healthy. Take the video game quiz at kidshealth.org to find out what role video games play in your life.

el: 1

Which item represents the most popular iPhone and iPad game app of 2013? (See p. 149.)

8

Top 10 Best-Selling Video Games of 2013 (Any Platform)

1. Grand Theft Auto V
2. Call of Duty: Ghosts
3. Madden NFL 25
4. Battlefield 4
5. Assassin's Creed 4: Black Flag
6. NBA 2K14
7. Call of Duty: Black Ops 2
8. Just Dance 2014
9. Minecraft
10. Disney Infinity

Top 10 Best-Reviewed Video Games of 2013

Title	Platform
Grand Theft Auto V	PS3
Grand Theft Auto V	Xbox 360
The Last of Us	PS3
BioShock Infinite	PS3
BioShock Infinite	PC
Super Mario 3D World	Wii U
BioShock Infinite	Xbox 360
Fire Emblem: Awakening	3DS
Rayman Legends	Wii U
Fez	PC

Popular Board Games of 2013

Carcassone
Settlers of Catan
Qwirkle
Ticket to Ride
Banangrams
Rummikub
Telestrations
Story Cubes
Pandemic
Dominion

Top 10 Games Played on Facebook
(March 5, 2014)

Candy Crush Saga
Farm Heroes Saga
8 Ball Pool
Bubble Witch Saga
Criminal Case
Diamond Dash
Dragon City
FarmVille 2
Hay Day
Papa Pear Saga

Top Free iPad Apps
for 2013

Candy Crush Saga

Temple Run 2

Despicable Me: Minion Rush

Subway Surfers

Real Racing 3

.ull Carrier   1:37 PM

Top Free iPhone Apps
for 2013

Candy Crush Saga

Temple Run 2

Despicable Me: Minion Rush

4 Pics 1 Word

Subway Surfers

GEOGRAPHY
WORLD & US

The Colorado River

Oh, Cut It Out

When you stand on the rim of the Grand Canyon, you are seeing much more than spectacular colors and shapes. You are seeing firsthand the incredible power of water on land. Working patiently for millions of years, the Colorado River carved out the steep canyon walls, revealing North America's geological history layer by layer.

The Paiute Indian tribe calls the canyon Kaibab, which means "mountain lying down" or "mountain turned upside down." The Grand Canyon has been called one of the seven natural wonders of the world. Here are the amazing stats:

Grand Canyon National Park

▶ Area: 1,904 square miles (4,931 sq km)

▶ Length: 277 miles (446 km)

▶ Width: 10 miles (16 km) to 18 miles (29 km)

▶ Depth: More than one mile (1.6 km) deep at its deepest point

▶ Age: The rocks at the bottom are 1.8 billion years old. The canyon itself is 5–6 million years old.

▶ Plants and Animals: Home to more than 1,500 plant, 355 bird, 89 mammal, 47 reptile, 9 amphibian, and 17 fish species. Some species are found nowhere else in the world.

Grand Canyon National Park was established in 1919. Close to 5 million people visit every year.

YOUR TURN

If you can't visit Grand Canyon in person, visit nps.gov/grca for tons of pictures, information, and an online tour.

What are some other US natural wonders? (See p. 174.)

How to Read a Map

Directions

When you're reading a map, how do you figure out which way is which? On most—but not all—maps:

 Up means north   Down means south   Left means west   Right means east

Some maps are turned or angled so that north is not straight up. Always look for a symbol called a compass rose to show you exactly where north is on the map you're reading.

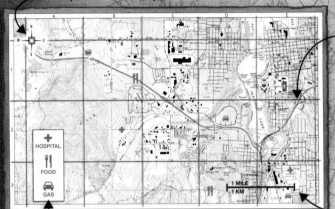

Location

Maps that show large areas such as countries and continents include lines of longitude and latitude. Maps of cities and streets are divided into blocks called grids. Grid maps have numbers on one side and letters on another. They also have an index that gives a number—letter combination for every place on the map.

Shapes and Symbols

Every picture, object, shape, and line on a map stands for something. A tiny red airplane stands for an airport. A thick line is one kind of road and a dotted line is another. A map's legend, or key, shows these symbols and explains what they stand for.

Distance

You can look at a map and think it's a hop, skip, and a jump from Maine to Maryland, but it's really a few million hops. The map scale shows you how many miles (or km) a certain length of map represents.

A Map Is a Map Is a Map . . .

All maps are not created equal. There are different maps for different purposes:

- A bathymetric map shows the depths and contours of the bottom of a body of water.
- A geological map shows earthquake faults, volcanoes, minerals, rock types, underground water, and landslide areas.
- A physical map shows mountains, lakes, and rivers.
- A planimetric map shows horizontal (not vertical, such as elevations) features.
- A political map shows boundaries of cities, states, countries, and provinces.
- A relief map uses different colors to show different elevations.
- A road map shows roads, highways, cities, and towns.
- A topographic map shows elevations.
- A weather map shows temperatures, fronts, rain, snow, sleet, storms, fog, and other weather conditions.

Geography—World & US

Geographical Terms

Term	Definition
Altitude	the distance above sea level
Archipelago	a group or chain of islands clustered together in an ocean or sea
Atlas	a book of maps
Atoll	an ocean island made out of an underwater ring of coral
Bay	a body of water protected and partly surrounded by land
Cartographer	a mapmaker
Compass rose	a four-pointed design on a map that shows north, south, east, and west
Continent	one of Earth's seven largest land masses
Degree	a unit of measurement used to calculate longitude and latitude
Delta	a flat, triangular piece of land that fans out at the mouth of a river
Elevation	the height of a point on the earth's surface above sea level
Equator	an imaginary circle around the earth halfway between the North Pole and the South Pole
Globe	a 3-D spherical map of the earth
GPS	short for Global Positioning System; finds longitude and latitude by bouncing information off satellites in space
Grid	a crisscross pattern of lines forming squares on a map
Hemisphere	one half of the world
Island	land that is surrounded by water on all sides
Isthmus	a narrow strip of land (with water on both sides) that connects two larger land areas
Latitude	distance north or south of the equator
Legend	a key to the symbols on a map
Longitude	distance east or west of the prime meridian
Map	a flat picture of a place drawn to scale
Meridian	an imaginary line running north and south and looping around the poles used to measure longitude
North Pole	the most northerly point on Earth
Ocean	the body of salt water surrounding the great land masses and divided by the land masses into several distinct portions
Parallel	an imaginary line parallel to the equator, used to measure latitude
Peninsula	a body of land surrounded by water on three sides
Scale	a tool on a map that helps calculate real distance
Sea level	the surface of the ocean
South Pole	the most southerly point on Earth
Strait	a narrow body of water that connects two larger bodies
Topography	the physical features of a place, such as mountains

Continental Drift

Maps are all well and good if things don't change. "Go east one mile and turn south and find Mt. Crumpet" works only if Mt. Crumpet doesn't decide to walk a few miles north. Sound ridiculous? Actually, the earth didn't always look like it does today. About 250 million years ago, all the continents were scrunched together in one lump called Pangaea.

Gradually the land drifted and changed into the seven continents we know today in a process called continental drift. And the land is still moving.

Pangaea

Journey to the Center of the Earth

Earth isn't just one big blue ball with the same stuff all the way through. It's made up of layers.

The part we walk around on is the crust, or lithosphere. It's only about 60 miles (100 km) deep.

Beneath the lithosphere is the mantle. It's a layer about 1,800 miles (2,897 km) deep.

Beneath that is the core, which is made of two parts:

The outer core (1,375 miles, or 2,200 km, thick) is almost as big as the Moon and made up of soupy molten iron.

The inner core is about 781 miles (1,250 km) thick and about as hot as the surface of the Sun.

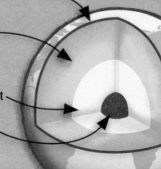

Earth's Layers

The Continents Today

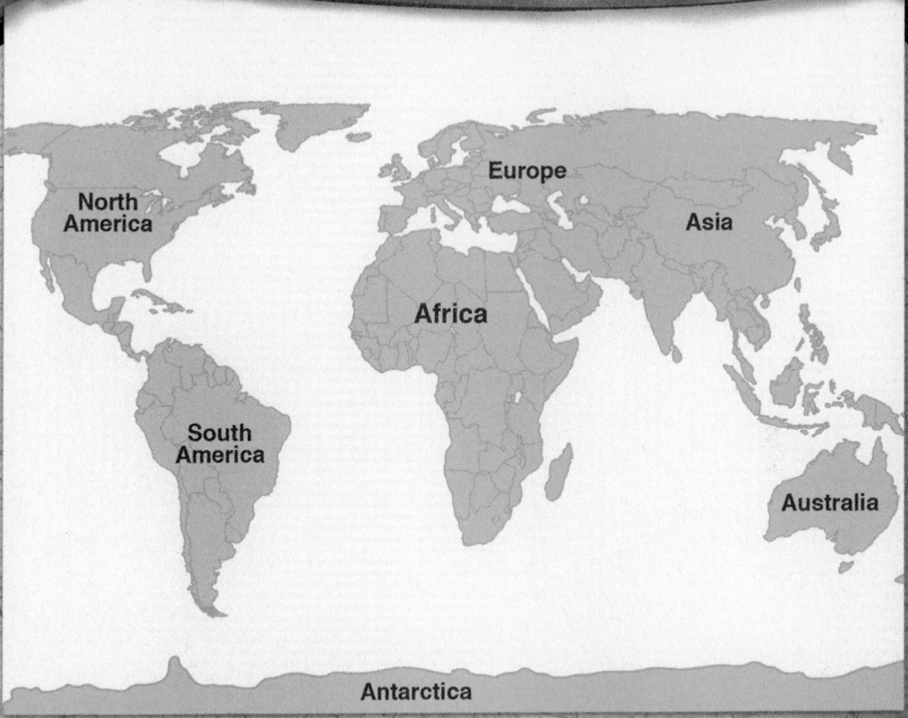

North
America

Europe

Asia

Africa

South
America

Australia

Antarctica

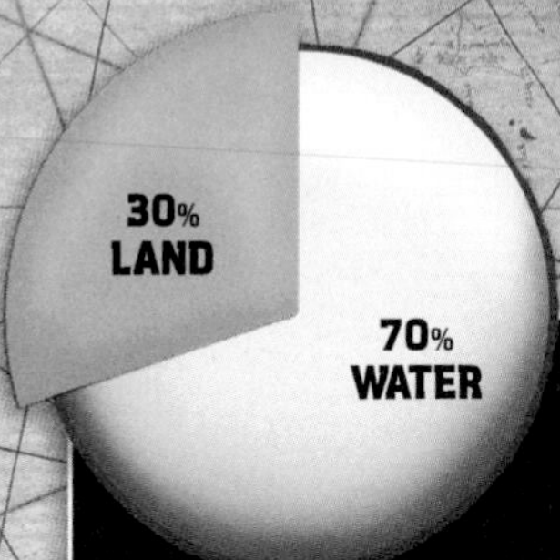

CHECK IT OUT !

30% LAND

70% WATER

The total surface area of the world is 196,937,583 square miles (510,066,000 sq km). However, about 70 percent of that is water. Turn the page to read about the continents in detail. Turn to pages 170—171 to read about the world's major oceans.

Arctic Ocean

Barents Sea

NOVAYA ZEMLYA

NEW SIBERIAN ISLANDS

East Siberian Sea

SEVERNAYA ZEMLYA

Kara Sea

Laptev Sea

Cherski

Tiksi

Yakutsk

Noril'sk

SIBERIA

RUSSIA

Nizhniy Novgorod

Kazan'

Perm'

Yekaterinburg

Chelyabinsk

Omsk

Novosibirsk

Krasnoyarsk

Irkutsk

Chita

Lake Baikal

Samara

Ufa

URAL MOUNTAINS

Astana

Qaraghandy (Karaganda)

Atyraū (Atyrau)

Aral Sea

Lake Balkhash

Ulaanbaatar

KAZAKHSTAN

MONGOLIA

GOBI DESERT

DA HINGAN LING

Shenyang

GEO.

Tbilisi

ARM.

Yerevan

AZERBAIJAN

Baku

Tabrīz

Caspian Sea

TURKMENISTAN

Ashgabat

UZBEKISTAN

Almaty

Ürümqi

Baotou

Beijing

Tianjin

Dalian

Qingdao

Tashkent

Bishkek

KYRGYZSTAN

Kashi

TIEN SHAN

Taiyuan

Jinan

Tehran

Mashhad

Dushanbe

TAJIKISTAN

TAKLA MAKAN DESERT

Lanzhou

Zhengzhou

Nanjing

Shanghai

IRAN

Eṣfahān

ZAGROS MTS.

Shīrāz

AFGHANISTAN

Kabul

Kandahār

KARAKUM

Line of Control

MOUNTAINS

QING ZANG GAOYUAN

Islamabad

Quetta

Faisalabad

Lahore

Ludhiāna

Mt. Everest highest point in the world 8850 m

Lhasa

Chengdu

CHINA

Xi'an

Chongqing

Wuhan

Hangzhou

Changsha

Nanchang

Persian Gulf

Bandar 'Abbās

Doha

QATAR

Abu Dhabi

U.A.E.

Muscat

SAUDI ARABIA

OMAN

PAKISTAN

New Delhi

Jaipur

Karachi

Ahmadābād

Indore

Surat

Mumbai

Pune

Hyderābād

DECCAN

WESTERN GHATS

EASTERN GHATS

Bengaluru

Chennai

Cochin

Jaffna

Kānpur

Lucknow

NEPAL

Kathmandu

Patna

BHUTAN

Thimphu

BANGLADESH

Dhaka

Kolkata

Chittagong

INDIA

Nāgpur

Vishākhapatnam

Bay of Bengal

Guiyang

Kunming

Xi Jiang

Nanning

Guangzhou

Hong Kong S.

Macau S.A.R.

Mandalay

Nay Pyi Taw

Hanoi

Haiphong

Hainan Dao

Da Nang

South China Sea

BURMA

LAOS

Vientiane

Rangoon

Bangkok

THAILAND

VIETNAM

Ho Chi Minh City

SPRATLY ISLANDS

Arabian Sea

LAKSHADWEEP (INDIA)

Laccadive Sea

MALDIVES

Male

Colombo

SRI LANKA

ANDAMAN ISLANDS (INDIA)

Andaman Sea

NICOBAR ISLANDS (INDIA)

CAMBODIA

Phnom Penh

Gulf of Thailand

Kuala Lumpur

MALAYSIA

MALAYSIA

Borneo

Bandar Seri Begawan

BRUNEI

SINGAPORE

Singapore

Medan

Pontianak

Sumatra

Palembang

INDON

Jakarta

Semarang

Surabaya

Bandung

Java

Christmas Island (AUSTL.)

Scale 1:48,000,000

Azimuthal Equal-Area Projection

0 — 800 Kilometers

0 — 800 Miles

Boundary representation is not necessarily authoritative.

ASIA can be described best in one word: BIG. It's the biggest continent in size, covering about 30 percent of Earth's land area. It's biggest in population, with about 60 percent of all the people in the world living there. And in terms of contributions to the world, it's enormous. Asians founded the first cities; set up the first legal system; invented writing paper, printing, the magnetic compass, and gunpowder; and much more. All of the world's major religions began in Asia.

Asia rules in world-class geographical features, too. It has:
- The highest mountain range, the Himalayas, as well as the most mountains of any continent
- The highest point on Earth, Mt. Everest, and the lowest, the Dead Sea

Asia at a Glance

Area
17,226,200 sq. mi. (44,614,000 sq km)

Population
4,347,630,000

Number of countries
50

Largest country
China
3,705,407 sq. mi. (9,596,960 sq km)

Most populated urban area
Tokyo, Japan
37,217,400 people

Longest river
Yangtze, China
3,915 mi. (6,300 km)

Largest lake
Lake Baikal, Russia
12,200 sq. mi. (31,500 sq km)

Highest point
Mt. Everest, Nepal/China
29,035 ft. (8,850 m) above sea level

Lowest point
Dead Sea, Israel/Jordan
1,380 ft. (421 m) below sea level

CHECK IT OUT!

Asia has some of the world's largest international business centers, such as Tokyo, Japan; Singapore; and Hong Kong. Yet about half of all Asians are farmers.

North
Atlantic
Ocean

London
GERMANY
POLAND
NETH.
Brussels
BEL.
LUX.
Prague
CZ. REP.
SLOV.
Paris
Vienna
AUS.
Budapest
HUNG.
ROM.
FRANCE
SWITZ.
Belgrade
BOS. &
HER.
SER.
Bucharest
Black Sea
KAZAR

AZORES
(PORTUGAL)

PORTUGAL
SLO.
CRO.
ITALY
Rome
MONT.
Sofia
BULG.
MACE.

Madrid
Corsica
Sardinia
ALB.
Ankara
TURKEY

Lisbon
SPAIN
GREECE
Athens
CYPRUS
LEB.
SYRIA
Damascus
GEOL
ARL

MADEIRA ISLANDS
(PORTUGAL)
Oran
Algiers
Tunis
MALTA
Mediterranean Sea
Beirut
ISRAEL
Jerusalem
Amman
JORDAN

Rabat
Fès
Constantine
TUNISIA
BAHR
QATAR
Riyadh

Casablanca
MOROCCO
Marrakech
Tripoli
Banghāzi
Alexandria
Cairo
Al Jīzah

CANARY ISLANDS
(SPAIN)

Laayoune
(El Aaiún)
Western
Sahara

ALGERIA
LIBYA
EGYPT
Aswān
Admin.
Boundary
SAUDI
ARABIA

Nouadhibou
S A H A R A
Al Jawf
Port
Sudan
Red
Sea
YEMEN
Sanaa

APE VERDE
Praia
Nouakchott
MAURITANIA
NIGER
Omdurman
Khartoum
ERITREA
Asmara
Lac Assal
(lowest point in
Africa; -155 m)
Djibouti
DJIBOUTI
Hargeysa

Dakar
SENEGAL
Tombouctou
Agadez
CHAD
SUDAN
Addis
Ababa
ETHIOPIA
Prov.
Admin.
Line

Banjul
THE GAMBIA
Bissau
GUINEA-BISSAU
MALI
BURKINA
FASO
Niamey
Zinder
N'Djamena
Moundou

Bamako
Kano
SOM

Conakry
GUINEA
Ouagadougou
BENIN
NIGERIA
Abuja
CENTRAL AFRICAN
REPUBLIC
SOUTH
SUDAN
Juba
Mogadi

Freetown
SIERRA LEONE
Monrovia
GHANA
TOGO
Ogbomoso
Ibadan
Lagos
Bangui
UGANDA
Kampala
KENYA
Nairobi

LIBERIA
CÔTE
D'IVOIRE
Yamoussoukro
Accra
Lomé
Porto-
Novo
CAMEROON
Douala
Yaoundé
CONGO
Congo
Kisangani
RWANDA
Kigali
Mt. Kilimanjaro
(highest point in
Africa; 5895 m)
Ind

Abidjan
Malabo
EQUATORIAL GUINEA
Libreville
REP. OF
THE
CONGO
BASIN
DEM. REP.
OF THE CONGO
Bukavu
BURUNDI
Bujumbura
Mombasa
Ocea

Equator
Gulf of Guinea
SAO TOME
AND PRINCIPE
GABON
Brazzaville
Pointe-Noire
Kinshasa
Mbuji-Mayi
Dodoma
Zanzibar
Dar es
Salaam

São Tomé
Annobón
(EQUA. GUI.)
ANGOLA
(Cabinda)
Luanda
Lubumbashi
TANZANIA
COMOROS
Moroni
Glorio
(FR

Ascension
(St. Helena)
ANGOLA
Namibe
Lubango
Kitwe
MALAWI
Lilongwe
Cidade
de Nacala
Mayotte
(admin. by France;
claimed by Comoros)
Mahajan

ZAMBIA
Lusaka
Blantyre
Juan de Nova
Island
(FRANCE)
Toamasina

Harare
ZIMBABWE
Beira
MOZAMBIQUE
Antar

Windhoek
BOTSWANA
KALAHARI
DESERT
Bassas
da India
(FRANCE)
Europa
Island
(FRANCE)
MADAGASC

Walvis Bay
Gaborone
NAMIBIA
Pretoria
Maputo
Mbabane
SWAZILAND

Johannesburg
SOUTH
AFRICA
Maseru
LESOTHO
Durban

Cape Town
Port Elizabeth
Indi

Scale 1:51,400,0

Azimuthal Equal-Area P

0   800 Kilom

Boundary representati
not necessarily authoritative.

AFRICA is second to Asia in area and population, but it tops all continents in other categories:

- Biggest desert: The Sahara, covering about 3.5 million square miles (9 million sq km), or about one-third of the continent
- Longest freshwater lake: Lake Tanganyika, 420 miles (680 km)
- Most independent countries: 54

Africa is a land of treasures, from the lions, giraffes, rhinos, and other spectacular wildlife that inhabit its rain forests and grasslands to its rich supplies of gold and diamonds. However, most Africans remain poor because of drought, famine, disease, and other ongoing serious problems.

Africa at a Glance

Area
11,684,000 sq. mi. (30,262,000 sq km)

Population
1,150,295,000

Largest country
Algeria
919,595 sq. mi. (2,381,740 sq km)

Most populated urban area
Cairo, Egypt
11,169,000 people

Longest river
Nile
4,132 mi. (6,650 km)

Largest lake
Lake Victoria, Tanzania/Uganda/Kenya
26,828 sq. mi. (69,484 sq km)

Highest point
Mount Kilimanjaro, Tanzania
19,340 ft. (5,895 m) above sea level

Lowest point
Lake Assal, Djibouti
509 ft. (155 m) below sea level

CHECK IT OUT !

From fossils found in Africa, scientists say that the earliest human beings lived here about 2 million years ago.

Geography—World & US

RUSSIA

Cherskiy
East Siberian Sea
Pevek
Anadyr'
Provideniya
Bering Strait
Nome
Bethel
Anchorage
Valdez

Arctic Ocean
Chukchi Sea
Barrow
Prudhoe Bay
Beaufort Sea

UNITED STATES
Mt. McKinley (highest point in North America, 6194 m)
Fairbanks
Inuvik
Dawson
Whitehorse
Juneau

BROOKS RANGE
ALASKA RANGE
ALEUTIAN TRENCH

Greenland
Ittoqqo (Scores

Greenland (DENMARK)
Qaanaaq (Thule)
Iluli (Jakob
(Ho

Alert
Ellesmere Island
QUEEN ELIZABETH ISLANDS
Resolute
Pond Inlet
Baffin Bay
Banks Island
Victoria Island
Cambridge Bay
Gjoa Haven
Baffin Island
Iqaluit
Davis Strait

Rankin Inlet

CANADA
Great Bear Lake
Great Slave Lake
Fort Nelson
Prince George
Fort McMurray
Edmonton
Saskatoon
Calgary
Regina
Winnipeg
Lake Athabasca
Churchill
Arviat
Hudson Bay
Chisasibi
Moosonee
Lake Winnipeg
Thunder Bay
Sudbury
Kuujju
Ha
Chicoutimi (Saguenay)
Québ
Montréal
Ottawa

North Pacific Ocean

Victoria
Vancouver
Seattle
Portland
Boise

ROCKY MOUNTAINS
CASCADES
SIERRA NEVADA

Fargo
Minneapolis
Milwaukee
Lake Superior
Lake Michigan
Lake Huron
Lake Ontario
Lake Erie
Toronto
Hamilton
London
Detroit
Buffalo
Cleveland
Pittsburgh

UNITED STATES

Sacramento
San Francisco
San Jose
Fresno
Las Vegas
Los Angeles
San Diego
Tijuana
Mexicali

Great Salt Lake
Salt Lake City
Death Valley (lowest point in North America, -86 m)
Denver
Omaha
Kansas City
Chicago
Indianapolis
Columbus
Cincinnati
Saint Louis
Louisville
Nashville
Memphis
Atlanta
Birmingham
Charl

APPALACHIAN MOUNTAINS

Albuquerque
Phoenix
Tucson
El Paso
Ciudad Juárez
Hermosillo
Chihuahua
Guadeloupe

Oklahoma City
Dallas
Austin
Houston
San Antonio
New Orleans
Jacksonville
Orlando
Tam

Gulf of Mexico

Torreón
Culiacán
La Paz
Monterrey
Matamoros

MEXICO
San Luis Potosí
Aguascalientes
León
Guadalajara
Morelia
Toluca
Mexico
Puebla
Querétaro
Veracruz
Oaxaca
Acapulco
Tampico
Mérida
Cancun
Bahía de Campeche

SIERRA MADRE ORIENTAL
SIERRA MADRE OCCIDENTAL
SIERRA MADRE DEL SUR
MIDDLE AMERICA TRENCH

BELIZE
Belmopan
HONDU
Teguciga
Guatemala
GUATEMALA
San Salvador
EL SALVADOR

ISLAS REVILLAGIGEDO (MEXICO)

Scale: 1:36,000,000

*Lambert Conformal Conic Projection,
standard parallels 25°N and 77°N*

0   300   600 Kilometers
0   300   600 Miles

NORTH AMERICA, the third-largest continent in area and the fourth-largest in population, is all about variety. The continent has an enormous mix of climates and habitats, from the frozen Arctic to warm, humid Central American rain forests, which support an amazing number of plants and animals. North American human inhabitants live in a variety of environments, too, from rural farms to such bustling, densely populated urban centers as Mexico City. Many—but not all—North Americans enjoy a high standard of living compared to inhabitants of the rest of the world.

Of all the continents, North America has:
- The world's largest island: Greenland,* 836,330 square miles (2,166,086, sq km)
- The world's largest freshwater lake: Lake Superior
- The longest coastline: 190,000 miles (300,000 km), or more than 60,000 times the distance across the Atlantic Ocean

*Except for Australia, which is classified as a continent as well as an island

North America at a Glance

Area
9,352,000 sq. mi. (24,220,000 sq km)

Population
564,073,000

Number of countries
23

Largest country
Canada
3,855,101 sq. mi. (9,984,670 sq km)

Most populated urban area
Mexico City, Mexico
20,445,800 people

Longest river
Mississippi-Missouri, United States
3,710 mi. (5,971 km) long

Largest lake
Lake Superior, United States/Canada
31,700 sq. mi. (82,100 sq km)

Highest point
Mt. McKinley, Alaska
20,320 ft. (6,194 m) above sea level

Lowest point
Death Valley, California
282 ft. (86 m) below sea level

CHECK IT OUT !

Nearly half of all Canadians and about a third of Americans come from English, Irish, Scottish, or Welsh ancestors. However, North America's first settlers were from Asia. Scientists say that these Native Americans, now sometimes called Indians, walked across the Bering Strait, which was dry land between 15,000 and 35,000 years ago. Before they came, there were no people on the continent.

Geography—World & US

Tegucigalpa
Providencia (COLOMBIA)
NICARAGUA
Managua
Isla de San Andrés (COLOMBIA)
Barranquilla
Aruba (NETH.)
Antilles (NETH.)
ST. VINCENT AND THE GRENADINES
GRENADA
BARBADOS
Port-of-Spain
TRINIDAD AND TOBAGO
San José
Panama
COSTA RICA
Cartagena
Maracaibo
Caracas
Valencia
Barcelona
PANAMA
Cúcuta
San Cristobal
Barquisimeto
Ciudad Guayana
VENEZUELA
Georgetown
Paramaribo
Cayenne
Medellín
Bucaramanga
GUYANA
SURINAME
French Guiana (FRANCE)
Isla de Malpelo (COLOMBIA)
Pereira
Ibagué
Bogotá
GUIANA HIGHLANDS
Cali
COLOMBIA
Boa Vista
Macapá
Equator
Río Orinoco
Río Negro
Quito
ECUADOR
Guayaquil
A M A Z O N
Amazon
Manaus
Santarém
Belém
São
Cuenca
Iquitos
Teresina
Piura
B A S I N
Río Madeira
Chiclayo
Pucallpa
Trujillo
Rio Branco
Pôrto Velho
BRAZIL
BRAZILIA
Huánuco
Huancayo
Lima
PERU
Cusco
Ica
Trinidad
MATO GROSSO PLATEAU
Cuiabá
Goiânia
Brasília
South Pacific Ocean
ANDES
PERU-CHILE TRENCH
Arequipa
La Paz
BOLIVIA
Cochabamba
Santa Cruz
HIGHLAND
Uberlândia
Con
Belo Horizon
Arica
Sucre
Potosí
Campo Grande
Iquique
ALTIPLANO
ATACAMA DESERT
Antofagasta
Salta
PARAGUAY
Londrina
Campinas
Campos
São Paulo
Vit
Rio de
Tropic of Capricorn
San Miguel de Tucumán
Asunción
Ciudad del Este
Curitiba
Joinvile
Santos
NAZCA RIDGE
Ambrosio (CHILE)
Resistencia
Florianópolis
CHILE
Cerro Aconcagua (highest point in South America, 6962 m)
Córdoba
Santa Fe
Porto Alegre
Salto
Valparaíso
Mendoza
Rosario
URUGUAY
Santiago
PAMPAS
Buenos Aires
La Plata
Montevideo
Concepcion
ARGENTINA
Bahía Blanca
Temuco
San Carlos de Bariloche
ANDES
South Atlan Ocea
Puerto Montt
PATAGONIA
Comodoro Rivadavia
Laguna del Carbón (lowest point in South America and the Western Hemisphere, -105 m)
SOUTH
Scale 1:35,000,000
Azimuthal Equal-Area Projection
Río Gallegos
Stanley
Falkland Islands (Islas Malvinas)
(administered by U.K., claimed by ARGENTINA)
0   500 Kilometers
0   500 Miles
Punta Arenas
Strait of Magellan
Ushuaia
Boundary representation is not necessarily authoritative.
Cape Horn

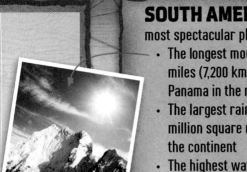

SOUTH AMERICA is dotted with some of the world's most spectacular physical features:

- The longest mountain range, the Andes, stretching 4,500 miles (7,200 km) from Chile in the south, to Venezuela and Panama in the north
- The largest rain forest, the Amazon, covering about 2 million square miles (5.2 million sq km), or two-fifths of the continent
- The highest waterfall, Angel Falls in Venezuela, plunging 3,212 feet (979 m)

South America is the fourth-largest continent, but only Australia and Antarctica have fewer people. About 80 percent of the people live in urban areas such as São Paulo, Brazil. South America's economy is growing fast, led by Brazil, Argentina, Colombia, and Chile.

Fortaleza

Natal

João
Pessoa

Recife

Maceió

Aracajú

Salvador

RIO
GRANDE
RISE

South America at a Glance

Area
6,887,000 sq. mi. (17,836,000 sq km)

Population
409,766,000

Number of countries
12

Largest country
Brazil
3,287,613 sq. mi. (8,514,877 sq km)

Most populated urban area
São Paulo, Brazil
19,924,458 people

Longest river
Amazon, Brazil
4,000 mi. (6,437 km)

Largest lake
Lake Maracaibo, Venezuela
5,217 sq. mi. (13,512 sq km)

Highest point
Aconcagua, Argentina
22,835 ft. (6,960 m) above sea level

Lowest point
Valdes Peninsula, Argentina
131 ft. (40 m) below sea level

CHECK
IT OUT
!

The Amazon rain forest is home to an estimated one in ten plant and animal species on Earth.

Jan Mayen (NORWAY)

Greenland Sea

Denmark Strait

Norwegian Sea

Nordkapp

Hammerfest

Tromsø

Murm

Reykjavik
ICELAND

Arctic Circle

Kiruna

NORWAY

Luleå

Oulu

Trondheim

Umeå

FINLAND

SWEDEN

Tampere

Faroe Islands (DENMARK)

Tórshavn

Bergen

Oslo

Gävle

Turku

Helsinki

ÅLAND ISLANDS

Tallinn

ESTONIA

SHETLAND ISLANDS

Stavanger

Stockholm

Gulf of Finland

ORKNEY ISLANDS

Göteborg

Gotland

Riga

LATVIA

HEBRIDES

Aberdeen

North Sea

Öland

Baltic Sea

LITHUANIA

Vilnius

Glasgow

Edinburgh

DENMARK

Malmö

Kaliningrad

RUSSIA

Hrodna

Belfast

UNITED

Copenhagen

Bornholm

Gdańsk

Dublin

Isle of Man (U.K.)

Leeds

Manchester

Hamburg

Poznań

Warsaw

Brest

IRELAND

Liverpool

KINGDOM

Birmingham

Bremen

Berlin

POLAND

Cardiff

Amsterdam

NETH.

Essen

Leipzig

Łódź

Wrocław

London

Rotterdam

Cologne

GERMANY

Prague

Kraków

Guernsey (U.K.)

Jersey (U.K.)

Brussels

BEL.

Lille

Bonn

Frankfurt

CZECH REPUBLIC

Brno

SLOVAKIA

Paris

Luxembourg

LUX.

Stuttgart

Bratislava

Nantes

Strasbourg

Munich

Vienna

Budapest

Bay of Biscay

MASSIF CENTRAL

Zürich

Vaduz

LIECH.

AUSTRIA

HUNGARY

Cluj-Napoc

FRANCE

Bern

SWITZ.

Geneva

Ljubljana

Zagreb

A Coruña

Bordeaux

Lyon

Turin

Milan

Venice

SLOVENIA

BOSNIA AND HERZEGOVINA

Belgrade

Bilbao

Genoa

CROATIA

SERBIA

Porto

Toulouse

MONACO

Florence

SAN MARINO

Sarajevo

Pristina

Zaragoza

Andorra la Vella

Marseille

ANDORRA

Corsica

ITALY

Podgorica

MONT.

KOS

S

PORTUGAL

Madrid

PYRENEES

Rome

VATICAN CITY

Tirana

MAC

Lisbon

Barcelona

Balearic Sea

Sardinia

Naples

ALB.

SPAIN

Valencia

BALEARIC ISLANDS

Cagliari

Tyrrhenian Sea

Ionian Sea

Sevilla

Mediterranean Sea

Palermo

Gibraltar (U.K.)

Málaga

Sicily

Ceuta (SPAIN)

Melilla (SPAIN)

Oran

Algiers

Tunis

Valletta

MALTA

Rabat

Casablanca

MOROCCO

ALGERIA

TUNISIA

Scale 1:19,30

Lambert Conformal Co
standard parallels 40°

0   300 KI

Irish Sea

Celtic Sea

English Channel

Oder

Vistula

Skagerrak

Kattegat

Gulf of Bothnia

Ligurian Sea

Adriatic Sea

Strait of Gibraltar

Alborán Sea

EUROPE is a small continent divided into many individual countries, with at least 50 different languages and up to 100 different dialects spoken. With the third-largest population and the second-smallest area of any continent, Europe is densely populated. Still, there's plenty of natural beauty in its rivers, lakes, canals, and towering mountain ranges such as the Urals and the Alps. Straddling the border between Europe and Asia is the largest inland body of water in the world, the saltwater Caspian Sea, which covers 149,200 square miles (386,400 sq km). European contributions in art, music, philosophy, and culture formed the basis for Western civilization.

Europe at a Glance

Area
4,033,000 sq. mi. (10,445,000 sq km)

Population
743,852,000

Number of countries
49

Largest country (entirely in Europe)
Ukraine
233,090 sq. mi. (603,628 sq km)

Most populated urban area
Moscow, Russia
11,620,600 people

Longest river
Volga, Russia
2,194 mi. (3,531 km) long

Largest lake
Lake Ladoga, Russia
6,835 sq. mi. (17,702 sq km)

Highest point
Mt. Elbrus, Russia
18,510 ft. (5,642 m) above sea level

Lowest point
Shore of the Caspian Sea
92 ft. (28 m) below sea level

CHECK IT OUT!

Europe has some of the world's longest railroad tunnels, including the Channel Tunnel, or Chunnel, which runs 31.1 miles (50 km) under the English Channel and connects the United Kingdom and France.

Boundary representation is not necessarily authoritative.

South Atlantic
Ocean

area of
enlargement

Queen Maud Land

Halley

Enderby
Land

Weddell Sea

Mac. Robertson
Land

Palmer
Land

Ronne
Ice Shelf

Bellingshausen
Sea

Ellsworth

Vinson Massif
(highest point in Antarctica, 4897 m)
Land

Peter I Island

South Pole
2800 m.

∇ **Bentley Subglacial Trench**
(lowest point in Antarctica, -2540 m)

Marie Byrd
Land

Ross
Ice Shelf

Amundsen
Sea

80

Wilkes Land

Ross Sea

average minimum
extent of sea ice

Victoria Land

70

Scott
Island

BALLENY
ISLANDS

Antarctic Circle

South
Pacific
Ocean

ANTARCTICA is the southernmost continent and the coldest place on Earth. It's almost entirely covered with ice that in some places is ten times as high as Chicago's Willis Tower, the tallest building in the United States. Gusts of wind up to 120 miles per hour (190 kph) make it feel even colder.

Antarctica is so cold, windy, and dry that humans never settled there. There are no countries, cities, or towns. However, researchers and scientists from different countries come to study earthquakes, the environment, weather, and more at scientific stations established by 19 countries. Some of these nations have claimed parts of Antarctica as their national territory, although other countries do not recognize the claims.

Few land animals can survive the continent's harsh conditions. The biggest one is a wingless insect called a midge, which is only one-half inch long. However, a great variety of whales, seals, penguins, and fish live in and near the surrounding ocean.

Ice Shelf

Shackleton
Ice Shelf

Antarctica at a Glance

Area
About 5,400,000 sq. mi. (14,000,000 sq km)

Population
No native people, but researchers come for various periods

Number of countries claiming territory
7

Number of research stations
60

Longest river
Onyx River 19 mi. (31 km) long

Highest point
Vinson Massif
16,050 ft. (4,892 m) above sea level

Lowest point
Bentley Subglacial Trench
8,383 ft. (2,555 m) below sea level

CHECK
IT OUT
!

The ice sheets covering Antarctica form the largest body of freshwater or ice in the world—7.25 million cubic miles (30 million cubic km), or about 70 percent of the world's freshwater.

Oceania
(Including Australia)

Equator

Yaren D

Samarinda • Palu
Ternate
Molucca
Sea
Balikpapan
Sorong • Biak
New
Ireland
Banjarmasin
Celebes
Ceram
Jayapura
Wewak
Bismarck Sea
Kendari
Buru
Ambon
Madang
PAPUA NEW GUINEA
Bougainville
Java Sea
Makassar
Banda Sea
Mount
Hagen
Lae
New Britain
Solomon
Sea
Surabaya
INDONESIA
Sumbawa
Flores
Dili
New Guinea
Java
Bali
Denpasar
Lombok
Sumba
Kupang
Timor
TIMOR-LESTE
Timor Sea
Arafura Sea
Torres
Strait
Awara
**Port
Moresby**
Gu

Indian
Ocean

Ashmore and
Cartier Island
(AUSTRALIA)
Darwin
Gulf of
Carpentaria

Cor
Isl.

C

Cairns

KING LEOPOLD
RANGE
MACDONNELL RANGE
GREAT
DIVIDING
RANGE

Townsville
Mackay
Rockhampton
Gladstone

20

Port
Hedland
HAMMERSLEY
RANGE
GREAT SANDY
DESERT
Mount Isa

Alice Springs
GIBSON
DESERT

AUSTRALIA
SIMPSON
DESERT

Toowoomba
Gold Coast
Brisbane

Geraldton
GREAT VICTORIA
DESERT
Lake Eyre
(lowest point
in Australia,
-15 m)
FLINDERS RANGE

Kalgoorlie

Perth
Rockingham
Bunbury
DARLING RANGE
Whyalla
Broken Hill
Newcastle
Sydney
Wollongong

Esperance
Adelaide
Canberra
Mount Kosciuszko
(highest point in Australia,
2229 m)
Melbourne

Great Australian
Bight
Geelong

LORD HOWE RIS

Tasman
Sea

40
Bass
Strait

Pacific Islands

Johnston Atoll
(U.S.)
North Pacific
Ocean
CLARION FRACTURE

Entwetok
MARSHALL
ISLANDS
Kwajalein
Majuro
Kingman Reef
(U.S.)
Palmyra Atoll
(U.S.)
CLIPPERTON FRACTURE ZONE

Pohnpei
Palikir
Kiritimati
(Christmas Island)
(KIRIBATI)
Equator
Tarawa
KIRIBATI
(GILBERT
ISLANDS)
Howland Island
(U.S.)
LINE ISLANDS

Yaren District
NAURU
Banaba
Baker Island
(U.S.)
Jarvis Island
(U.S.)

Bougainville
KIRIBATI
RAWAKI
(PHOENIX
ISLANDS)
KIRIBATI
ÎLES
MARQUISES

**SOLOMON
ISLANDS**
SANTA CRUZ
ISLANDS
TUVALU
Funafuti
Tokelau
(N.Z.)
Honiara
Guadalcanal
Rotuma
Swains Island

Coral Sea
Wallis and
Futuna
(FRANCE)
Mata-
Utu
SAMOA
Apia
Pago
Pago
American
Samoa
(U.S.)
Cook
Islands
(N.Z.)
SOCIETY
ISLANDS
Papeete
ARCHIPEL DES TUAMOTU
Tahiti

VANUATU
FIJI
Vanua
Levu
TONGA
Alofi
Niue
(N.Z.)
Avarua
French Polynesia
(FRANCE)
Mururoa

New
Caledonia
(FRANCE)
Port-Vila
Suva
Viti
Levu
Ceva-i-Ra

Noumea
Nuku'Alofa
Tropic of Capricorn
ÎLES TUBUAI
Adamstown

Minerva Reefs

sbane

KERMADEC
ISLANDS
(N.Z.)
Kingston
Norfolk Island
(AUSTRALIA)

LORD HOWE

OCEANIA is a large geographical area that includes Australia, New Zealand, Papua New Guinea, 11 other independent countries, and thousands of smaller islands. Australia is the world's smallest continent and the only continent that is also a country. Because Australia is surrounded by water, it is also technically an island.

Most of Australia is low and flat, with deserts covering about one-third of the continent. The world's largest coral reef, the Great Barrier Reef, is in the Coral Sea off the coast of Queensland in northeast Australia. Huge cattle and sheep ranches make Australia a leading producer of beef, mutton, and wool. Still, 90 percent of Australians live in cities and towns.

Oceania at a Glance

Area
3,300,000 sq. mi. (8,600,000 sq km)

Population
37,143,000

Number of countries
14

Most populated urban area
Sydney, Australia
4,543,205 people

Longest river
Murray-Darling, Australia
2,094 mi. (3,376 km) long

Largest lake
Lake Eyre, Australia
3,708 sq. mi. (9,399 sq km)

Highest point
Mount Wilhelm, Papua New Guinea
14,793 ft. (4,509 m)

Lowest point
Lake Eyre
−52 ft. (−16 m)

CHECK IT OUT!

All of Australia is located below the equator. This is why the continent is called "the land Down Under."

The Continents and Major Oceans

HOW MANY oceans are there? Actually, there's only one. Although the seven continents split the ocean into five major parts, the ocean is one huge connected body of water. This *world ocean* has an average depth of 13,000 feet (4,000 m), with parts plunging almost three times that deep. On the ocean floor is a landscape of valleys and ridges that is constantly changing, as magma from underwater volcanoes seeps out and forms new land.

The ocean provides food, energy, medicines, minerals, and most of the precipitation that falls to the earth. It regulates the world's climate by storing and releasing heat from the Sun. Without the ocean, there could be no life on our planet.

North America

Atlantic Ocean

South America

Pacific Ocean

Area
About 66 million sq. mi. (171 million sq km)

Greatest depth
35,840 ft. (10,924 m), in the Challenger Deep

Surface temperature
Highest: 82°F (28° C), near the equator in August
Lowest: 30°F (−1° C), in the polar region in winter

Area
About 34 million sq. mi. (88 million sq km)

Greatest depth
28,232 ft. (8,605 m) in the Puerto Rico Trench

Surface temperature
Highest: About 86°F (30° C), near the equator in summer
Lowest: 28°F (−2° C), at and near the boundary with the Southern Ocean in winter

Area
About 3,680,000 sq. mi. (9,530,000 sq km)

Greatest depth
18,399 ft. (5,608 m), in Molloy Hole, northwest of Svalbard

Surface temperature
Highest: 29°F (–1.5°C), in July
Lowest: 28°F (–2°C), in January

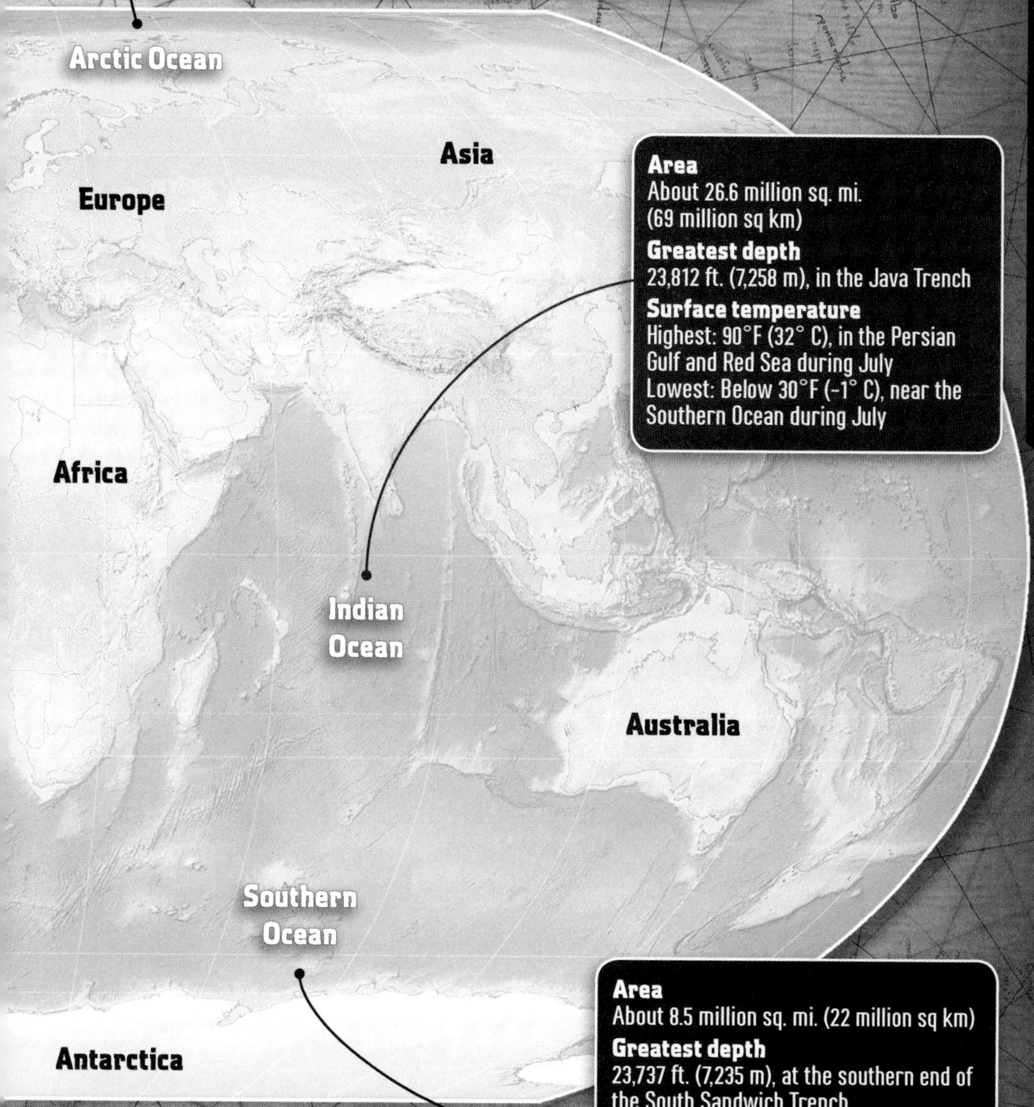

Arctic Ocean

Asia

Europe

Area
About 26.6 million sq. mi. (69 million sq km)

Greatest depth
23,812 ft. (7,258 m), in the Java Trench

Surface temperature
Highest: 90°F (32° C), in the Persian Gulf and Red Sea during July
Lowest: Below 30°F (–1° C), near the Southern Ocean during July

Africa

Indian Ocean

Australia

Southern Ocean

Antarctica

Area
About 8.5 million sq. mi. (22 million sq km)

Greatest depth
23,737 ft. (7,235 m), at the southern end of the South Sandwich Trench

Surface temperature
Highest: 30 to 43°F (–1 to 6°C), near 60° south latitude in February
Lowest: 28 to 30°F (–2 to–1°C), near Antarctica in August

World's **5** Deepest Oceans and Seas

(Ranked by average depth)

Pacific Ocean
14,040 ft. (4,279 m)

Indian Ocean
12,800 ft. (3,900 m)

Atlantic Ocean
11,810 ft. (3,600 m)

Caribbean Sea
8,448 ft. (2,575 m)

Sea of Japan
5,468 ft. (1,666 m)

World's **5** Largest Lakes

Caspian Sea
Azerbaijan/Iran/Kazakhstan/
Russia/Turkmenistan
146,101 sq. mi.
(378,401 sq km)

Lake Superior
Canada/United States
31,699 sq. mi.
(378,401 sq km)

Lake Victoria
Kenya/Tanzania/Uganda
26,828 sq. mi.
(69,485 sq km)

Lake Huron
Canada/United States
23,004 sq. mi.
(59,580 sq km)

Lake Michigan
United States
22,278 sq. mi.
(57,700 sq km)

World's 5 Highest Waterfalls

Angel
Venezuela
Tributary of Caroni River
3,212 ft. (979 m)

Tugela
South Africa
Tugela River
3,110 ft. (948 m)

Tres Hermanas
Peru
Cutivireni River
3,000 ft. (914 m)

Olo'upena
United States
2,953 ft. (900 m)

Yumbilla
Peru
2,938 ft. (896 m)

World's 5 Longest River Systems

Nile
Tanzania/Uganda/Sudan/Egypt
4,145 mi.
(6,670 km)

Amazon
Peru/Brazil
4,007 mi.
(6,448 km)

Yangtze-Kiang
China
3,915 mi.
(6,300 km)

Mississippi-Missouri-Red
United States
3,710 mi.
(5,971 km)

Yenisey-Angara-Selenga
Mongolia/Russia
2,500 mi.
(4,000 km)

World's 5 Highest Mountains

(Height of principal peak; lower peaks of same mountain excluded)

Mt. Everest
Nepal/Tibet
29,035 ft. (8,850 m)

K2
Kashmir/China
28,250 ft. (8,611 m)

Kanchenjunga
Nepal/Sikkim
28,208 ft. (8,598 m)

Lhotse
Tibet
27,923 ft. (8,511 m)

Makalu
Nepal/Tibet
27,824 ft. (8,480 m)

Grand Canyon
Location: Arizona

Redwood Forest
Location: California

Yellowstone
Location: Wyoming

Bryce Canyon
Location: Utah

Crater Lake
Location: Oregon

Geography—World & US

10 Largest States in Total Area

1. Alaska	663,267 sq. mi. (1,717,854 sq km)
2. Texas	268,581 sq. mi. (695,622 sq km)
3. California	163,696 sq. mi. (423,971 sq km)
4. Montana	147,042 sq. mi. (380,837 sq km)
5. New Mexico	121,589 sq. mi. (314,914 sq km)
6. Arizona	113,998 sq. mi. (295,253 sq km)
7. Nevada	110,561 sq. mi. (286,352 sq km)
8. Colorado	104,094 sq. mi. (269,602 sq km)
9. Oregon	98,381 sq. mi. (254,806 sq km)
10. Wyoming	97,814 sq. mi. (253,337 sq km)

10 Smallest States in Total Area

1. Rhode Island	1,545 sq. mi. (4,002 sq km)
2. Delaware	2,489 sq. mi. (6,446 sq km)
3. Connecticut	5,543 sq. mi. (14,356 sq km)
4. New Jersey	8,721 sq. mi. (22,587 sq km)
5. New Hampshire	9,350 sq. mi. (24,216 sq km)
6. Vermont	9,614 sq. mi. (24,900 sq km)
7. Massachusetts	10,555 sq. mi. (27,337 sq km)
8. Hawaii	10,931 sq. mi. (28,311 sq km)
9. Maryland	12,407 sq. mi. (32,134 sq km)
10. West Virginia	24,230 sq. mi. (62,755 sq km)

5 Highest US Mountains

Mt. McKinley
Alaska
20,320 ft. (6,194 m)

Mt. St. Elias
Alaska—Yukon
18,008 ft. (5,489 m)

Mt. Foraker
Alaska
17,400 ft. (5,304 m)

Mt. Bona
Alaska
16,550 ft. (5,044 m)

Mt. Blackburn
Alaska
16,390 ft. (4,996 m)

10 Longest US Rivers

Mississippi
2,348 mi. (3,779 km)

Missouri
2,315 mi. (3,726 km)

Yukon
1,979 mi. (3,186 km)

Rio Grande
1,900 mi. (3,058 km)

Arkansas
1,459 mi. (2,348 km)

Red
1,290 mi. (2,076 km)

Columbia
1,243 mi. (2,000 km)

Snake
1,038 mi. (1,670 km)

Ohio
981 mi. (1,579 km)

St. Lawrence
800 mi. (1,287 km)

10 Largest US National Historical Parks

(By total acreage and hectares)

Chaco Culture
New Mexico
33,960 acres (13,743 h)

Cumberland Gap
Kentucky/Tennessee/Virginia
22,365 acres (9,050 h)

Jean Lafitte
Louisiana
20,001 acres (8,094 h)

Chesapeake & Ohio Canal
Maryland/West Virginia/
Washington, DC
19,615 acres (7,938 h)

Klondike Gold Rush
Alaska/Washington
12,996 acres (5,259 h)

Colonial
Virginia
8,676 acres (3,511 h)

Pecos
New Mexico
6,669 acres (2,699 h)

Nez Perce
Idaho/Montana/
Oregon/Washington
4,570 acres (1,849 h)

Harpers Ferry
West Virginia/Maryland/Virginia
3,647 acres (1,476 h)

Cedar Creek & Belle Grove
Virginia
3,712 acres (1,502 h)

The Great Lakes—Facts and Figures

Lake Superior
Area	31,700 sq. mi. (82,103 sq km)
Borders	Minnesota, Wisconsin, Michigan (United States); Ontario (Canada)
Major Ports	Duluth, Superior, Sault Ste. Marie (United States); Sault Ste. Marie, Thunder Bay (Canada)

Lake Huron
Area	23,000 sq. mi. (59,570 sq km)
Borders	Michigan (United States); Ontario (Canada)
Major Ports	Port Huron (United States); Sarnia (Canada)

Lake Michigan
Area	22,300 sq. mi. (57,570 sq km)
Borders	Illinois, Indiana, Michigan, Wisconsin (United States)
Major Ports	Milwaukee, Racine, Kenosha, Chicago, Gary, Muskegon (United States)

Lake Erie
Area	9,940 sq. mi. (25,745 sq km)
Borders	Michigan, New York, Ohio, Pennsylvania (United States); Ontario (Canada)
Major Ports	Toledo, Sandusky, Lorain, Cleveland, Erie, Buffalo (United States)

Lake Ontario
Area	7,340 sq. mi. (19,011 sq km)
Borders	New York (United States); Ontario (Canada)
Major Ports	Rochester, Oswego (United States); Toronto, Hamilton (Canada)

The Great Lakes from Space

An easy way to remember the names of the Great Lakes is the mnemonic *HOMES*:

H URON
O NTARIO
M ICHIGAN
E RIE
S UPERIOR

CHECK IT OUT !

National Parks by State

Alaska
Denali
Gates of the Arctic
Glacier Bay
Katmai
Kenai Fjords
Kobuk Valley
Lake Clark
Wrangell-St. Elias

Arizona
Grand Canyon
Petrified Forest
Saguaro

Arkansas
Hot Springs

California
Channel Islands
Death Valley
Joshua Tree
Kings Canyon
Lassen Volcanic
Redwood
Sequoia
Yosemite

Colorado
Black Canyon of the Gunnison
Great Sand Dunes
Mesa Verde
Rocky Mountain

Florida
Biscayne
Dry Tortugas
Everglades

Hawaii
Haleakala
Hawaii Volcanoes

Idaho
Yellowstone

Kentucky
Mammoth Cave

Maine
Acadia

Michigan
Isle Royale

Minnesota
Voyageurs

Montana
Glacier
Yellowstone

Nevada
Death Valley
Great Basin

New Mexico
Carlsbad Caverns

North Carolina
Great Smoky Mountains

North Dakota
Theodore Roosevelt

Ohio
Cuyahoga Valley

Oregon
Crater Lake

South Carolina
Congaree

South Dakota
Badlands
Wind Cave

Tennessee
Great Smoky Mountains

Texas
Big Bend
Guadalupe Mountains

Utah
Arches
Bryce Canyon
Capitol Reef
Canyonlands
Zion

Virginia
Shenandoah

Washington
Mount Rainier
North Cascades
Olympic

Wyoming
Grand Teton
Yellowstone

10 Most Visited US National Parks

In 2013, total visitation at national parks dropped by 9.1 million, due to a two-week government shutdown and the effects of Hurricane Sandy.

Park (Location)	Visitors in 2013
Great Smoky Mountains (Tennessee/North Carolina)	9,354,695
Grand Canyon (Arizona)	4,564,840
Yosemite (California)	3,691,191
Yellowstone (Wyoming)	3,188,030
Olympic (Washington)	3,085,340
Rocky Mountain (Colorado)	2,991,141
Zion (Utah)	2,807,387
Grand Teton (Wyoming)	2,688,794
Acadia (Maine)	2,254,922
Glacier (Montana)	2,190,374

US National Memorials

Memorial	State	Description
Arkansas Post	Arkansas	First permanent French settlement in the lower Mississippi River valley
Arlington House (Robert E. Lee Memorial)	Virginia	Lee's home overlooking the Potomac
Chamizal	Texas	Commemorates 1963 settlement of 99-year border dispute with Mexico
Coronado	Arizona	Commemorates first European exploration of the Southwest
De Soto	Florida	Commemorates 16th-century Spanish explorations
Father Marquette	Michigan	Commemorates Father Jacques Marquette, a French Jesuit missionary who helped establish Michigan's first European settlement at Sault Ste. Marie in 1668
Federal Hall	New York	First seat of US government under the Constitution
Flight 93	Pennsylvania	Commemorates the passengers and crew of Flight 93, who lost their lives to bring down a plane headed to attack the nation's capital on September 11, 2001
Fort Caroline	Florida	On St. Johns River; overlooks site of a French Huguenot colony
Fort Clatsop	Oregon	Lewis and Clark encampment, 1805–1806
Franklin Delano Roosevelt	DC	Statues of President Roosevelt and First Lady Eleanor Roosevelt, as well as waterfalls and gardens; dedicated May 2, 1997
General Grant	New York	Grant's Tomb
Hamilton Grange	New York	Home of Alexander Hamilton
Jefferson National Expansion Monument	Missouri	Commemorates westward expansion
Johnstown Flood	Pennsylvania	Commemorates tragic flood of 1889
Korean War Veterans	DC	Dedicated in 1995; honors those who served in the Korean War
Lincoln Boyhood	Indiana	Site of Lincoln cabin, boyhood home, and grave of Lincoln's mother
Lincoln Memorial	DC	Marble statue of the 16th US president
Lyndon B. Johnson Grove on the Potomac	DC	Honors the 36th president; overlooks the Potomac River vista of the capital
Martin Luther King Jr. Memorial	DC	Dedicated October 16, 2011; honors the civil rights leader with a sculpture, the "Stone of Hope"
Mount Rushmore	South Dakota	World-famous sculpture of four presidents
Oklahoma City	Oklahoma	Commemorates the April 19, 1995, bombing of the Alfred P. Murrah Federal Building
Perry's Victory and International Peace Memorial	Ohio	The world's largest Doric column, constructed 1912–1915, promotes pursuit of international peace through arbitration and disarmament
Roger Williams	Rhode Island	Memorial to founder of Rhode Island
Thaddeus Kosciuszko	Pennsylvania	Memorial to Polish hero of the American Revolution
Theodore Roosevelt Island	DC	Statue of the 26th president in wooded island sanctuary
Thomas Jefferson Memorial	DC	Statue of the 3rd president in a circular, colonnaded structure
USS *Arizona*	Hawaii	Memorializes American losses at Pearl Harbor
Vietnam Veterans	DC	Black granite wall inscribed with names of those missing or killed in action in the Vietnam War
Washington Monument	DC	Obelisk honoring the 1st US president
World War II	DC	Oval plaza with central pool commemorating those who fought and died in World War II
Wright Brothers	North Carolina	Site of first powered flight

US National Battlefields

Stones River, Tennessee
Scene of battle that began Union offensive to trisect Confederacy

Fort Donelson, Tennessee
Site of first major Union victory

Antietam, Maryland
Battle here ended first Confederate invasion of North, Sept. 17, 1862

Big Hole, Montana
Site of major battle between Nez Perce and US Army

Petersburg, Virginia
Scene of 10-month Union campaigns, 1864–1865

Fort Necessity, Pennsylvania
Some of the first battles of French and Indian War

Wilson's Creek, Missouri
Scene of Civil War battle for control of Missouri

Tupelo, Mississippi
Site of crucial Civil War battle over Sherman's supply line

Cowpens, South Carolina
American Revolution battlefield

Monocacy, Maryland
Civil War battle in defense of Washington, DC, fought here July 9, 1864

Moores Creek, North Carolina
1776 battle between Patriots and Loyalists commemorated here

Stats on the Statue of Liberty

The Statue of Liberty was designed by French sculptor Frederic Auguste Bartholdi and arrived in 214 packing cases from Rouen, France, in June 1885. The completed statue was dedicated on October 28, 1886, by President Grover Cleveland. It was designated a National Monument in 1924 and is one of America's most famous symbols of freedom.

Part of Statue	Measurement
Height from heel to torch	151 ft. 1 in. (45.3 m)
Height from base of pedestal to torch	305 ft. 1 in. (91.5 m)
Length of hand	16 ft. 5 in. (5 m)
Length of index finger	8 ft. 0 in. (2.4 m)
Circumference at second finger joint	3 ft. 6 in. (1 m)
Size of fingernail	13 x 10 in. (33 x 25 cm)
Height of head from chin to cranium	17 ft. 3 in. (5 m)
Thickness of head from ear to ear	10 ft. 0 in. (3 m)
Distance across eye	2 ft. 6 in. (0.76 m)
Length of nose	4 ft. 6 in. (1.4 m)
Length of right arm	42 ft. 0 in. (12.8 m)
Thickness of right arm at thickest point	12 ft. 0 in. (3.7 m)
Thickness of waist	35 ft. 0 in. (10.7 m)
Width of mouth	3 ft. 0 in. (1 m)
Length of tablet	23 ft. 7 in. (7.2 m)
Width of tablet	13 ft. 7 in. (4.1 m)
Thickness of tablet	2 ft. 0 in. (0.6 m)

Geography—World & US

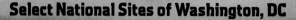

Select National Sites of Washington, DC

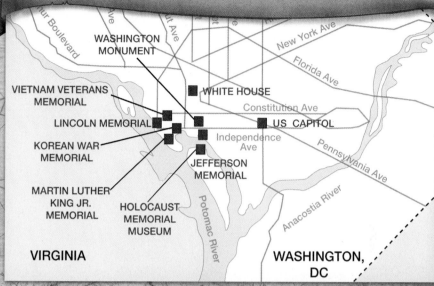

WASHINGTON MONUMENT

VIETNAM VETERANS MEMORIAL

WHITE HOUSE

LINCOLN MEMORIAL

Constitution Ave

US CAPITOL

KOREAN WAR MEMORIAL

Independence Ave

JEFFERSON MEMORIAL

New York Ave

Florida Ave

Pennsylvania Ave

Anacostia River

MARTIN LUTHER KING JR. MEMORIAL

HOLOCAUST MEMORIAL MUSEUM

Potomac River

VIRGINIA

WASHINGTON, DC

US Capitol
The Capitol is open to the public for guided tours 8:50 AM to 3:20 PM, Monday through Saturday. Tickets are available at tour kiosks at the east and west fronts of the Capitol.
Phone: (202) 226-8000

Holocaust Memorial Museum
The museum is open daily, beginning at 10:00 AM, except Yom Kippur and December 25. 100 Raoul Wallenburg Pl., SW (formerly 15th St., SW) near Independence Ave.
Phone: (202) 488-0400

Jefferson Memorial
The memorial, which is located on the south edge of the Tidal Basin, is open 8 AM to 11:45 PM every day except Christmas Day. An elevator and curb ramps for the disabled are in service.
Phone: (202) 426-6841

Korean War Memorial
The $18 million military memorial, which was funded by private donations, is open 24 hours a day.
Phone: (202) 426-6841

Lincoln Memorial
The memorial, which is located in West Potomac Park, is open 8 AM to 11:45 PM every day except Christmas Day. An elevator and curb ramps for the disabled are in service.
Phone: (202) 426-6841

Martin Luther King Jr. Memorial
This memorial features a sculpture of the late civil rights leader that seems to be rising from a mountain of granite and a wall inscribed with some of his famous quotes. It is open 24 hours a day throughout the year.
Phone: (202) 426-6841

Vietnam Veterans Memorial
The memorial is open 24 hours a day.
Phone: (202) 426-6841

Washington Monument
The memorial is open 9:00 AM–4:45 PM daily, except July 4 and December 25. Tickets are required for entry and can be either reserved ahead of time or picked up same day. The monument was closed in 2011 for repairs of damages caused by an earthquake, but it reopened on May 12, 2014.
Phone: (202) 426-6841

The White House
Free reserved tickets for guided tours can be obtained up to six months in advance. Contact your senators or representatives for tickets.
Phone: (202) 456-7041

HEALTH & WELLNESS

DON'T SKIP THIS!

Every year, hundreds of young athletes gather from around the world at the Apollo Theatre in Harlem to compete in the Double Dutch Holiday Classic (left). In Double Dutch, two people turn ropes in opposite directions while a third person jumps, doing tricks and stunts. The game came over from Europe with Dutch settlers in the 1600s and became a popular street game in cities, especially New York. A New York City police detective named David A. Walker helped develop it into a competitive team sport in 1973. Today there are national and international events with about 100,000 girls and boys competing, mostly middle-schoolers.

Double Dutch jumpers compete in standard, compulsory, and freestyle events. Freestyle accompanied by music is called fusion. Some of the coolest Double Dutch stunts look like gymnastics or break-dancing: the criss-cross, the pop-up, the 360, the hand plant, the backflip, the high-step, and the push-up. Competitive jumpers are rated on technical difficulty, artistic quality, accuracy, and other standards.

YOUR TURN

Learn more about Double Dutch at worldjumprope.org.

What is your body's largest organ? (See p. 187.)

Systems of the Human Body

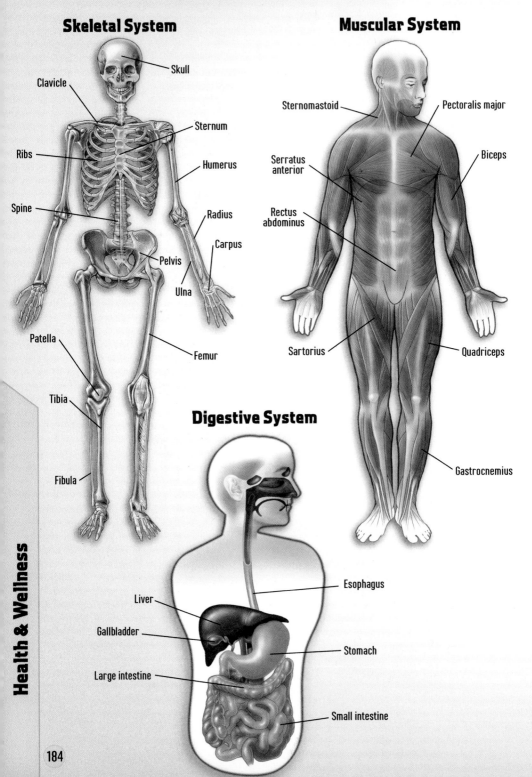

Skeletal System

- Skull
- Clavicle
- Sternum
- Ribs
- Humerus
- Spine
- Radius
- Pelvis
- Carpus
- Ulna
- Patella
- Femur
- Tibia
- Fibula

Muscular System

- Sternomastoid
- Pectoralis major
- Serratus anterior
- Biceps
- Rectus abdominus
- Sartorius
- Quadriceps
- Gastrocnemius

Digestive System

- Esophagus
- Liver
- Gallbladder
- Stomach
- Large intestine
- Small intestine

Health & Wellness

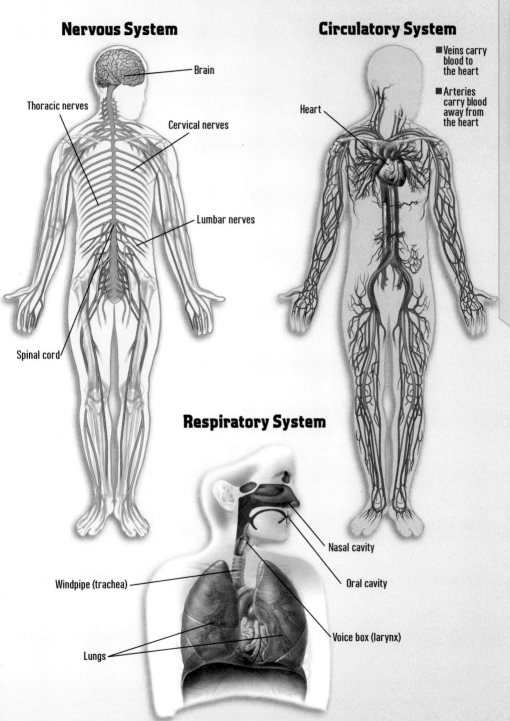

Nervous System

Brain

Thoracic nerves

Cervical nerves

Lumbar nerves

Spinal cord

Circulatory System

- Veins carry blood to the heart
- Arteries carry blood away from the heart

Heart

Respiratory System

Windpipe (trachea)

Lungs

Nasal cavity

Oral cavity

Voice box (larynx)

The New Food Pyramid

In 2005, the US Department of Agriculture (USDA) created a new food pyramid. The colored parts of the pyramid stand for different food groups. The width of each part shows what portion of your daily diet should be from that food group.

The amounts shown below are based on what a 12-year-old boy of average height and weight who is moderately active should eat every day. To figure out your own personal food pyramid plan, go to **mypyramid.gov**.

The most popular fruit in the world is one you may think is a vegetable—the tomato. Scientifically speaking, a tomato is considered a fruit because it comes from a flowering plant that contains seeds. Sixty million tons of tomatoes are produced every year.

CHECK IT OUT !

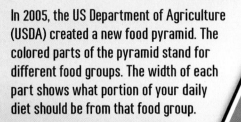

Health & Wellness

Grains	Vegetables	Fruits	Milk	Meat & Beans
Seven ounces of bread, cereal, crackers, rice, or pasta every day. At least half should be whole grains.	Three cups every day, fresh or frozen. Dark green, orange, light green—mix it up!	Two cups of nature's sweet treats a day. Go easy on the fruit juice.	Three cups a day. Choose nonfat or lowfat milk products.	Six ounces of lean protein a day: meat, fish, or poultry, or nuts, seeds, beans, and peas.

Oils Oils aren't a food group, but you need some for good health. Nuts and fish are good sources. Be sure to limit sugars and solid fats such as butter. Read the labels—you might be surprised!

Kids' Top 5 Favorite Activities

According to a study by the Outdoor Foundation, these are the favorite activities of kids between the ages of 6 and 17:

1. Running/ Jogging
2. Biking
3. Skateboarding
4. Fishing
5. Camping

While millions of kids love outdoor activities, millions of others don't get enough exercise. What are they doing instead? According to Let's Move!, the kid's health program started by First Lady Michelle Obama, young people spend an average of 7.5 hours a day watching TV or movies, using computers, playing video games, and talking or texting on cell phones. To control weight and limit risk of certain diseases, experts recommend at least 60 minutes of exercise every day. Find an activity you love and start moving in a healthy direction!

Your Amazing Body, by the Numbers

Your heart pumps blood along 60,000 miles (97,000 km) of veins and arteries. It beats 100,000 times a day—that's 40 million times a year and more than 3 billion times in an average lifetime.

Your brain weighs only about 3 pounds (1.4 kg), but it has about 100 billion nerve cells. Nerves help you think, move, dream, feel happy or sad, and regulate unconscious activities such as digesting food and breathing.

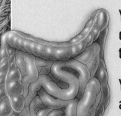

Your digestive system consists of about 30 feet (9 m) of tubes that carry food along a journey from top to bottom, squeezing out nutrients to keep you healthy and processing waste materials.

Your skin is your body's largest organ, weighing about 8 pounds (3.6 kg) and measuring about 22 square feet (2 sq m). Be good to your skin by keeping it clean and well protected from the sun.

Inventors & Inventions

This Teen's Invention Could Save Thousands of Lives. Every Year.

Pancreatic cancer kills about 40,000 people a year. It is one of the deadliest forms of cancer because there are often no symptoms. By the time doctors find it, the cancer has spread and become untreatable. But thanks to a Maryland teenager named Jack Andraka, early detection could soon be an option.

For seven months, Jack spent every day after school, including his 15th birthday, working in a nearby university lab. What he came up with was a simple five-minute test that uses one-sixth of a drop of blood to show the presence of pancreatic cancer. Scientists say Jack's test has the potential to save thousands of lives.

YOUR TURN

Young inventors and scientists like Jack Andraka are changing the world. How about you? The National Museum of Education offers competitions and opportunities for students in grades K-12. Check out nmoe.org for more information.

Which came first? (See pp. 190-191.)

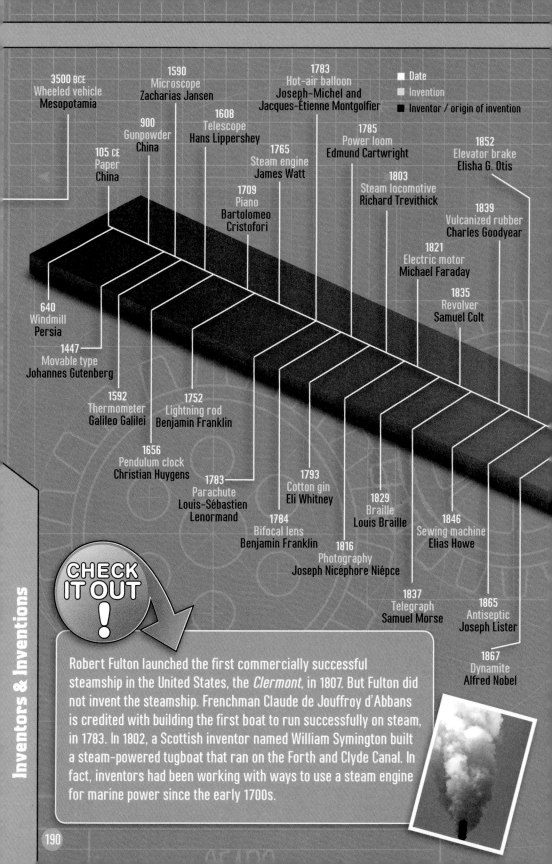

3500 BCE
Wheeled vehicle
Mesopotamia

1590
Microscope
Zacharias Jansen

1783
Hot-air balloon
Joseph-Michel and
Jacques-Étienne Montgolfier

■ Date
■ Invention
■ Inventor / origin of invention

900
Gunpowder
China

1608
Telescope
Hans Lippershey

1785
Power loom
Edmund Cartwright

1852
Elevator brake
Elisha G. Otis

105 CE
Paper
China

1765
Steam engine
James Watt

1803
Steam locomotive
Richard Trevithick

1709
Piano
Bartolomeo
Cristofori

1839
Vulcanized rubber
Charles Goodyear

1821
Electric motor
Michael Faraday

640
Windmill
Persia

1835
Revolver
Samuel Colt

1447
Movable type
Johannes Gutenberg

1592
Thermometer
Galileo Galilei

1752
Lightning rod
Benjamin Franklin

1656
Pendulum clock
Christian Huygens

1783
Parachute
Louis-Sébastien
Lenormand

1793
Cotton gin
Eli Whitney

1829
Braille
Louis Braille

1846
Sewing machine
Elias Howe

1784
Bifocal lens
Benjamin Franklin

1816
Photography
Joseph Nicéphore Niépce

1865
Antiseptic
Joseph Lister

1837
Telegraph
Samuel Morse

1867
Dynamite
Alfred Nobel

CHECK
IT OUT
!

Robert Fulton launched the first commercially successful
steamship in the United States, the *Clermont*, in 1807. But Fulton did
not invent the steamship. Frenchman Claude de Jouffroy d'Abbans
is credited with building the first boat to run successfully on steam,
in 1783. In 1802, a Scottish inventor named William Symington built
a steam-powered tugboat that ran on the Forth and Clyde Canal. In
fact, inventors had been working with ways to use a steam engine
for marine power since the early 1700s.

Important Inventions and Their Inventors

These are just a few of the inventions that have shaped our world and changed our lives. The inventors listed are either those who received patents for the invention or the ones widely credited with introducing the version of the invention we use today. But in many cases, other inventors contributed to the invention by doing experiments or making earlier versions. Do some additional research for the whole story behind these inventions and others.

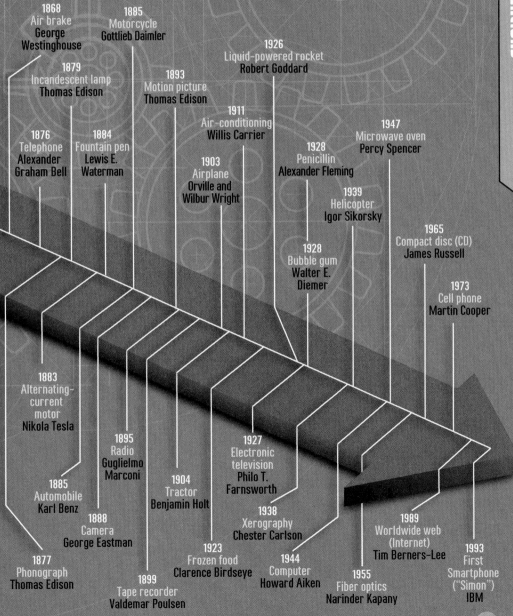

1868
Air brake
George Westinghouse

1885
Motorcycle
Gottlieb Daimler

1926
Liquid-powered rocket
Robert Goddard

1879
Incandescent lamp
Thomas Edison

1893
Motion picture
Thomas Edison

1947
Microwave oven
Percy Spencer

1876
Telephone
Alexander Graham Bell

1884
Fountain pen
Lewis E. Waterman

1911
Air-conditioning
Willis Carrier

1928
Penicillin
Alexander Fleming

1903
Airplane
Orville and Wilbur Wright

1939
Helicopter
Igor Sikorsky

1965
Compact disc (CD)
James Russell

1928
Bubble gum
Walter E. Diemer

1973
Cell phone
Martin Cooper

1883
Alternating-current motor
Nikola Tesla

1895
Radio
Guglielmo Marconi

1927
Electronic television
Philo T. Farnsworth

1885
Automobile
Karl Benz

1904
Tractor
Benjamin Holt

1888
Camera
George Eastman

1938
Xerography
Chester Carlson

1989
Worldwide web (Internet)
Tim Berners-Lee

1877
Phonograph
Thomas Edison

1923
Frozen food
Clarence Birdseye

1944
Computer
Howard Aiken

1993
First Smartphone ("Simon")
IBM

1899
Tape recorder
Valdemar Poulsen

1955
Fiber optics
Narinder Kapany

LANGUAGES

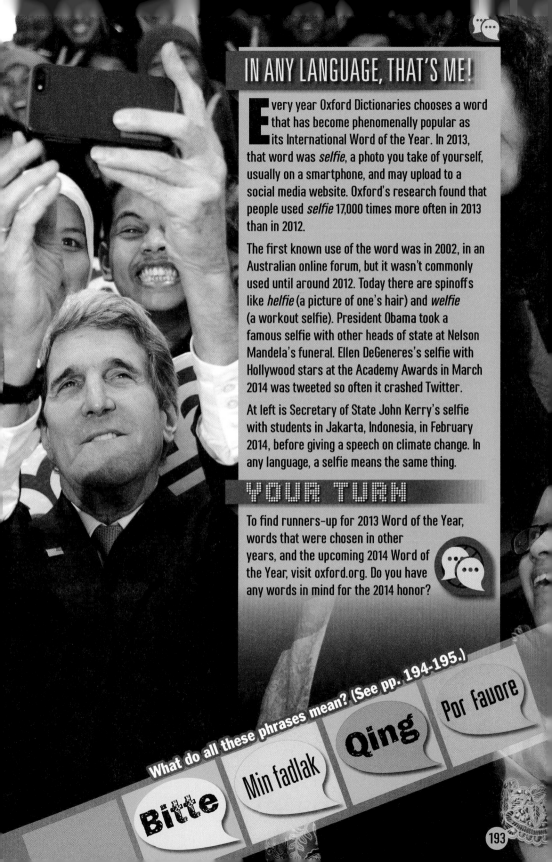

IN ANY LANGUAGE, THAT'S ME!

Every year Oxford Dictionaries chooses a word that has become phenomenally popular as its International Word of the Year. In 2013, that word was *selfie*, a photo you take of yourself, usually on a smartphone, and may upload to a social media website. Oxford's research found that people used *selfie* 17,000 times more often in 2013 than in 2012.

The first known use of the word was in 2002, in an Australian online forum, but it wasn't commonly used until around 2012. Today there are spinoffs like *helfie* (a picture of one's hair) and *welfie* (a workout selfie). President Obama took a famous selfie with other heads of state at Nelson Mandela's funeral. Ellen DeGeneres's selfie with Hollywood stars at the Academy Awards in March 2014 was tweeted so often it crashed Twitter.

At left is Secretary of State John Kerry's selfie with students in Jakarta, Indonesia, in February 2014, before giving a speech on climate change. In any language, a selfie means the same thing.

YOUR TURN

To find runners-up for 2013 Word of the Year, words that were chosen in other years, and the upcoming 2014 Word of the Year, visit oxford.org. Do you have any words in mind for the 2014 honor?

What do all these phrases mean? (See pp. 194-195.)

Bitte

Min fadlak

Qing

Por favore

193

Common Words and Phrases in Select Languages

MANDARIN CHINESE

Hello	Ni hao (nee how)
Good-bye	Zai jian (zay gee-en)
Yes	Shide (sure-due)
No	Bu shi (boo sure)
Please	Qing (ching)
Thank you	Xiexie (shieh-shieh)
You're welcome	Bukeqi (boo-keh-chee)
Excuse me	Duibuqi (doo-ee-boo-chee)

SPANISH

Hello	Hola (OH-lah)
Good-bye	Adiós (ah-dee-OHSS)
Good morning	Buenos días (BWAY-nohs DEE-ahs)
Good afternoon	Buenas tardes (BWAY-nahs TAHR-dehs)
Good evening	Buenas noches (BWAY-nahs NOH-chehs)
Yes	Sí (SEE)
No	No (NOH)
Please	Por favor (por fa-VOHR)
Thank you	Gracias (GRAH-see-ahs)
You're welcome	De nada (DE nada)
What's going on?	¿Qué pasa? (kay PAH-sah)
How are you?	¿Cómo está usted? (COH-mo es-TAH oo-STEHD)

GERMAN

Hello	Guten Tag (GOO-tin TAHK)
Good-bye	Auf Wiedersehen (ahf VEE-dehr-zeh-hehn)
Good morning	Guten Morgen (GOO-tin MOR-gun)
Yes	Ja (yah)
No	Nein (nine)
Please	Bitte (BIT-uh)
Thank you	Danke (DAHN-keh)
You're welcome	Bitte schön (BIT-uh shane)

Privet!

góðan dag

salut

ITALIAN

Hi, 'bye (informal)	Ciao (chow)
Good-bye	Arrivederci (ah-ree-vay-DEHR-chee)
Good morning, good afternoon, or a general hello	Buon giorno (bwohn JOOR-noh)
Yes	Sì (SEE)
No	No (NOH)
Please	Per favore (purr fa-VO-ray)
Thank you	Grazie (GRAH-tsee-ay)
You're welcome	Prego (PRAY-go)
How are you?	Come sta? (KOH-may STAH)
Fine, very well	Molto bene (MOHL-toh BAY-nay)
Excuse me	Scusi (SKOO-zee)

EGYPTIAN ARABIC

Good morning	Sabah el khair (sa-BAH el KHAIR)
Good-bye	Ma salama (MA sa-LA-ma)
Yes	Aiwa (AYE-wa)
No	La (la)
Please	Min fadlak (min FAD-lak)
Thank you	Shukran (SHU-kran)
No problem	Ma fee mushkila (ma FEE mush-KI-la)
How are you?	Izzayak? (iz-ZAY-ak)
What is your name?	Ismak ay? (IS-mak AY)

JAPANESE

Hi	Konnichiwa (koh-nee-chee-wah)
Good-bye	Ja mata (jahh mah-tah)
Yes	Hai (hah-ee)
No	Iie (EE-eh)
Good morning	Ohayō gozaimasu (oh-hah-yohh goh-zah-ee-mahs)
Excuse me	Sumimasen (soo-mee-mah-sehn)
Pleased to meet you	Yoroshiku (yoh-roh-shee-koo)
One	Ichi (ee-chee)
Thank you	Dōmo arigatō (dohh-moh ah-ri-gah-toh)

hoi

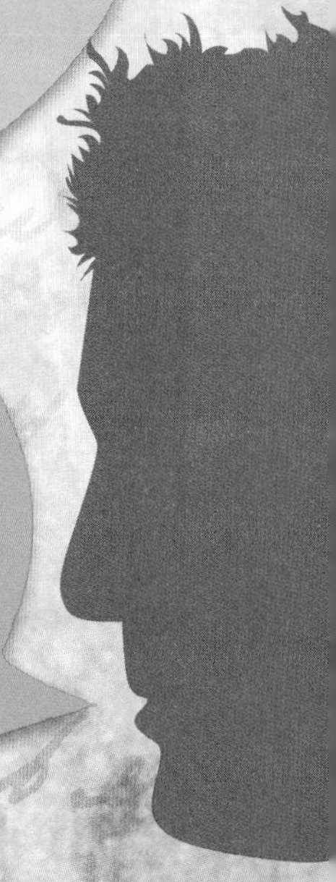

Common Words and Phrases in Select Languages (continued)

FRENCH

Hello	Bonjour (bohn-ZHOOR)
Good-bye	Au revoir (oh reh-VWAH)
Yes	Oui (wee)
No	Non (no)
Excuse me	Pardonnez-moi (par-dough-nay MWAH)
Please	S'il vous plaît (see voo PLAY)
Thank you	Merci (mare-SEE)
How are you?	Comment allez-vous? (co-mahn-tah-lay VOO)

KOREAN

Hello	Anyŏng haseyo (ahn-n'yohng hah-say-yoh)
Good-bye	Anyŏng-hi kyeseyo (ahn-n'yohng-he kuh-say-yoh)
Please	Jwe-song-ha-ji-mahn (chey-song-hah-gee-mon)
Thank you	Kamsahamnida (kahm-sah-hahm-need-dah)
Excuse me	Miam hamnida (Me-ahn hahm-nee-dah)
One	Hana (hah-nah)
Ten	Yeol (yuhl)

xin chào

Hi

NIGERIAN
(four of the major Nigerian language groups)

English	Fulani	Hausa	Ibo	Yoruba
I'm fine	Jam tan (JAM-taan)	Kalau (KA-lay-U)	Adimnma (ah-DEE-mm-NMAA)	A dupe (ah-DEW-pay)
one	gogo (GO-quo)	daya (DA-ya)	otu (o-TOO)	eni (EE-nee)
two	didi (DEE-dee)	biyu (BEE-you)	abua (ah-BOO-ah)	eji (EE-gee)
three	tati (TA-tea)	uku (OO-coo)	ato (ah-TOE)	eta (EE-ta)
nine	jeenayi (gee-NA-yee)	tara (TAA-ra)	iteghete (IT-egg-HE-tee)	esan (EE-san)
ten	sappo (SAP-poe)	goma (GO-ma)	iri (EE-ree)	ewa (EE-wa)

Which Languages Are Spoken Most?

The following languages have the most speakers in the world. The languages combine individual varieties and dialects that may have different names. The numbers include only first-language (mother-tongue) speakers.

Language	Estimated Number of Speakers (in millions)
Chinese	1,197
Spanish	406
English	335
Hindi	260
Arabic	223
Portuguese	202
Bengali	193
Russian	162
Japanese	122
Javanese	84
German	84
Lahnda	83
Telugu	74
Marathi	72
Tamil	69
French	69
Vietnamese	68
Korean	66
Urdu	63
Italian	61

اَبحرم

dzień dobry

talofa

hej

alô

CHECK IT OUT !

Portugal isn't the only place where people speak Portuguese. About 150 million people speak it in Brazil, where it is the official language.

MATH

Block Party

Teenagers, adults, little kids—everyone loves LEGOs! Luckily, there are enough to go around. In 2012, the LEGO Group produced 5.2 million bricks every *hour*. That's 45.7 billion a year—more than enough to reach the Moon if they were stacked up in a tower.

In 2013, students at Red Clay Consolidated School District near Wilmington, DE, created a LEGO tower tall enough to break records, if not reach the Moon. Their structure, shown at left, was named Tallest Freestanding LEGO Tower in the World by the *Guinness Book of World Records*.

Here are the stats:

▶ **Number of LEGO blocks:** More than 500,000

▶ **Height:** 113 feet (34 m), about the size of an eleven-story building

▶ **Weight:** Over a ton

Working with teachers and community members, students had fun while using math skills such as estimating and ratios. The coolest jobs of the future will need math. Figure out fun ways to put more math in your life!

YOUR TURN

According to the LEGO company, on average every person in the world owns 86 LEGOs. Grab a few and try these brain teasers!

▶ How many ways can you combine two eight-stud LEGO blocks?

▶ How many ways can you combine three eight-stud LEGO blocks?

▶ How many ways can you combine six eight-stud LEGO blocks? (It's okay to take a guess at this one!)

(Answers are on p. 350.)

NOTE: As we went to press, we learned that the Red Clay students' record had just been broken by a 114-foot (34.76 m) tower built in Budapest, Hungary.

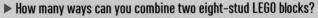

Which of these are polygons? (See p. 205.)

MULTIPLICATION TABLE

	1	2	3	4	5	6	7	8	9	10	11	12
1	1	2	3	4	5	6	7	8	9	10	11	12
2	2	4	6	8	10	12	14	16	18	20	22	24
3	3	6	9	12	15	18	21	24	27	30	33	36
4	4	8	12	16	20	24	28	32	36	40	44	48
5	5	10	15	20	25	30	35	40	45	50	55	60
6	6	12	18	24	30	36	42	48	54	60	66	72
7	7	14	21	28	35	42	49	56	63	70	77	84
8	8	16	24	32	40	48	56	64	72	80	88	96
9	9	18	27	36	45	54	63	72	81	90	99	108
10	10	20	30	40	50	60	70	80	90	100	110	120
11	11	22	33	44	55	66	77	88	99	110	121	132
12	12	24	36	48	60	72	84	96	108	120	132	144

Math

Squares and Square Roots

Multiplying a number by itself is also called squaring it (or raising it to its second power). For example, 3 squared (3^2) is 9. By the same token, the square root of 9 is 3. The symbol for square root is called a radical sign ($\sqrt{}$).

Examples of squaring
2 squared: $2^2 = 2 \times 2 = 4$
3 squared: $3^2 = 3 \times 3 = 9$
4 squared: $4^2 = 4 \times 4 = 16$

Examples of Square Roots
Square root of 16: $\sqrt{16} = 4$
Square root of 9: $\sqrt{9} = 3$
Square root of 4: $\sqrt{4} = 2$

SQUARE ROOTS TO 40

$\sqrt{1} = 1$ $\sqrt{36} = 6$ $\sqrt{121} = 11$ $\sqrt{256} = 16$ $\sqrt{441} = 21$ $\sqrt{676} = 26$ $\sqrt{961} = 31$ $\sqrt{1,296} = 36$

$\sqrt{4} = 2$ $\sqrt{49} = 7$ $\sqrt{144} = 12$ $\sqrt{289} = 17$ $\sqrt{484} = 22$ $\sqrt{729} = 27$ $\sqrt{1,024} = 32$ $\sqrt{1,369} = 37$

$\sqrt{9} = 3$ $\sqrt{64} = 8$ $\sqrt{169} = 13$ $\sqrt{324} = 18$ $\sqrt{529} = 23$ $\sqrt{784} = 28$ $\sqrt{1,089} = 33$ $\sqrt{1,444} = 38$

$\sqrt{16} = 4$ $\sqrt{81} = 9$ $\sqrt{196} = 14$ $\sqrt{361} = 19$ $\sqrt{576} = 24$ $\sqrt{841} = 29$ $\sqrt{1,156} = 34$ $\sqrt{1,521} = 39$

$\sqrt{25} = 5$ $\sqrt{100} = 10$ $\sqrt{225} = 15$ $\sqrt{400} = 20$ $\sqrt{625} = 25$ $\sqrt{900} = 30$ $\sqrt{1,225} = 35$ $\sqrt{1,600} = 40$

Some Mathematical Formulas

π (pi) = 3.1416
(See page 204.)

To find the CIRCUMFERENCE of a:
- Circle—Multiply the diameter by π

To find the AREA of a:
- Circle—Multiply the square of the radius by π
- Rectangle—Multiply the base by the height
- Sphere (surface)—Multiply the square of the radius by π and multiply by 4
- Square—Square the length of one side
- Trapezoid—Add the two parallel sides, multiply by the height, and divide by 2
- Triangle—Multiply the base by the height and divide by 2

To find the VOLUME of a:
- Cone—Multiply the square of the radius of the base by π, multiply by the height, and divide by 3
- Cube—Cube (raise to the third power) the length of one edge
- Cylinder—Multiply the square of the radius of the base by π and multiply by the height
- Pyramid—Multiply the area of the base by the height and divide by 3
- Rectangular prism—Multiply the length by the width by the height
- Sphere—Multiply the cube of the radius by π, multiply by 4, and divide by 3

LARGE NUMBERS AND HOW MANY ZEROS THEY CONTAIN

million	6	1,000,000
billion	9	1,000,000,000
trillion	12	1,000,000,000,000
quadrillion	15	1,000,000,000,000,000
quintillion	18	1,000,000,000,000,000,000

sextillion	21	1,000,000,000,000,000,000,000
septillion	24	1,000,000,000,000,000,000,000,000
octillion	27	1,000,000,000,000,000,000,000,000,000
nonillion	30	1,000,000,000,000,000,000,000,000,000,000
decillion	33	1,000,000,000,000,000,000,000,000,000,000,000

NUMBERS GLOSSARY

COUNTING NUMBERS
Counting numbers, or natural numbers, begin with the number 1 and continue into infinity.

WHOLE NUMBERS
Whole numbers are the same as counting numbers, except that the set of whole numbers begins with 0.

INTEGERS
Integers include 0, all counting numbers (called positive whole numbers), and all whole numbers less than 0 (called negative whole numbers).

RATIONAL NUMBERS
Rational numbers include any number that can be written in the form of a fraction (or a ratio), as long as the denominator (the bottom number of the fraction) is not equal to 0. All counting numbers and whole numbers are also rational numbers because all counting numbers and whole numbers can be written as fractions with a denominator equal to 1.

PRIME NUMBERS
Prime numbers are counting numbers that can be divided by only two numbers: 1 and themselves.

Prime numbers between 1 and 1,000
2, 3, 5, 7, 11, 13, 17, 19, 23, 29, 31, 37, 41, 43, 47, 53, 59, 61, 67, 71, 73, 79, 83, 89, 97, 101, 103, 107, 109, 113, 127, 131, 137, 139, 149, 151, 157, 163, 167, 173, 179, 181, 191, 193, 197, 199, 211, 223, 227, 229, 233, 239, 241, 251, 257, 263, 269, 271, 277, 281, 283, 293, 307, 311, 313, 317, 331, 337, 347, 349, 353, 359, 367, 373, 379, 383, 389, 397, 401, 409, 419, 421, 431, 433, 439, 443, 449, 457, 461, 463, 467, 479, 487, 491, 499, 503, 509, 521, 523, 541, 547, 557, 563, 569, 571, 577, 587, 593, 599, 601, 607, 613, 617, 619, 631, 641, 643, 647, 653, 659, 661, 673, 677, 683, 691, 701, 709, 719, 727, 733, 739, 743, 751, 757, 761, 769, 773, 787, 797, 809, 811, 821, 823, 827, 829, 839, 853, 857, 859, 863, 877, 881, 883, 887, 907, 911, 919, 929, 937, 941, 947, 953, 967, 971, 977, 983, 991, 997

COMPOSITE NUMBERS
Composite numbers are all counting numbers that are not prime numbers. In other words, composite numbers are numbers that have more than two factors. The number 1, because it has only one factor (itself), is not a composite number.

Composite numbers between 1 and 100
4, 6, 8, 9, 10, 12, 14, 15, 16, 18, 20, 21, 22, 24, 25, 26, 27, 28, 30, 32, 33, 34, 35, 36, 38, 39, 40, 42, 44, 45, 46, 48, 49, 50, 51, 52, 54, 55, 56, 57, 58, 60, 62, 63, 64, 65, 66, 68, 69, 70, 72, 74, 75, 76, 77, 78, 80, 81, 82, 84, 85, 86, 87, 88, 90, 91, 92, 93, 94, 95, 96, 98, 99, 100

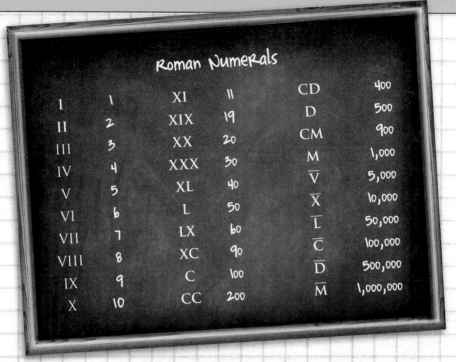

Roman Numerals

I	1	XI	11	CD	400
II	2	XIX	19	D	500
III	3	XX	20	CM	900
IV	4	XXX	30	M	1,000
V	5	XL	40	V̄	5,000
VI	6	L	50	X̄	10,000
VII	7	LX	60	L̄	50,000
VIII	8	XC	90	C̄	100,000
IX	9	C	100	D̄	500,000
X	10	CC	200	M̄	1,000,000

Fractions, Decimals, and Percents

To find the equivalent of a fraction in decimal form, divide the numerator (top number) by the denominator (bottom number). To change from a decimal to a percent, multiply by 100. To change from a percent to a decimal, divide by 100.

Fraction	Decimal	Percent
1/16 (= 2/32)	0.0625	6.25
1/8 (= 2/16)	0.125	12.5
3/16 (= 6/32)	0.1875	18.75
1/4 (= 2/8; = 4/16)	0.25	25.0
5/16 (= 10/32)	0.3125	31.25
1/3 (= 2/6; = 4/12)	0.333	33.3
3/8 (= 6/16)	0.375	37.5
7/16 (= 14/32)	0.4375	43.75
1/2 (= 2/4; = 4/8; = 8/16)	0.5	50.0
9/16 (= 18/32)	0.5625	56.25
5/8 (= 10/16)	0.625	62.5
2/3 (= 4/6; = 8/12)	0.666	66.6
11/16 (= 22/32)	0.6875	68.75
3/4 (= 6/8; = 12/16)	0.75	75.0
13/16 (= 26/32)	0.8125	81.25
7/8 (= 14/16)	0.875	87.5
15/16 (= 30/32)	0.9375	93.75
1 (= 2/2; = 4/4; = 8/8; = 16/16)	1.0	100.0

Geometry Glossary

Acute angle	Any angle that measures less than 90°
Angle	Two rays that have the same endpoint form an angle
Area	The amount of surface inside a closed figure
Chord	A line segment whose endpoints are on a circle
Circumference	The distance around a circle
Congruent figures	Geometric figures that are the same size and shape
Degree (angle)	A unit for measuring angles
Diameter	A chord that passes through the center of a circle
Endpoint	The end of a line segment
Line of symmetry	A line that divides a figure into two identical parts if the figure is folded along the line
Obtuse angle	Any angle that measures greater than 90°
Perimeter	The distance around the outside of a plane figure
Pi (π)	The ratio of the circumference of a circle to its diameter; when rounded to the nearest hundredth, pi equals 3.14
Polygon	A simple closed figure whose sides are straight lines
Protractor	An instrument used to measure angles
Quadrilateral	A polygon with four sides
Radius	A straight line that connects the center of a circle to any point on the circumference of the circle
Ray	A straight line with one endpoint
Rectangle	A four-sided figure with four right angles
Right angle	An angle that measures 90°
Square	A rectangle with congruent sides and 90° angles in all four corners
Surface area	The total outside area of an object
Symmetrical	Referring to a figure that, when folded along a line of symmetry, has two halves that superimpose exactly on each other
Triangle	A three-sided figure
Vertex	The common endpoint of two or more rays that form angles
Vertices	The plural of vertex

All About Polygons

Polygons are two-dimensional, or flat, shapes formed from three or more line segments.

Examples

Triangles

Triangles are polygons that have three sides and three vertices.

- **Right triangles** are formed when two of three line segments meet in a 90° angle. In a right triangle, the longest side has a special name: the hypotenuse.

- **Isosceles triangles** have two sides of equal length.

- **Scalene triangles** have no sides of equal length.

- **Equilateral triangles** have three sides of equal length.

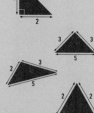

Quadrilaterals

Quadrilaterals are polygons that have four sides and four vertices.

- **Trapezoids** are quadrilaterals that have one pair of parallel sides.

- **Parallelograms** are quadrilaterals that have parallel line segments in both pairs of opposite sides.

- **Rectangles** are parallelograms formed by line segments that meet at right angles. A rectangle always has four right angles.

- **Squares** are rectangles that have sides of equal length and four right angles.

- **Rhombuses** are parallelograms that have sides of equal length but don't meet at right angles.

Circles

A circle is a set of points within a plane. Each point on the circle is at an equal distance from a common point inside the circle called the center.

The distance from the center of the circle to any point on the circle is called the radius (r = radius).

A line segment drawn through the center of the circle to points on either side of the circle is called the diameter (d = diameter). The circle is bisected, or cut in two equal parts, along the diameter line. Diameter is equal to two times the radius (2r = diameter).

The distance around the circle is called the circumference (πd or π2r = circumference).

MILITARY

Welcome Home, Warriors!

The men and women who wear the uniform of the United States are America's finest. When they return from combat, many face special challenges. They deserve the finest care and honor. The Wounded Warrior Project, woundedwarriorproject.org, was formed in 2003 to help veterans returning from Afghanistan and Iraq. The Project celebrated its 10th anniversary in 2013.

The Wounded Warrior Project offers programs and services that help injured service members and their families cope with immediate challenges and plan for a successful, happy future.

In 2013, Warrior Games track and field events at the United States Air Force Academy in Colorado Springs, CO, gathered injured and disabled service men and women from all branches of the military, plus Special Operations and members of the British Armed Forces.

YOUR TURN

If you or a friend are part of a military family, you need to know about the programs offered by Operation Military Kids. Visit operationmilitarykids.org to learn more.

Is the medal featured here the Silver Star, the Distinguished Flying Cross, the Purple Heart, or the Legion of Merit? (See p. 209.)

Top 10 Best-Armed Nations

The world's strongest militaries are built with manpower, financial resources, training, and equipment.

Country	Active Troops	Annual Defense Budget ($ in billions, rounded)	Tanks	Ships	Combat Aircraft
China	2,285,000	$1024	7430 +	141	1,385 +
United States	1,520,000	$645.7	5,838	173	1,105
India	1,325,000	$38.5	3,274 +	38	799
North Korea	1,190,000	Not Available	3,500 +	75	489 +
Russia	840,000	$59.9	2,800 +	96	953
South Korea	655,000	$29.0	2414	43	468
Pakistan	642,000	$5.9	2,411 +	18	374
Iran	523,000	$24.0	1,663 +	29	295 +
Turkey	511,000	$17.0	2494	32	354
Vietnam	482,000	$3.3	1,315	4	97

Bring in the 'Bots

In today's military, high-tech devices help keep soldiers out of harm's way.

Explosive Ordinance Disposal (EOD) is a military unit that consists of robots designed to handle chemical, biological, radiological, nuclear, and explosive threats.

Precision Urban Hopper is a GPS-guided robot that can hop more than 25 feet (7.6 m) in the air, allowing it to jump over fences and barricades. It's designed especially to be used in cities.

MQ-1 Predator is a plane that can be piloted remotely for surveillance and attack.

Branches of the US Military

Army
The oldest and largest branch of the United States military serves to defend and protect the nation at home and abroad. The most elite units, Army Rangers and Special Forces, train in advanced combat methods.

Navy
Members are especially skilled to handle any operations on and under the sea and in the air. Navy Divers and SEALs undergo specialized training for the most complex warfare operations.

Marines
The smallest branch of the nation's military is known for being the first on the ground in combat. Marines live by a strict code of honor, courage, and commitment.

Air Force
The technologically advanced members of the Air Force specialize in air and space operations to protect American interests.

Coast Guard
During peacetime, this branch protects national waterways, providing law enforcement, environmental cleanup, as well as search and rescue operations. During wartime, Coast Guard members serve with the Navy.

Beyond the Call of Duty

Military medals, or decorations, are awarded for bravery in and out of combat, loss of life or injury in combat, and other reasons. Most medals can be awarded to a member of any branch of the armed forces. The top 12 awards are listed in order, beginning with the highest.

Military Medals
1. Medal of Honor
2. Army Distinguished Service Cross, Navy Cross, Air Force Cross
3. Distinguished Service Medal
4. Silver Star
5. Defense Superior Service Medal
6. Legion of Merit
7. Distinguished Flying Cross
8. Soldier's Medal, Navy and Marine Corps Medal, Airman's Medal, Coast Guard Medal
9. Gold Lifesaving Medal
10. Bronze Star
11. Purple Heart
12. Defense Meritorious Service Medal

CHECK IT OUT!

Liquid Body Armor is made of Kevlar soaked with Shear Thickening Fluid (STF), silica particles mixed with polyethylene glycol. The material's liquid form makes it lightweight and flexible, but it hardens in milliseconds if struck by a bullet or shrapnel.

MOVIES & TV

THE HUNGER G
MOCKING
PART I

IN A BLEAK FUTURE, TEENS BEAT THE BAD GUYS.

The worldwide phenomenon of *The Hunger Games* continues to set the world on fire with *The Hunger Games: Mockingjay—Part 1,* which finds Katniss Everdeen in District 13 after she literally shatters the games forever. Under the leadership of President Coin and the advice of her trusted friends, Katniss spreads her wings as she fights to save Peeta and a nation moved by her courage. The novel on which the film is based is the third in a trilogy written by Suzanne Collins that has over 65 million copies in print in the U.S. alone.

The Hunger Games movies have created a trend of films based on books about teens in a grim future world or dystopia. The movie based on Veronica Roth's *Divergent*, starring Shailene Woodley, came out in March 2014. Save these dates for the sequels:

▶ The Divergent Series: *Insurgent* —March 20, 2015

▶ The Divergent Series: *Allegiant, Part 1* —March 18, 2016

▶ The Divergent Series: *Allegiant, Part 2* —March 24, 2017

Watch for more popular dystopian-themed books to hit the screen soon.

YOUR TURN

What are your favorite books, movies, TV shows, bands? Cast your vote in Nickelodeon's 2015 Kids' Choice Awards. Visit nick.com and click on KCA.

Which of these actors won both a 2013 Emmy and a Teen Choice award? (See pp. 214-215.)

10 Top-Grossing Movies of 2013

Movie	Box-Office Receipts
1. *Iron Man 3*	$1.2 billion
2. *Frozen*	$985.1 million
3. *Despicable Me 2*	$970.8 million
4. *The Hobbit: The Desolation of Smaug*	$893.8 million
5. *The Hunger Games: Catching Fire*	$863.5 million
6. *Fast & Furious 6*	$788.7 million
7. *Monsters University*	$743.6 million
8. *Gravity*	$703.9 million
9. *Man of Steel*	$668.0 million
10. *Thor: The Dark World*	$641.1 million

Lupita Nyong'o

2014 Oscar Winners

Best Picture: *12 Years a Slave*

Best Director: Alfonso Cuaron, *Gravity*

Best Actor: Matthew McConaughey, *Dallas Buyers Club*

Best Supporting Actor: Jared Leto, *Dallas Buyers Club*

Best Actress: Cate Blanchett, *Blue Jasmine*

Best Supporting Actress: Lupita Nyong'o, *12 Years a Slave*

Best Animated Film: *Frozen*

Best Foreign Film: *The Great Beauty*

Best Original Screenplay: Spike Jonze, *Her*

Best Adapted Screenplay: John Ridley, *12 Years a Slave*

2014 Golden Globe Winners

Best Picture, Drama: *12 Years a Slave*
Best Actor, Drama: Matthew McConaughey, *Dallas Buyers Club*
Best Actress, Drama: Cate Blanchett, *Blue Jasmine*
Best Picture, Comedy or Musical: *American Hustle*
Best Actor, Comedy or Musical: Leonardo DiCaprio, *The Wolf of Wall Street*
Best Actress, Comedy or Musical: Amy Adams, *American Hustle*
Best Director: Alfonso Cuaron, *Gravity*
Best Supporting Actor: Jared Leto, *Dallas Buyers Club*
Best Supporting Actress: Jennifer Lawrence, *American Hustle*
Best Animated Film: *Frozen*
Best Foreign Film: *The Great Beauty*
Best Screenplay: Spike Jonze, *Her*

2014 Nickelodeon Kids' Choice Awards Movie Winners

Favorite Movie: *Frozen*
Favorite Movie Actor: Adam Sandler
Favorite Movie Actress: Jennifer Lawrence
Favorite Animated Movie: *Frozen*
Favorite Voice from an Animated Movie:
Miranda Cosgrove, *Despicable Me 2*

Jennifer Lawrence

2013 Teen Choice Awards Movie Winners

Action: *Iron Man 3*
Actor, Action: Robert Downey Jr., *Iron Man 3*
Actress, Action: Anne Hathaway, *The Dark Knight Rises*
Comedy: *Pitch Perfect*
Actor, Comedy: Skylar Astin, *Pitch Perfect*
Actress, Comedy: Rebel Wilson, *Pitch Perfect*
Drama: *The Perks of Being a Wallflower*
Actor, Drama: Logan Lerman, *The Perks of Being a Wallflower*
Actress, Drama: Emma Watson, *The Perks of Being a Wallflower*
Romance: *The Twilight Saga: Breaking Dawn—Part 2*
Actor, Romance: Robert Pattinson, *The Twilight Saga: Breaking Dawn—Part 2*
Actress, Romance: Kristen Stewart, *The Twilight Saga: Breaking Dawn—Part 2*
Sci-Fi/Fantasy: *The Twilight Saga: Breaking Dawn—Part 2*
Actor, Sci-Fi/Fantasy: Taylor Lautner, *The Twilight Saga: Breaking Dawn—Part 2*
Actress, Sci-Fi/Fantasy: Kristen Stewart, *The Twilight Saga: Breaking Dawn—Part 2*
Breakout Star: Nicholas Hoult, *Warm Bodies*
Villain: Adam Devine, *Pitch Perfect*

Robert Downey Jr.

Television

Most-Watched Primetime Shows of 2013

NCIS
NBC NFL Sunday Night Football
The Big Bang Theory
NCIS: Los Angeles
Blacklist
Person of Interest
NBC NFL Sunday Night Pre-Kick
Dancing with the Stars
OT (NFL Post-Show)
The Voice

Jim Parsons

2013 Emmy Award Winners

Outstanding Series, Drama: *Breaking Bad*
Outstanding Series, Comedy: *Modern Family*
Outstanding Reality Program, Competition: *The Voice*
Outstanding Actor, Drama: Jeff Daniels, *The Newsroom*
Outstanding Actress, Drama: Claire Danes, *Homeland*
Outstanding Actor, Comedy: Jim Parsons, *The Big Bang Theory*
Outstanding Actress, Comedy: Julia Louis-Dreyfus, *Veep*
Outstanding Supporting Actor, Drama: Dan Bucatinsky, *Scandal*
Outstanding Supporting Actress, Drama: Carrie Preston, *The Good Wife*
Outstanding Supporting Actor, Comedy: Tony Hale, *Veep*
Outstanding Supporting Actress, Comedy: Merritt Weaver, *Nurse Jackie*

2014 Nickelodeon Kids' Choice Awards TV Winners

Favorite TV Show: *Sam & Cat*
Favorite Reality Show: *Wipeout*
Favorite TV Actor: Ross Lynch
Favorite TV Actress: Ariana Grande
Favorite Cartoon: *SpongeBob SquarePants*

Ariana Grande

2013 Teen Choice Awards
TV Winners

Animated Show: *The Simpsons*
Action: *NCIS: Los Angeles*
Actor, Action: LL Cool J, *NCIS: Los Angeles*
Actress, Action: Lucy Liu, *Elementary*
Comedy: *Glee*
Actor, Comedy: Jim Parsons, *The Big Bang Theory*
Actress, Comedy: Lea Michele, *Glee*
Drama: *Pretty Little Liars*
Actor, Drama: Ian Harding, *Pretty Little Liars*
Actress, Drama: Troian Bellisario, *Pretty Little Liars*
Fantasy/Sci-Fi: *The Vampire Diaries*
Actor, Fantasy/Sci-Fi: Ian Somerhalder, *The Vampire Diaries*
Actress, Fantasy/Sci-Fi: Nina Dobrev, *The Vampire Diaries*
Reality Show: *Keeping Up With the Kardashians*
Female, Reality/Variety: The Kardashians & Jenners, *Keeping up with the Kardashians*
Male, Reality/Variety: Kevin Jonas, *Married to Jonas*
Reality Competition: *The X Factor*
Breakout Star: Blake Jenner, *Glee*
Personality, Male: Simon Cowell, *The X Factor*
Personality, Female: Demi Lovato, *The X Factor*
Villain: Janel Parish, *Pretty Little Liars*

Selena Gomez

Multitalented Selena Gomez is a singer and a TV and movie star, has her own fashion line and fragrance, and was the youngest-ever ambassador appointed for UNICEF.

CHECK IT OUT!

MUSIC

POP MUSIC'S NEWEST ROYALTY

Her stage name is just one word: Lorde. She's a singer and songwriter from New Zealand who shot into superstardom at age 17 with her song "Royals." The tune was named Song of the Year at the 2014 Grammy Awards and was the fifth most digitally downloaded song of 2013, even beating out Katy Perry's "Roar."

Lorde's real name is Ella Yelich-O'Connor. She describes her family as "middle-class" and says her middle-class upbringing gave her the background to write moving lyrics about real, normal teenage concerns. Critics have praised her voice and musical talent, and her words talk about things other teens can relate to.

"The Love Club" talks about high school cliques: "There are fights for being my best friend. And the girls get their claws out. . . ."

"Bravado" is about being shy around others who are outgoing and confident. Lorde says she wrote it as kind of a "personal pep talk" to prepare herself for a life onstage in the fast-paced music industry. She writes, ". . . when the lights go on, I'll be ready for this."

Ready or not, Lorde is sure to rule for some time.

YOUR TURN

Did you know that the Grammys offer programs and a summer music camp for young people aiming for a musical career? You can learn about it at grammy.org.

Which of these artists had the top album of 2013? (See p. 21

Top 10 Albums of 2013

Album	Artist
20/20	Justin Timberlake
The Marshall Mathers LP 2	Eminem
Crash My Party	Luke Bryan
Night Visions	Imagine Dragons
Unorthodox Jukebox	Bruno Mars
Here's to the Good Times	Florida Georgia Line
Nothing Was the Same	Drake
Beyoncé	Beyoncé
Based on a True Story	Blake Shelton
Magna Carta . . . Holy Grail	Jay-Z

Top 10 Digitally Downloaded Songs of 2013

Song	Artist
"Blurred Lines"	Robin Thicke, featuring Pharrell and T.I.
"Thrift Shop"	Macklemore & Ryan Lewis
"Radioactive"	Imagine Dragons
"Cruise"	Florida Georgia Line
"Royals"	Lorde
"Roar"	Katy Perry
"Just Give Me a Reason"	Pink, featuring Nate Ruess
"Can't Hold Us"	Macklemore & Ryan Lewis
"When I Was Your Man"	Bruno Mars
"Stay"	Rihanna, featuring Mikky Ekko

2014 Grammy Award Winners

Record of the Year: "Get Lucky," Daft Punk, featuring Pharrell Williams and Nile Rodgers

Album of the Year: *Random Access Memories,* Daft Punk

Song of the Year: "Royals," Joel Little and Ella Yelich-O'Connor (Lorde), songwriters

Best New Artist: Macklemore & Ryan Lewis

Best Rap Album: *The Heist,* Macklemore & Ryan Lewis

Best Rap Song: "Thrift Shop," Ben Haggerty & Ryan Lewis, songwriters (Macklemore & Ryan Lewis)

Best R & B Album: *Girl On Fire,* Alicia Keys

Best R & B Song: "Pusher Love Girl," James Fauntleroy, Jerome Harmon, Timothy Mosley, and Justin Timberlake, songwriters (Justin Timberlake)

Best Rock Album: *Celebration Day,* Led Zeppelin

Best Rock Song: "Cut Me Some Slack," Dave Grohl, Paul McCartney, Krist Novoselic & Pat Smear, songwriters (Paul McCartney, Dave Grohl, Krist Novoselic, Pat Smear)

Best Alternative Music Album: *Modern Vampires of the City,* Vampire Weekend

Best Pop Vocal Album: *Unorthodox Jukebox,* Bruno Mars

Best Country Song: "Merry Go 'Round," Shane McAnally, Kacey Musgraves & Josh Osborne, songwriters (Kacey Musgraves)

2013 Teen Choice Awards

Rock Track: "Radioactive," Imagine Dragons

Rock Group: Paramore

R & B/Hip-Hop Track: "Can't Hold Us," Macklemore & Ryan Lewis

R & B/Hip-Hop Artist: Macklemore & Ryan Lewis

Love Song: "Little Things," One Direction

Breakout Artist: Ed Sheeran

Female Artist: Demi Lovato

Male Artist: Justin Bieber

Group: One Direction

Single, Female: "Heart Attack," Demi Lovato

Single, Male: "Beauty And A Beat," Justin Bieber, featuring Nicki Minaj

2014 Nickelodeon Kids' Choice Awards

Favorite Music Group: One Direction

Favorite Song: "Story Of My Life," One Direction

Favorite Male Singer: Justin Timberlake

Favorite Female Singer: Selena Gomez

PLANTS

LEAF ME ALONE!

Are your tomatoes talking to your turnips behind your back?

A May 2013 scientific study says that plants may be able to use sound vibrations to "listen" to other plants. Researchers found that chili seedlings growing next to a good neighbor such as basil, which helps keep away weeds and pests, sprouted faster than other chilis growing alone. Most scientists had already agreed that plants can "smell" chemicals and "see" reflected light from nearby plants. But in this experiment, researchers separated the chilis and basils with black plastic, blocking chemical and light signals. Somehow the chilis still could tell what kinds of plants were living next door. Dr. Monica Gagliano, the head of the project, suggested that they were responding to sound vibrations created inside the plant cells.

In a different sound-related study, a recording of a caterpillar munching a leaf triggered a plant to produce defense chemicals, even though the plant was perfectly safe.

Gagliano and other scientists think that learning more about plant communication could bring big benefits. For instance, farmers could use sound instead of pesticides to encourage or discourage certain plants.

YOUR TURN

Do you want to know more about the secret lives of plants—and tons of other stuff about how the world works? Visit exploratorium.edu for experiments, videos, games, and the coolest science you can imagine.

How are the plants below related? (See p. 222.)

Biological Classification of Plants

PLANT KINGDOM

Filicinophyta	Ginkgophyta	Bryophyta
FERNS	GINKGO	BRYOPHYTES

Lycopodophyta	Gnetophyta	Sphenophyta
CLUB MOSSES	WELWITSCHIA, EPHEDRA, GNETUM	HORSETAILS

	Psilophyta	Coniferophyta
	WHISKFERNS	CONIFERS

KEY
These colors show the classification groupings in the chart.

- PHYLUM or DIVISION
- CLASS
- ORDER

	Cycadophyta	Angiospermophyta
	CYCADS	FLOWERING PLANTS

		Hepaticae
		LIVERWORTS

	Monocotyledoneae	Musci
	MONOCOTYLEDONS	MOSSES

	Dicotyledoneae	Anthocerotae
	DICOTYLEDONS	HORNWORTS

Liliaceae	LILY, TULIP	Rosaceae	APPLE, ROSE
Orchidaceae	ORCHIDS	Fabaceae	BEAN, PEANUT
Poaceae	WHEAT, BAMBOO	Magnoliaceae	MAGNOLIA, TULIP TREE
Iridaceae	IRIS, GLADIOLUS	Apiaceae	CARROT, PARSLEY
Arecaceae	COCONUT PALM, DATE PALM	Solonaceae	POTATO, TOMATO
Bromeliaceae	BROMELIAD, PINEAPPLE	Lamiaceae	MINT, LAVENDER
Cyperaceae	SEDGES	Asteraceae	SUNFLOWER, DANDELION
Juncaceae	RUSHES	Salicaceae	WILLOW, POPLAR
Musaceae	BANANA	Cucurbitaceae	MELON, CUCUMBER
Amaryllidaceae	DAFFODIL, AMARYLLIS	Malvaceae	HIBISCUS, HOLLYHOCK
Ranunculaceae	BUTTERCUP, DELPHINIUM	Cactaceae	CACTUS
Brassicaceae	CABBAGE, TURNIP		

Plants

Where Do Plants Grow?

Plants grow everywhere in the world, except where there is permanent ice. However, different types of plants grow best in different regions. A region's plant life depends on the climate, the amount of water and sun, the type of soil, and other features. For instance, plants in the tundra grow close to the ground, away from the region's icy winds. Desert plants have thick skins to hold in every drop of water. This map shows five major regions where certain kinds of plants grow best, and the areas where the climate is too harsh for any plant life at all.

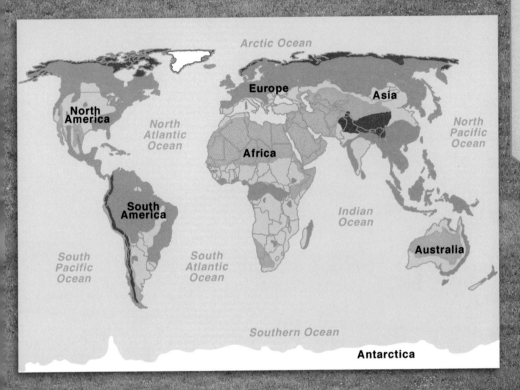

Region	Types of Plants
Aquatic	Cattails, seaweed
Grassland	Short and tall grasses
Forest	Trees, shrubs, ferns, wildflowers
Tundra	Small shrubs, mosses
Desert	Many kinds of cacti
Permanent ice	No plant life

POPULATION

Tiny Town Where Mermaids Live

Huge population centers such as New York City and Tokyo always have plenty of exciting things going on. However, even the tiniest town can be full of surprises. Take Weeki Wachee, FL. Only four people live there, but the place is swimming with mermaids.

Twice a day, swimmers dressed as mermaids perform 16–20 feet (52–66 m) under the surface of a deep spring in Weeki Wachee Springs State Park. Visitors cheer and wave through a Plexiglas screen. The mermaids do tricky timed ballet stunts and shows with props and music, including The Little Mermaid fairy tale. They use air hoses hidden in the scenery to grab extra breaths. Sometimes a turtle or a manatee floats into the act.

Weeki Wachee is not the smallest town in America. Buford, WY, claims to have only one full-time resident. Regardless of size, every city and town in the world has a unique personality that comes from its people, its activities, its history, and its geography. Read about US and world populations in this chapter and in Flags & Facts: Countries of the World, Flags & Facts: States of the United States, and Geography.

YOUR TURN

How many people live in your area? Visit QuickFacts at census.gov for stats on every state and county, and for cities and towns with more than 5,000 people. To explore current and projected world populations, visit census.gov's International Data Base.

Which one of these is NOT one of the three most populous states? (See p. 228.)

CALIFORNIA 1850
JOHN MUIR
YOSEMITE VALLEY
2005

NEW YORK 1788
GATEWAY TO FREEDOM
2001
E PLURIBUS UNUM

FLORIDA 1845
GATEWAY TO DISCOVERY
2004
E PLURIBUS UNUM

TEX
18

Population by Continent

Country	Population
Asia	4,347,630,000
Africa	1,150,295,000
Europe	743,852,000
North America	564,073,000
South America	402,047,000
Oceania*	37,143,000

*Includes Australia, New Zealand, Tasmania, Papua New Guinea, and thousands of other smaller islands

CHECK IT OUT !

The continent of Antarctica is not listed above because it has no permanent population. Scientists, researchers, and tourists come and go.

5 Most Populous Countries

Country	Population
China	1,361,512,535
India	1, 251,695,584
United States	321,362,789
Indonesia	255,993,674
Brazil	204,259,812

5 Least Populous Countries

Country	Population
Holy See (Vatican City)	842
Nauru	9,540
Tuvalu	10,869
Palau	21,265
Monaco	30,535

Population

*Country and continent populations based on US Census International Data Base 2015 projections.

5 Most Densely Populated Countries

Country	Persons per sq. mi. (persons per sq km)
Monaco	39,497.3 (15,250)
Singapore	20,585.3 (7,948)
Holy See (Vatican City)	4,938.6 (1,906.8)
Bahrain	4,366.6 (1,686)
Maldives	3,424.2

5 Most Sparsely Populated Countries

Country	Persons per sq. mi. (persons per sq km)
Mongolia	5.4 (2.1)
Namibia	6.9 (2.7)
Australia	7.5 (2.9)
Iceland	8.1 (3.1)
Libya	8.6 (3.3)

5 Largest World Urban Centers

City	Population (includes surrounding densely populated areas)
Tokyo, Japan	37,217,400
New Delhi, India	22,653,600
Mexico City, Mexico	20,445,800
New York, NY, United States	20,351,700
Shanghai, China	20,207,600

CHECK IT OUT !

You can figure out population density by dividing the population by the land area. Land areas for all countries can be found on pages 90–121. Land areas for each state of the United States, Puerto Rico, and Washington, DC, can be found on pages 128–145.

10 Most Populous States

State	Population
California	38,332,521
Texas	26,448,193
New York	19,651,127
Florida	19,552,860
Illinois	12,882,135
Pennsylvania	12,773,801
Ohio	11,570,808
Georgia	9,992,167
Michigan	9,895,622
North Carolina	9,848,060

10 Least Populous States

State	Population
Wyoming	582,658
Vermont	626,630
North Dakota	723,393
Alaska	735,132
South Dakota	844,877
Delaware	925,749
Montana	1,015,165
Rhode Island	1,051,511
New Hampshire	1,323,459
Maine	1,328,302

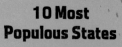

US Population Growth 1790–2013

Year	Population (in millions)
1790	3.9
1830	12.9
1870	38.6
1890	62.9
1910	92.2
1930	123.2
1950	151.3
1970	203.2
1990	248.7
2000	281.4
2010	308.7
2013	316.4

Population

10 Most Populous US Cities

City	Population
New York, NY	8,336,697
Los Angeles, CA	3,857,799
Chicago, IL	2,714,856
Houston, TX	2,160,821
Philadelphia, PA	1,547,607
Phoenix, AZ	1,488,750
San Antonio, TX	1,359,758
San Diego, CA	1,338,348
Dallas, TX	1,241,162
San Jose, CA	982,765

10 Fastest-Growing US Cities

City	Percentage increase 2012–2013
Austin, TX	2.50
Provo, UT	2.48
Cape Coral, FL	2.41
Raleigh, NC	2.15
Ogden, UT	2.05
Charlotte, NC	1.92
Dallas, TX	1.91
San Antonio	1.83
Orlando, FL	1.82
Houston, TX	1.82

US Racial Makeup

White	77.9
Black	13.1
Asian	5.1
American Indian, Native Alaskan	1.2
Native Hawaiian, other Pacific Islander	0.2
Two or more races	2.4

Hispanic is an ethnic background, not a race. Hispanic people can be of any race. Researchers use both "Latino" and "Hispanic" to describe people with origins in Spain or Latin America.

Top 10 States in Hispanic Population Percentage

According to the Pew Research Center's Hispanic Project, there were approximately 53 million Hispanic people living in the United States in 2012. The 10 states below have the highest percentage of Hispanics in their total population.

State	Percent Hispanic
New Mexico	47.0
California	38.2
Texas	38.2
Arizona	30.2
Nevada	27.3
Florida	23.2
Colorado	21.0
New Jersey	18.5
New York	18.2
Illinois	16.3

(Figures from 2010 US Census)

Our Foreign-Born Residents

According to the US Census Bureau, about 40 million US residents were born in a different country. That's about 13 percent of the population.

Where Do They Come from?

Continent or Region	Percentage of foreign-born
Latin America and the Caribbean	53
Asia	28
Europe	12
Africa	4
Northern America	2
Oceania	Less than 1

10 Top Countries of Origin

Country	Percentage of foreign-born
Mexico	28.9
China	5.5
India	4.6
Philippines	4.5
El Salvador	3.1
Vietnam	3.1
Cuba	2.7
North and South Korea	2.7
Dominican Republic	2.2
Guatemala	2.1

Where Do They Live?

Foreign-born residents live in every state, but more than half live in California, New York, Texas, and Florida.

10 States with Highest Foreign-Born Percentage

State	Percentage
California	27.2
New York	21.8
New Jersey	20.6
Florida	19.2
Texas	16.2
Massachusetts	14.7
Arizona	13.9
Illinois	13.7
Washington	12.8
Virginia	11.0

Foreign-Born Percentage in 10 Most Populous US Cities

City	Percentage
Los Angeles	39.4
San Jose	38.6
New York City	36.8
Houston	28.4
San Diego	25.6
Dallas	24.6
Phoenix	21.5
Chicago	21.0
San Antonio	13.7
Philadelphia	11.6

CHECK IT OUT!

More than one in four California residents and more than one in five residents of New York and New Jersey were born in another country. In Miami, FL, 56.4 percent of residents are foreign-born, the highest percentage of any major US city.

RELIGION

Heavenly Wheels

Archbishop Jorge Bergoglio of Buenos Aires, Argentina, became Pope Francis, the spiritual leader of the world's 1.2 billion Roman Catholics, on March 13, 2013. From the beginning, this pope has been anything but traditional.

He is the first pope since 731 who hasn't come from a country in Europe. He worked as a janitor and a security guard in a nightclub to help pay for college. His official car is a 10-year old economy model, instead of the expensive Mercedes-Benz that goes with his position.

Another vehicle the pope owned briefly was a Harley-Davidson motorcycle, a Dyna Super Glide model. The grandson of a Harley-Davidson founder gave it to him in honor of the company's 110th anniversary.

Pope Francis put the bike up for sale at an auction in Paris, and it sold for about $327,000. A new Dyna Super Glide sells for $16,000–$22,000, but Pope Francis signed this one's gas tank, making the motorcycle a collector's item. He included a leather motorcycle jacket, also signed, which sold for $77,485. All the money went to a shelter and a soup kitchen.

YOUR TURN

You can visit the Sistine Chapel and St. Peter's Cathedral in Vatican City, the official center of the Roman Catholic Church, without ever leaving home. Log on to vatican.com/tour for a 3-D tour of some of the most magnificent art and architecture on Earth.

Which religion has the most members? Turn the page.

Major Religions of the World

Buddhism

Buddhism began about 525 BCE, reportedly in India. This religion is based on the teachings of Gautama Siddhartha, the Buddha, who achieved enlightenment through intense meditation. The Buddha taught that though life is full of pain, you can break the cycle and achieve peace by being mindful, meditating, and doing good deeds. There are Buddhists all over the world, but mostly in Asia. The Buddha's teachings can be read in spiritual texts, or scriptures, called sutras.

Christianity

Christianity is the world's biggest religion, with over 2 billion worshippers. It is based on the teachings of Jesus Christ, who lived between 8 BCE and 29 CE. The Old and New Testaments of the Bible are the key scriptures. Christians believe that Jesus Christ is the son of God, who died on the cross to save humankind and later rose from the dead.

Hinduism

To Hindus, there is one overarching divine principle, with a variety of gods such as Vishnu, Shiva, and Shakti representing different parts of it. Hindus believe that by being mindful and doing good deeds you can break meaningless cycles and improve the purity of your actions, known as your karma. Hinduism was founded about 1500 BCE. The main scriptures are called Vedas.

Islam

Islam was founded in 610 CE by Muhammad. People who practice Islam are called Muslims. They believe in one God, Allah, who gave the spiritual writings of the Qur'an (also known as the Koran) to Muhammad so he could teach truth and justice to all people. There are two major Muslim groups, the Shiites and the Sunni.

Judaism

Judaism was founded about 2000 BCE. The prophet Abraham is recognized as the founder. Jews believe in one god. They believe God created the universe, and they believe in being faithful to God and in following God's laws as outlined in key scriptures such as the Torah and the Hebrew Bible. There are people practicing Judaism all over the world. Many of them are in Israel and the United States.

5 Largest World Religions

Religion	Members
Christianity	2,319,839,000
Islam	1,609,200,900
Hinduism	967,164,000
Buddhism	504,784,000
Chinese folk religions	437,133,000

CHECK IT OUT!

The first Muslim settlers began arriving in America in the late 1800s. Many of these first immigrants bypassed big population centers and settled in the Midwest. The Mother Mosque in Cedar Rapids, Iowa, claims to be the first mosque in the United States. It was built in 1934.

SCIENCE

FLYING HIGH, NO FEATHERS

When he was 13, Yves (EAVES) Rossy saw a jet team perform at an air show near his home in Switzerland and knew that he wanted to fly. He grew up to become an airline pilot, but soon that wasn't enough. He wanted to fly without the airplane—like a bird.

Today Rossy does fly like a bird. In fact, he was once attacked by an eagle that thought he was a bird. He uses a carbon-fiber wing and four small jet engines strapped to its back, which earned him the nickname "Jetman." He averages 125 mph (183 kph) and controls the machine by shifting his body.

Rossy has flown over the Grand Canyon, the English Channel, and Lake Geneva in Switzerland. In November 2013 he flew around 12,388 ft. (3,776 m) Mount Fuji, Japan's highest peak, nine times at 190 mph (306 kph).

The jetpack doesn't have enough power to get him off the ground, so he rides up to elevation in a plane or helicopter then jumps out and starts flying. He ends his flights by powering down his engines and parachuting.

YOUR TURN

Did you know that May 26 is National Paper Airplane Day? Have an uplifting celebration on that day or anytime with your own custom paper airplane or kite. Get video directions at schooltube.com.

What was the first element discovered? (See p. 242.)

15
P
Phosphorus
30.973761

11
Na
Sodium
22.989770

10
Ne
Neon
20.1797

1
H
Hydrogen
1.00794

The 5 Kingdoms of Life

To understand living things, life scientists divide them into groups that share certain features. This process is called classification. A classification system created in 1735 by Carolus Linnaeus divides life-forms into five kingdoms: animals, plants, fungi, protista, and monera. Here are some (not all) of the types of life-forms within each kingdom.

ANIMAL KINGDOM	Vertebrates (such as mammals, birds, and reptiles), sponges, worms, insects and arthropods, crustaceans, and jellyfish
PLANT KINGDOM	Ferns, mosses, ginkgos, horsetails, conifers, flowering plants, liverworts, and bladderworts
FUNGI KINGDOM	Molds, mildews, blights, smuts, rusts, mushrooms, puffballs, stinkhorns, lichens, dung fungi, yeasts, morels, and truffles
PROTISTA KINGDOM	Yellow-green algae, golden algae, protozoa, green algae, brown algae, and red algae
MONERA KINGDOM	Bacteria and blue-green algae

The kingdoms are subdivided into smaller and more specific groups.

Most general

Most specific

Category	Example: Human Being
Kingdom	Animal
Phylum	Chordate
Subphylum	Vertebrate (animals with backbones)
Superclass	Vertebrate with jaws
Class	Mammal
Subclass	Advanced mammal
Infraclass	Placental mammal
Order	Primate
Family	Hominid
Genus	*Homo*
Species	*Homo sapiens*

The Domain System

In 1990, biologist Carl R. Woese and other scientists proposed a slightly different classification system. They suggested dividing living things into three domains, based on their cell structure. Domain Eukaryota includes multi-celled organisms: animals, plants, fungi, and protista. Domains Archaea and Bacteria are made up of microscopic one-celled organisms. The huge majority of all living things belong to these two domains. Scientists believe that Archaea are among the oldest forms of life on Earth.

Science

Some Major Discoveries in Life Science

Year	Discovery
400 BCE	Aristotle classifies 500 species of animals into 8 classes.
1628 CE	William Harvey discovers how blood circulates in the human body.
1683	Anton van Leeuwenhoek observes bacteria.
1735	Carolus Linnaeus introduces the classification system.
1859	Charles Darwin publishes *On the Origin of Species*, which explains his theories of evolution.
1860	Gregor Mendel discovers the laws of heredity through experiments with peas and fruit flies.
1861	Louis Pasteur, the "father of bacteriology," comes up with a theory that certain diseases are caused by bacteria.
1953	James D. Watson and Francis H. Crick develop the double helix model of DNA, which explains how traits are inherited. Jonas Salk invents the polio vaccine.
1996	Dolly the sheep is cloned in Scotland.
2009	Doctors successfully treat blindness, brain disorders, and immune system deficiencies by inserting genes into patients' cells and tissues. However, the procedure remains controversial because of dangerous side effects.
2011	Early tests of a vaccine for malaria give scientists hope the disease can someday be wiped out. Malaria is carried by certain types of mosquitoes and is a leading cause of death for children in many countries.
2012	Scientists create artificial compounds called XNAs that can copy and store information and evolve, like DNA.
2013	Scientists recover the oldest human DNA ever found, from a 400,000-year-old thighbone.

CHECK IT OUT!

Companies around the world are using 3-D printers to make everything from toys to food to airplane parts. Now medical researchers are applying this technology to print out body parts. Artificial noses, bones, ears, joints, and blood vessels have all been created with bioprinters. Scientists say this is only the beginning.

The Rock Cycle

Rocks don't grow like plants and animals, but they change from one form to another in a never-ending process called the **rock cycle**. Geologists, or scientists who study rocks, divide them into three groups.

Igneous

Igneous rock makes up about 95 percent of the upper part of Earth's crust. There are two kinds:

> **Intrusive** igneous rock forms when melted rock, or magma, cools beneath Earth's surface. Granite is a common type of intrusive igneous rock. Intrusive igneous rocks are constantly being pushed up to the surface by natural forces.

> **Extrusive** igneous rock forms when the melted rock erupts as lava and cools on Earth's surface. Basalt is a common type of extrusive igneous rock.

Granite

Basalt

Sedimentary

Igneous rocks on Earth's surface can be broken down into tiny pieces and moved around by wind, rain, and ocean waves. These little pieces, called sediments, pile up in water and are squeezed into layers with other sediments such as bits and pieces of plants or dead animals. Limestone is a common type of sedimentary rock.

Limestone

Metamorphic

Pressure and heat can flatten and fold igneous or sedimentary rock into a whole new shape, color, and mineral structure. Marble is a metamorphic rock that often comes from limestone.

Marble

CHECK IT

Plymouth Rock in Plymouth, Massachusetts, is made of granite scientists think was formed more than 600 million years ago. The famous landmark is much smaller today than it was in 1620, when the Pilgrims arrived from England. It has been worn down by erosion and chipped away by souvenir-hunting tourists.

What's the Difference Between Rocks and Minerals?

The difference is simple: Rocks are made of minerals, but minerals are not made of rocks. Minerals are chemical compounds found on, in, and below Earth's crust. There are about 4,000 known minerals on Earth.

Quartz is one of the most common minerals, making up about 12 percent of Earth's crust. Some quartz is so clear you can see straight through it. Other types are pink, green, yellow, or purple. The color varies depending on how the quartz was formed. But quartz does more than look pretty. Under certain conditions, quartz can generate electricity to power clocks, computers, TVs, heaters, and other devices.

A Scratch Test for Minerals

The Mohs scale, invented by German mineralogist Frederich Mohs, ranks ten minerals on hardness based on their resistance to scratches. Minerals with higher numbers can scratch minerals with lower numbers.

Mineral	Rank
Talc	1
Gypsum	2
Calcite	3
Fluorite	4
Apatite	5
Orthoclase feldspar	6
Quartz	7
Topaz	8
Corundum	9
Diamond	10

Hard to Say

Here's how certain items would rank in hardness on the Mohs scale.

Fingernails	2.5
Gold, silver	2.5–3
Copper penny	3
Iron	4–5
Knife blade	5.5
Glass	6–7
Hardened steel file	7+

Periodic Table of Elements

If rocks are made of minerals, what are minerals made of? Elements! Everything in the world is made of elements, which are found in nature or made by scientists. The first element discovered was phosphorus, in 1669. Since then 114 elements have been added. Some elements are named for scientists. Some are named for places or characters in mythology. Others are named after a certain feature of the element. Scientists put elements in groups called periods on the periodic table.

Period

IA

| 1 **H** Hydrogen 1.00794 |

IIA

| 3 **Li** Lithium 6.941 | 4 **Be** Beryllium 9.012182 |

| 11 **Na** Sodium 22.989770 | 12 **Mg** Magnesium 24.3050 |

IVB **VB** **VIB** **VIIB** **VIII**

| 19 **K** Potassium 39.0983 | 20 **Ca** Calcium 40.078 | 21 **Sc** Scandium 44.955910 | 22 **Ti** Titanium 47.867 | 23 **V** Vanadium 50.9415 | 24 **Cr** Chromium 51.9961 | 25 **Mn** Manganese 54.938049 | 26 **Fe** Iron 55.845 | 27 **Co** Cobalt 58.933200 |

| 37 **Rb** Rubidium 85.4678 | 38 **Sr** Strontium 87.62 | 39 **Y** Yttrium 88.90585 | 40 **Zr** Zirconium 91.224 | 41 **Nb** Niobium 92.90638 | 42 **Mo** Molybdenum 95.94 | 43 **Tc** Technetium (98) | 44 **Ru** Ruthenium 101.07 | 45 **Rh** Rhodium 102.90550 |

| 55 **Cs** Cesium 132.90545 | 56 **Ba** Barium 137.327 | | 72 **Hf** Hafnium 178.49 | 73 **Ta** Tantalum 180.9479 | 74 **W** Tungsten 183.84 | 75 **Re** Rhenium 186.207 | 76 **Os** Osmium 190.23 | 77 **Ir** Iridium 192.217 |

| 87 **Fr** Francium (223) | 88 **Ra** Radium (226) | | 104 **Rf** Rutherfordium (261) | 105 **Db** Dubnium (262) | 106 **Sg** Seaborgium (266) | 107 **Bh** Bohrium (264) | 108 **Hs** Hassium (277) | 109 **Mt** Meitnerium (268) |

Atomic Number

Symbol

Name

Atomic Weight

| 58 **Ce** Cerium 140.116 |

Lanthanides

| 57 **La** Lanthanum 138.9055 | 58 **Ce** Cerium 140.116 | 59 **Pr** Praseodymium 140.90765 | 60 **Nd** Neodymium 144.24 | 61 **Pm** Promethium (145) | 62 **Sm** Samarium 150.36 |

Actinides

| 89 **Ac** Actinium (227) | 90 **Th** Thorium 232.0381 | 91 **Pa** Protactinium 231.03588 | 92 **U** Uranium 238.02891 | 93 **Np** Neptunium (237) | 94 **Pu** Plutonium (244) |

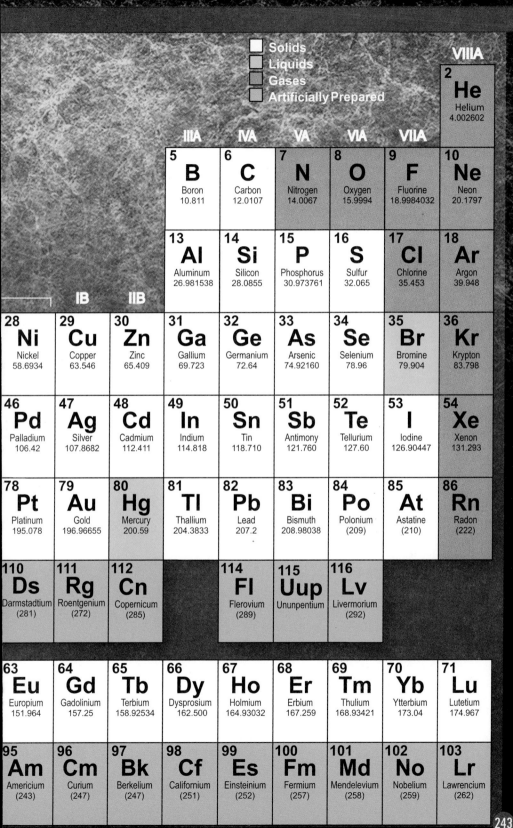

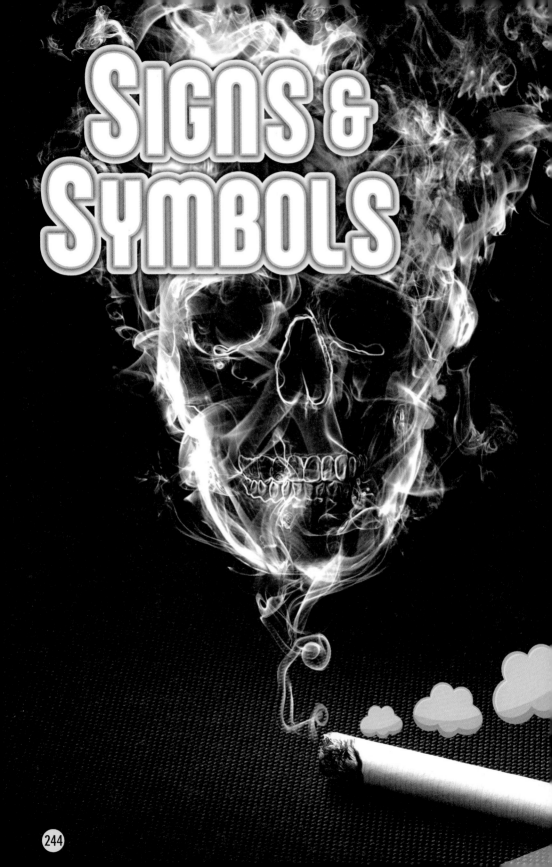

Signs & Symbols

Caution: These Signs Can Save Your Life

Before 1964, more than half of US adults smoked cigarettes. People smoked at home, at work, in schools and grocery stores—almost anywhere they wanted. Then the US Surgeon General issued an alarming report that said there was a proven link between cigarette smoking and cancer.

America began to kick the habit. Businesses put out signs saying "Thank You for Not Smoking." Congress passed laws forbidding smoking in certain places. Congress also passed a law requiring cigarette manufacturers to print a warning label on every pack.

Over the years, anti-smoking laws have grown tougher. The language on warning labels has gotten stronger. Combined with other actions, the labels have helped raise public awareness of smoking's dangers. Today, less than 20 percent of adults smoke cigarettes.

YOUR TURN

Fewer people smoke than in 1964, but more than 400,000 Americans still die from smoking-related causes every year. The American Lung Association (ALA) has asked every state and Washington, DC, to make public places and workplaces 100% smoke free. Where does your state stand? Visit stateoftobaccocontrol.org.

2014
Smoking can kill you.

1970
The Surgeon General has determined that cigarette smoking is dangerous to your health.

1966
Caution—cigarette smoking may be hazardous to your health.

What do these signs spell? (See p. 247.)

Basic Signs

Fire extinguisher

Women's room

Men's room

First aid

Elevator

Information

Disabled (parking, restrooms, access)

Bus

Recycle

Fallout shelter

No smoking

No admittance

No parking

Danger

Poison

Stop

Yield

Do not enter

No left turn

Falling rock

Stop ahead

Bicycle path

Traffic light ahead

Railroad crossing

Pedestrian crossing

Intersection ahead

Left turn

Right turn

Two-way traffic

Slippery when wet

Signs & Symbols

American Sign Language

In the manual alphabet of the hearing impaired, the fingers of the hand are moved to positions that represent the letters of the alphabet. Whole words and ideas are also expressed in sign language.

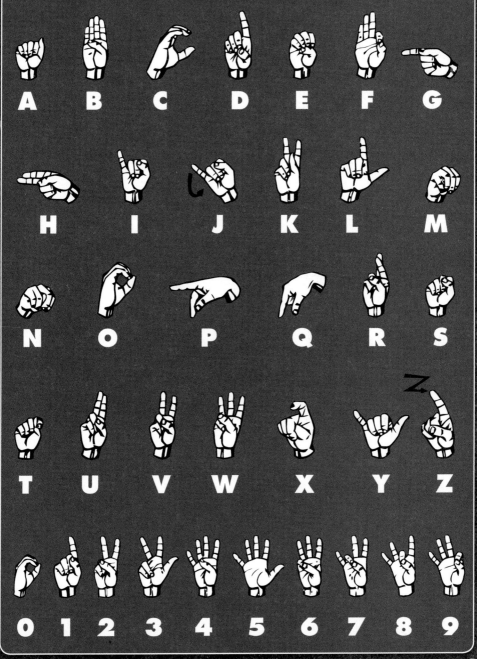

SPACE

A New National Park That's Over the Moon

Planning a family vacation to a national park? Forget packing up the camper. You may need a spaceship and lots and lots of travel time. Congress is considering a bill to create a new national park on the Moon.

The two US Representatives who sponsored the bill thought creating a national park would be a good way to protect historic sites like Tranquility Base, where humans first walked on the Moon. With more and more countries becoming able to land on the Moon, the representatives were concerned that significant features such as Neil Armstrong's footprints could be destroyed.

The park would be on the Moon, but that doesn't mean the United States would own a piece of the Moon. The Moon is international territory. No one country can own it. The park could be up and running by the end of 2015.

YOUR TURN

NASA has two exciting missions planned for 2015:

▶ February 1: The spacecraft *Dawn* will go into orbit around Asteroid 1 Ceres

▶ July 14: The spacecraft *New Horizons* will fly by Pluto and Charon

Log onto nasa.gov for updates and information. Did you know that nasa.gov also has activities, projects, and educational opportunities for students?

Which of these is not a planet? (See p. 253.)

The Solar System

(with distances from the Sun*)

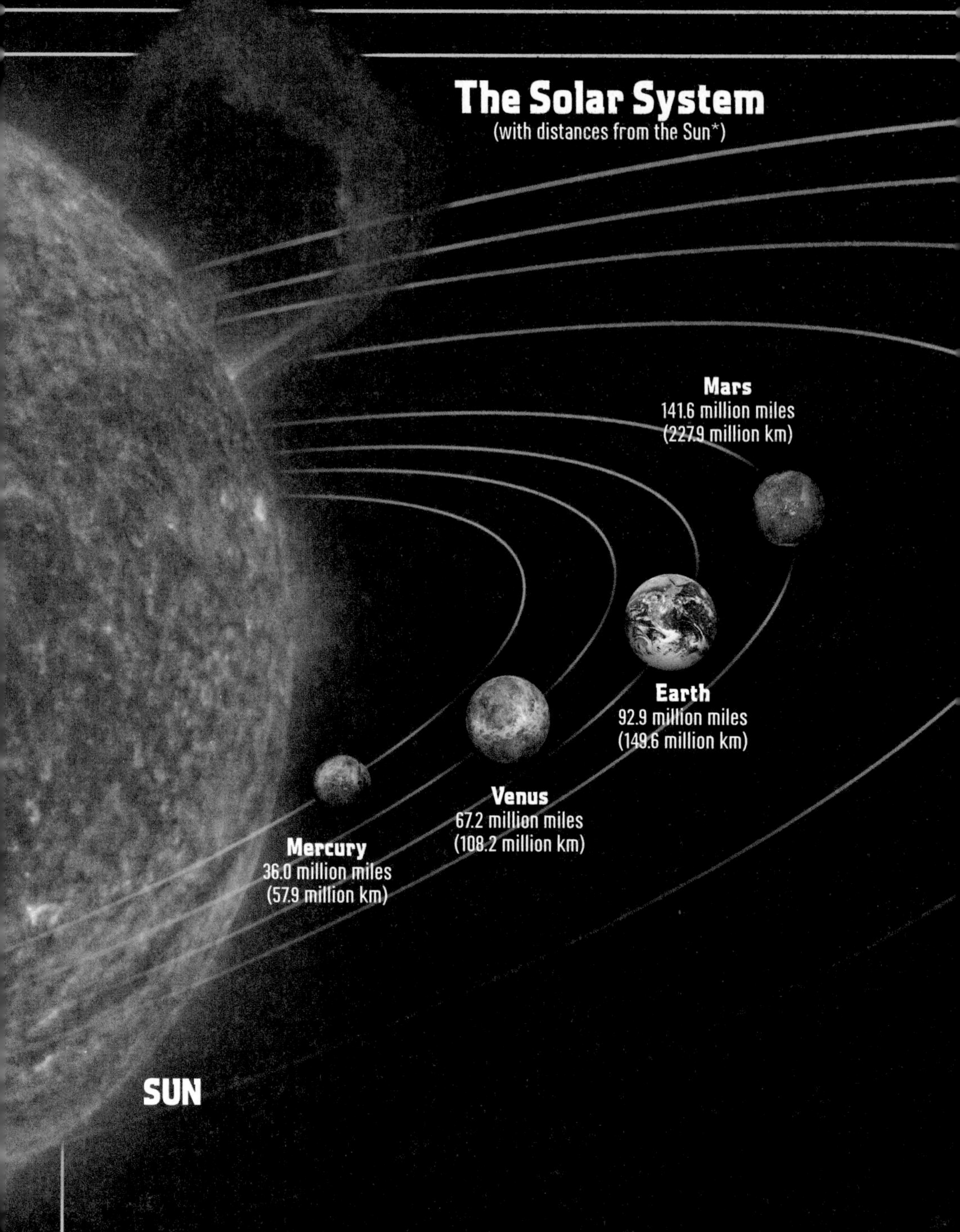

Mars
141.6 million miles
(227.9 million km)

Earth
92.9 million miles
(149.6 million km)

Venus
67.2 million miles
(108.2 million km)

Mercury
36.0 million miles
(57.9 million km)

SUN

*Distances rounded to nearest tenth

Neptune
2.8 billion miles
(4.5 billion km)

Uranus
1.8 billion miles
(2.9 billion km)

Saturn
885.9 million miles
(1.4 billion km)

Jupiter
483.7 million miles
(778.4 million km)

CHECK
IT OUT
!

Space Rocks!

- **Asteroid**: Rocky object that orbits the Sun
- **Comet**: Ball of dirt and ice with a tail that orbits the Sun
- **Meteoroid**: Small particle from an asteroid or comet
- **Meteor**: Meteoroid that enters Earth's atmosphere, burns up, and is visible as a streak of light
- **Meteorite**: Meteoroid that falls to Earth

In February 2013, 13-year-old Jansen Lyons found a 2-lb. meteorite near his New Mexico home, using a homemade metal detector. Experts at nearby University of New Mexico estimate the space object landed 10,000 years ago.

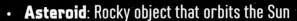

Basic Facts About the Planets in Our Solar System

Planet	Average distance from Sun	Rotation period (hours)	Period of revolution (in Earth days)	Diameter relative to Earth	Average surface or effective temperature	Planetary satellites (moons)
Mercury	36.0 million miles (57.9 million km)	1,407.5 hours	88 days	38.2%	332°F (166°C)	0
Venus	67.2 million miles (108.2 million km)	5,832.2 hours*	224.7 days	94.9%	864°F (462°C)	0
Earth	92.9 million miles (149.6 million km)	23.9 hours	365.24 days	100%	59°F (15°C)	1
Mars	141.6 million miles (227.9 million km)	24.6 hours	687 days	53.2%	−80°F (−62°C)	2
Jupiter	483.7 million miles (778.4 million km)	9.9 hours	4,330.6 days	1,121%	−234°F (−148°C)	66
Saturn	885.9 million miles (1.4 billion km)	10.7 hours	10,755.7 days	944%	−288°F (−178°C)	at least 62
Uranus	1.8 billion miles (2.9 billion km)	17.2 hours*	30,687.2 days	401%	−357°F (−216°C)	at least 27
Neptune	2.8 billion miles (4.5 billion km)	16.1 hours	60,190 days	388%	−353°F (−214°C)	at least 13

Space

*Retrograde rotation; rotates backward, or in the opposite direction from most other planetary bodies.

Basic Facts About the Sun

Position in the solar system	center
Average distance from Earth	92,955,820 miles (149,597,891 km)
Distance from center of Milky Way galaxy	27,710 light-years
Rotation period	25.38 days
Equatorial diameter	864,400 miles (1,391,117 km)
Diameter relative to Earth	109 times larger
Temperature at core	27,000,000°F (15,000,000°C)
Temperature at surface	10,000°F (5,538°C)
Main components	hydrogen and helium
Expected life of hydrogen fuel supply	6.4 billion years

Top 10 Largest Bodies in the Solar System

Ranked by size of equatorial diameter

1. Sun
864,400 miles
(1,391,117 km)

2. Jupiter
88,846 miles
(142,984 km)

3. Saturn
74,898 miles
(120,536 km)

4. Uranus
31,764 miles
(51,118 km)

5. Neptune
30,776 miles
(49,528 km)

6. Earth
7,926 miles
(12,755 km)

7. Venus
7,521 miles
(12,104 km)

8. Mars
4,222 miles
(6,794 km)

9. Ganymede
(moon of Jupiter)
3,280 miles
(5,262 km)

10. Titan
(moon of Saturn)
3,200 miles
(5,149 km)

Astronomy Terms and Definitions

Light-year (distance traveled by light in one year)	5.880 trillion miles (9.462 trillion km)
Velocity of light (speed of light)	186,000 miles/second (299,338 km/s)
Mean distance, Earth to Moon	238,855 miles (384,400 km)
Radius of Earth (distance from Earth's center to the equator)	3,963.19 miles (6,378 km)
Equatorial circumference of Earth (distance around the equator)	24,901 miles (40,075 km)
Polar circumference of Earth (distance around the poles)	24,860 miles (40,008 km)
Earth's mean velocity in orbit (how fast it travels)	18.5 miles/second (29.8 km/sec)

Fast Facts About the Moon

Age	4.6 billion years
Location	solar system
Mean distance from Earth	238,855 miles (384,400 km)
Diameter	2,160 miles (3,476 km)
Period of revolution	27 Earth days

Interesting features:
The Moon has no atmosphere or magnetic field. Most rocks on the surface of the Moon seem to be between 3 billion and 4.6 billion years old. Thus the Moon provides evidence about the early history of our solar system.

Top 10 Known Closest Comet Approaches to Earth Prior to 2014

5. Biela
December 9, 1805
3,402,182.5 miles
(5,475,282 km)

6. Comet of 1743
February 8, 1743
3,625,276.5 miles
(5,834,317 km)

4. Halley
April 10, 837
3,104,724.0 miles
(4,996,569 km)

7. Pons-Winnecke
June 26, 1927
3,662,458.7 miles
(5,894,156 km)

3. IRAS-Araki-Alcock
May 11, 1983
2,900,221.5 miles
(4,667,454 km)

8. Comet of 1014
February 24, 1014
3,783,301.1 miles
(6,088,633 km)

2. Tempel-Tuttle
October 26, 1366
2,128,687.8 miles
(3,425,791 km)

9. Comet of 1702
April 20, 1702
4,062,168.8 miles
(6,537,427 km)

1. Lexell
July 1, 1770
1,403,632.1 miles
(2,258,927 km)

10. Comet of 1132
October 7, 1132
4,155,124.7 miles
(6,687,025 km)

The Phases of the Moon

The Moon's appearance changes as it moves in its orbit around Earth.

First quarter

Waxing gibbous

Waxing crescent

Full moon

New moon

Waning gibbous

Waning crescent

Last quarter

Major Constellations

Latin	English	Latin	English
Aries	Ram	Lynx	Lynx
Camelopardalis	Giraffe	Lyra	Harp
Cancer	Crab	Microscopium	Microscope
Canes Venatici	Hunting Dogs	Monoceros	Unicorn
Canis Major	Big Dog	Musca	Fly
Canis Minor	Little Dog	Orion	Orion
Capricornus	Goat	Pavo	Peacock
Cassiopeia	Queen	Pegasus	Pegasus
Centaurus	Centaur	Phoenix	Phoenix
Cetus	Whale	Pictor	Painter
Chamaeleon	Chameleon	Pisces	Fish
Circinus	Compass	Piscis Austrinus	Southern Fish
Columba	Dove	Sagitta	Arrow
Corona Australis	Southern Crown	Sagittarius	Archer
Corona Borealis	Northern Crown	Scorpius	Scorpion
Corvus	Crow	Sculptor	Sculptor
Crater	Cup	Scutum	Shield
Crux	Southern Cross	Serpens	Serpent
Cygnus	Swan	Sextans	Sextant
Delphinus	Dolphin	Taurus	Bull
Dorado	Goldfish	Telescopium	Telescope
Draco	Dragon	Triangulum	Triangle
Equuleus	Little Horse	Triangulum Australe	Southern Triangle
Gemini	Twins	Tucana	Toucan
Grus	Crane	Ursa Major	Big Bear
Hercules	Hercules	Ursa Minor	Little Bear
Horologium	Clock	Virgo	Virgin
Lacerta	Lizard	Volans	Flying Fish
Leo	Lion	Vulpecula	Little Fox
Leo Minor	Little Lion		

Galaxies Nearest to the Sun

1. Canis Major Dwarf Galaxy
25,000 light-years

2. Sagittarius Dwarf Elliptical Galaxy
70,000 light-years

3. Large Magellanic Cloud
179,000 light-years

4. Small Magellanic Cloud
210,000 light-years

CHECK IT OUT !

It would take the spacecraft *Voyager* about 749,000,000 years to get to Canis Major Dwarf Galaxy, the closest galaxy to ours.

Stars Closest to Earth *

1. Proxima Centauri
4.22 light-years

2. Alpha Centauri A and B
4.35 light-years

3. Barnard's Star
5.9 light-years

4. Wolf 359
7.6 light-years

5. Lalande 21185
8.0 light-years

6. Sirius A and B
8.6 light-years

7. Luyten 726-8A and 726-8B
8.9 light-years

*besides the Sun

SPORTS

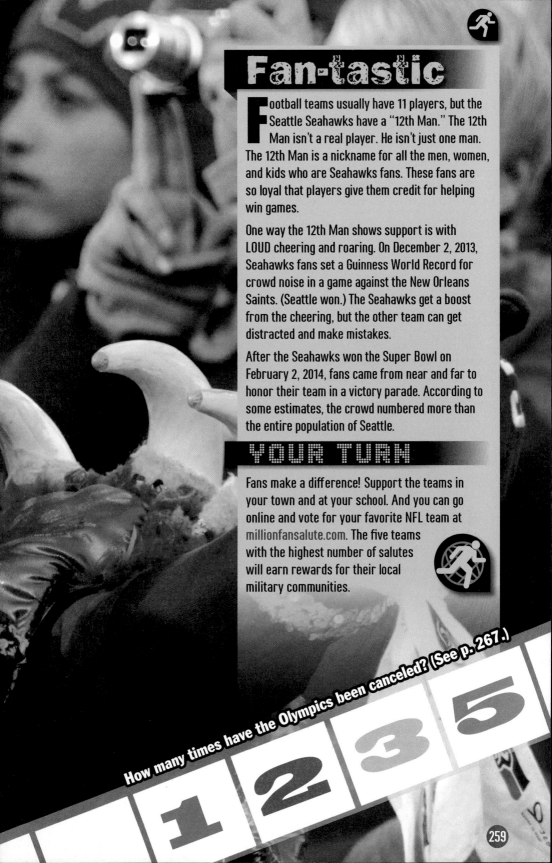

Fan-tastic

Football teams usually have 11 players, but the Seattle Seahawks have a "12th Man." The 12th Man isn't a real player. He isn't just one man. The 12th Man is a nickname for all the men, women, and kids who are Seahawks fans. These fans are so loyal that players give them credit for helping win games.

One way the 12th Man shows support is with LOUD cheering and roaring. On December 2, 2013, Seahawks fans set a Guinness World Record for crowd noise in a game against the New Orleans Saints. (Seattle won.) The Seahawks get a boost from the cheering, but the other team can get distracted and make mistakes.

After the Seahawks won the Super Bowl on February 2, 2014, fans came from near and far to honor their team in a victory parade. According to some estimates, the crowd numbered more than the entire population of Seattle.

YOUR TURN

Fans make a difference! Support the teams in your town and at your school. And you can go online and vote for your favorite NFL team at millionfansalute.com. The five teams with the highest number of salutes will earn rewards for their local military communities.

How many times have the Olympics been canceled? (See p. 267.)

1 2 3 5

PRO FOOTBALL

League Leaders 2013

Passing Yards
Peyton Manning, Denver Broncos — 5,477

Rushing Yards
LeSean McCoy, Philadelphia Eagles — 1,607

Receiving Yards
Josh Gordon, Cleveland Browns — 1,646

Touchdowns
Jamaal Charles, Kansas City Chiefs — 19

Kick Returns
Devin Hester, Chicago Bears — 52 Returns for 1,436 yards

Super Bowl XLVIII

On February 2, 2014, the National Football League (NFL) staged its championship football game, Super Bowl XLVIII, between National Football Conference (NFC) leaders Seattle Seahawks and American Football Conference (AFC) leaders Denver Broncos at MetLife Stadium in East Rutherford, New Jersey. The Seahawks won 43–8. Seahawks linebacker Malcolm Smith was named MVP, the first defender to win the honor in 11 years. Smith returned an interception for a touchdown, recovered a fumble, and had nine tackles. Seattle forced 4 turnovers.

Seattle Seahawks (NFC) 43
Denver Broncos (AFC) 8

The Pittsburgh Steelers made NFL history in February 2009 when Pittsburgh won the Super Bowl for the sixth time—the most Super Bowl victories by any single team. They claimed the Lombardi Trophy in Super Bowls IX, X, XIII, XIV, XL, and XLIII. The San Francisco 49ers (XVI, XIX, XXIII, XXIV, XXIX) and the Dallas Cowboys (VI, XII, XXVII, XXVIII, XXX) are the other league leaders, with five championships each.

CHECK IT OUT!

Sports

Bowl Championship Series (BCS)

National Championship Game 2013
Florida State 34, Auburn 31

Major Bowl Games 2013–2014

Game	Location	Teams/Score
Capital One Bowl	Orlando, FL	South Carolina 34, Wisconsin 24
Chick-fil-A Bowl	Atlanta, GA	Texas A&M 52, Duke 48
Russell Athletic Bowl	Orlando, FL	Louisville 36, Miami 9
Fiesta Bowl	Glendale, AZ	UCF 52, Baylor 42
Gator Bowl	Jacksonville, FL	Nebraska 24, Georgia 19
Outback Bowl	Tampa, FL	LSU 21, Iowa 14
Cotton Bowl	Arlington, TX	Missouri 41, Oklahoma State 31
Orange Bowl	Miami, FL	Clemson 40, Ohio State 35
Rose Bowl	Pasadena, CA	Michigan State 24, Stanford 20
Sugar Bowl	New Orleans, LA	Oklahoma 45, Alabama 31

Heisman Trophy 2013

James Winston, Florida State University, is the 34th quarterback to receive the award, the second freshman, and the third winner from Florida State. He completed 237 of 349 passes this year for 3,820 yards and 38 touchdowns, both of which are freshman records (only throwing 8 interceptions). He led the Seminoles to an undefeated regular season, an ACC Championship, and won the National Championship.

Top Players 2013

Rookies of the Year
American League — Wil Myers, Tampa Bay Rays
National League — Jose Fernandez, Miami Marlins

Managers of the Year
American League — Terry Fancona, Cleveland Indians
National League — Clint Hurdle, Pittsburgh Pirates

Most Valuable Player Awards
American League — Miguel Cabrera, Detroit Tigers
National League — Andrew McCutchen, Pittsburgh Pirates

Cy Young Awards
American League — Max Scherzer, Detroit Tigers
National League — Clayton Kershaw, Los Angeles Dodgers

Gold Glove Winners 2013
(selected by managers and players)

American League

Pitcher	R.A. Dickey, Toronto Blue Jays
Catcher	Salvador Perez, Kansas City Royals
First Baseman	Eric Hosmer, Kansas City Royals
Second Baseman	Dustin Pedroia, Boston Red Sox
Third Baseman	Manny Machado, Baltimore Orioles
Shortstop	JJ Hardy, Baltimore Orioles
	Alex Gordon, Kansas City Royals
	Adam Jones, Baltimore Orioles
Outfielders	Shane Victorino, Boston Red Sox

National League

Pitcher	Adam Wainwright, St. Louis Cardinals
Catcher	Yadier Molina, St. Louis Cardinals
First Baseman	Paul Goldschmidt, Arizona Diamondbacks
Second Baseman	Brandon Phillips, Cincinatti Reds
Third Baseman	Nolan Arenado, Colorado Rockies
Shortstop	Andrelton Simmons, Atlanta Braves
	Carlos González, Colorado Rockies
	Carlos Gomez, Milwaukee Brewers
Outfielders	Gerardo Parra, Arizona Diamondbacks

League Leaders 2013

American League

Batting Average	Miguel Cabrera, Detroit Tigers
Home Runs	Chris Davis, Baltimore Orioles
Runs Batted In	Chris Davis, Baltimore Orioles
Wins	Max Scherzer, Detroit Tigers
Earned Run Average	Anibal Sanchez, Detroit Tigers
Saves	Jim Johnson, Oakland A's

National League

Batting Average	Michael Cuddyer, Colorado Rockies
Home Runs	Pedro Alvarez, Pittsburgh Pirates
Runs Batted In	Paul Goldschmidt, Arizona Diamondbacks
Wins	Adam Wainwright, St. Louis Cardinals
Earned Run Average	Clayton Kershaw, Los Angeles Dodgers
Saves	Craig Kimbrel, Atlanta Braves

World Series 2013

On October 31, 2013, the Boston Red Sox won the World Series after six games. This was the first time that the Red Sox won the World Series at their home field of Fenway Park since 1918. The Red Sox staged an incredible comeback after finishing last in 2012 with 93 losses. David Ortiz was named MVP. "I think that this may be the most special of all the World Series that I have been a part of," said Ortiz, who finished the series with a .688 batting average (11 for 16) and a .760 on-base percentage (19 for 25). The win came a little over six months after explosions at the Boston Marathon killed 3 and injured 26.

Little League World Series 2013

Japan Region defeated the United States Champs from the West Region 6-4, in a series played in South Williamsport, PA, August 15-August 25. The Little Leaguers from Japan had to battle back late to capture the crown, scoring the go-ahead runs in the fifth inning thanks to Ryusei Hirooka's double down the left-side line, scoring Takuma Gomi and Kyousuke Kobayashi.

NBA Championship Finals 2013

On June 20, 2013, the Miami Heat won the NBA Championship with a 95-88 win over the San Antonio Spurs. It was Game 7 of 7, and it was played in the American Airlines Arena in Miami, FL. LeBron James was MVP, scoring 37 points, 4 assists, and 12 rebounds.

NBA Top Scorers 2013

NAME	TEAM	GAMES	AVG. POINTS
1. Carmelo Anthony	NYK	67	28.7
2. Kevin Durant	OKC	81	28.1
3. Kobe Bryant	LA	78	27.3
4. LeBron James	MIA	76	26.8
5. James Harden	HOU	78	25.9

WNBA Championship Finals 2013

On October 10, 2013, the Minnesota Lynx faced the Atlanta Dream at Gwinnett Center in Duluth, GA. The Lynx won 86-77 in Game 3 (of a 5-game series). It was their second WNBA Championship in three years. Maya Moore was named MVP, scoring 23 points. Minnesota had been undefeated in seven playoff games.

WNBA Top Scorers 2013

NAME	TEAM	GAMES	AVG. POINTS (per game)
1. Angel McCoughtry	Atlanta Dream	33	21.5
2. Diana Taurasi	Phoenix Mercury	32	20.3
3. Maya Moore	Minnesota Lynx	34	18.5
4. Elena Delle Donne	Chicago Sky	30	18.0
5. Tina Charles	Connecticut Sun	29	18.0

COLLEGE BASKETBALL

NCAA Men's Division I Championship 2014

The University of Connecticut Huskies beat the University of Kentucky Wildcats to win the National Collegiate Athletic Association (NCAA) championship on April 7, 2014, at the AT&T Stadium in Arlington, TX. The final score was 60–54.

Connecticut made 100% of their free throws in the championship game, an NCAA record. Shabazz Napier, who was named the Final Four's Most Outstanding Player, scored 22 points and added 6 rebounds for the Huskies. This is the fourth National Championship for UConn since 1999.

NCAA Men's Championship Game Leaders

	CONNECTICUT		KENTUCKY	
Points	Shabazz Napier	22	James Young	20
Rebounds	Shabazz Napier	6		
	DeAndre Daniels	6		
	Lasan Kromah	6	James Young	7
Assists	Shabazz Napier	3		
	Ryan Boatwright	3	Andrew Harrison	5

NCAA Women's Division I Championship 2014

In the women's division of the NCAA, the University of Connecticut Huskies defeated the Notre Dame Fighting Irish 79-58 on April 8, 2014, to win the national championship game at Bridgestone Arena in Nashville, TN. It was the ninth time the UConn women, led by Coach Geno Auriemma, have made it to the finals—and the ninth time they've won. Connecticut Sophomore Breanna Stewart scored 21 points and was named Most Outstanding Player of the Final Four.

This is the second time UConn men and women have taken the top collegiate basketball title. Both teams won in 2004 too. The men's and women's teams have a combined 17 appearances in the Final Four.

Sochi 2014 Winter Olympics

The 2014 Winter Olympics took place in Sochi, Russian Federation, February 7-23. An estimated 2,800 athletes from 88 countries competed in 15 sports. Among many highlights, Meryl Davis and Charlie White won the first US gold medal ever in ice dancing. Colorado's 18-year-old Mikaela Shiffrin became the youngest female to win an Alpine skiing gold medal.

Approximately 1,300 medals were to be awarded at the Olympics and the Paralympic Games hosted by Sochi in March. Russia won 33 medals, the most for any country. Dutch speedskater Ireen Wust won the most medals for any athlete: two golds and three silvers.

Medal Count Leaders

Country	Gold	Silver	Bronze	Total
Russia	13	11	9	33
United States	9	7	12	28
Norway	11	5	10	26
Canada	10	10	5	25
Netherlands	8	7	9	24
Germany	8	6	5	19
Austria	4	8	5	17
France	4	4	7	15
Sweden	2	7	6	15
Switzerland	6	3	2	11
China	3	4	2	9
South Korea	3	3	2	8
Czech Republic	2	4	2	8
Slovenia	2	2	4	8
Japan	1	4	3	8
Italy	0	2	6	8
Belarus	5	0	1	6

Locations of the Modern-Day Olympics

Year	Location
1896	Athens, Greece
1900	Paris, France
1904	St. Louis, Missouri, USA
1906	Athens, Greece
1908	London, UK
1912	Stockholm, Sweden
1916	Canceled
1920	Antwerp, Belgium
1924	Chamonix, France
1924	Paris, France
1928	Amsterdam, Holland
1928	St. Moritz, Switzerland
1932	Los Angeles, California, USA
1932	Lake Placid, New York, USA
1936	Berlin, Germany
1936	Garmisch-Partenkirchen, Germany
1940	Canceled
1944	Canceled
1948	London, UK
1948	St. Moritz, Switzerland
1952	Helsinki, Finland
1952	Oslo, Norway
1956	Melbourne, Australia
1956	Cortina d'Ampezzo, Italy
1960	Rome, Italy
1960	Squaw Valley, California, USA
1964	Tokyo, Japan
1964	Innsbruck, Austria
1968	Mexico City, Mexico
1968	Grenoble, France
1972	Munich, Germany
1972	Sapporo, Japan
1976	Montreal, Canada
1976	Innsbruck, Austria
1980	Moscow, USSR
1980	Lake Placid, New York, USA
1984	Los Angeles, California, USA
1984	Sarajevo, Yugoslavia
1988	Seoul, South Korea
1988	Calgary, Alberta, Canada
1992	Barcelona, Spain
1992	Albertville, France
1994	Lillehammer, Norway
1996	Atlanta, Georgia, USA
1998	Nagano, Japan
2000	Sydney, Australia
2002	Salt Lake City, Utah, USA
2004	Athens, Greece
2006	Turin, Italy
2008	Beijing, China
2010	Vancouver, Canada
2012	London, UK
2014	Sochi, Russian Federation
2016	Rio de Janeiro, Brazil
2018	Pyeong Chang, South Korea

TECHNOLOGY & COMPUTERS

Happy 25th Birthday, Worldwide Web!

Today most Americans are online every day, but 25 years ago few people had even heard of the Internet. At that time the Internet was a network of linked computers used only by major universities and the military. It was like a highway closed off to all but a few special travelers.

On March 12, 1989, a scientist named Tim Berners-Lee suggested a way to open up the highway to everyone. His idea involved coding and typing letters and symbols into a browser window. Tim Berners-Lee's suggestion became the worldwide web.

The Internet is available almost everywhere in the United States and many other countries, but four billion people around the world have no way to go online. Technology leaders such as Google and Facebook are working on ways to deliver Internet access to remote areas using satellites, drones, and even balloons. They hope making the Internet available everywhere will help bring the world together for everyone's good.

YOUR TURN

Discover the history behind the Internet, cable, cell phones, satellite TV, and more at transition.fcc.gov/cgb/kidszone/history.html.

Which country has the most Internet users? (See p. 271)

RUSSIA

UNITED STATES

CHINA

JAPAN

Internet Usage 1995-2014

According to the Pew Research Internet Project, 87% of Americans use the Internet as of January 2014. This chart shows how Internet use has increased since 1995.

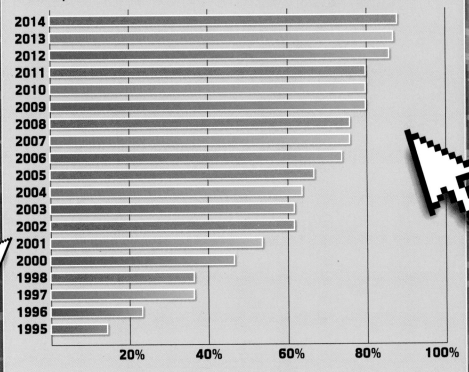

Top US Internet Activities

What do Americans spend time doing online?

Online Activity	Several Times a Day	Daily
Check e-mail	55%	32%
Browse (surf)	29%	30%
Look for News	15%	33%
Instant Message	9%	11%
Find or check a fact	8%	21%
Play games	8%	14%
Listen/download music	7%	10%
Watch/download videos	6%	10%
Listen to online radio	6%	8%
Look up a definition	5%	10%
Online banking	3%	17%

Top 10 Worldwide Internet Users

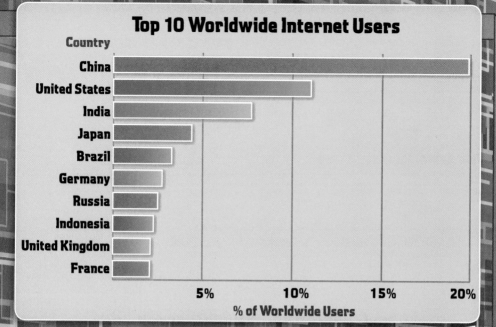

Country

Country	% of Worldwide Users
China	▇▇▇▇▇▇▇▇ ~20%
United States	▇▇▇▇ ~10.5%
India	▇▇▇ ~7.5%
Japan	▇▇ ~4.5%
Brazil	▇▇ ~4%
Germany	▇ ~3.5%
Russia	▇ ~3%
Indonesia	▇ ~2.5%
United Kingdom	▇ ~2.5%
France	▇ ~2.5%

% of Worldwide Users

Top 10 US Internet Destinations

1. Google sites (YouTube, Blogger)
2. Yahoo! sites (Flickr, Rivals.com)
3. Microsoft sites (Bing, Xbox Live)
4. Facebook.com (Instagram)
5. AOL Inc. (Moviefone; Patch, Huffington Post)
6. Amazon sites (Zappos, Audible, IMDb)
7. Glam Media (Glam, Brash)
8. Wikipedia Foundation sites (Wikipedia)
9. CBS Interactive (CNET, GameSpot)
10. Apple Inc. (iTunes)

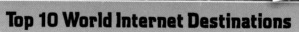

Top 10 World Internet Destinations

1. Google sites (YouTube, Blogger)
2. Microsoft sites (Bing, Xbox Live)
3. Facebook.com
4. Yahoo! sites (Yahoo! Voices, Rivals.com)
5. Wikimedia Foundation sites (Wikipedia)
6. Amazon sites (Zappos, Audible, IMDb, LoveFilm)
7. Baidu.com Inc
8. Tencent Inc. (QQ)
9. Alibaba.com Corp
10. Sohu.com Inc

Top 5 US E-mail Websites

Website	Visitors (in thousands)
Yahoo! Mail	83,249
Google Gmail	75,312
Outlook	30,771
AOL Email	19,358
Xfinity.com WebMail	7,294

*Number of persons age 2 and older in any US location, in thousands, who visited the website at least once in June 2013.

Top 5 Search and Navigation Websites

Website	Searches (millions)	% of Searches
Google sites	12,823	66.7
Microsoft sites (Bing)	3,434	17.9
Yahoo! Sites	2,197	114
Ask Network	524	2.7
AOL, Inc.	253	1.3

CHECK IT OUT !

Emoticons are symbols formed from computer characters and used to show the sender's feelings in texts and e-mails. The first emoticon was invented in 1982 by Scott Fahlman, a professor at Carnegie Mellon University in Pittsburgh, PA. Falhman used three keystrokes to create a smiley face. : -)

A newer kind of emoticon is called an emoji, which means "picture" and "letter" in Japanese. Emojis are tiny images of faces, animals, hearts, and other things. More and more people are using them in e-mail and texts to substitute for words or add punctuation and feeling.

Top 5 Most-Visited US Video Sites

Website	Visitors (in thousands)
Google sites (YouTube)	154,609
Yahoo! sites	54,273
Vevo	47,980
Facebook.com	45,870
Microsoft site (Xbox Live)	41,770

*Number of persons age 2 and older in any US location, in thousands, who visited the website at least once in June 2013.

VIDEOS

BLOGS

FORU

CHECK IT OUT !

YouTube by the numbers:
- ▶ More than 1 billion unique visits (not counting multiple visits by the same user) each month
- ▶ Over 6 billion hours of video are watched each month
- ▶ 100 hours of video are uploaded to YouTube every minute

Mobile Internet

According to the Pew Internet Project, as of May 2013, 63% of adult cell owners use their phones to go online. About 34% of cell Internet users go online mostly using their phones, instead of some other device such as a desktop or laptop computer.

America Gets Smart(phones)

According to Pew, as of January 2014:

- ▶ 91% of American adults have a cell phone
- ▶ 58% of American adults have a smartphone
- ▶ 32% of American adults own an e-reader
- ▶ 42% of American adults own a tablet computer

An estimated 14 billion smartphones were projected to be in use at the end of 2013. The three top suppliers were:

- ▶ Android   798 million
- ▶ Apple   294 million
- ▶ Windows Phone   45 million

Top Activities on Mobile Phones

Send or receive a text message

Go online

Send or receive e-mail

Download apps

Get directions, recommendations, or other location-based information

Listen to music

Participate in a video call or video chat

"Check in" or share your location

About 91% of Americans have cell phones, but China leads the world with 95% cell phone ownership. In Pakistan, slightly more than half the people have a cell phone. Researchers think the rapid rise in cell phone ownership in emerging countries like Pakistan could be because these nations have bypassed land lines and gone straight to mobile.

CHECK IT OUT !

All About Apps

Device	Total Number of Free and Costing App Downloads
Apple	50 billion (as of May 2013)
Google	48 billion (as of May 2013)
Blackberry	5 billion (as of July 2013)
Windows	3 billion (as of November 2013)

Free iPhone Apps:
Top Downloaded Apps of 2013

Candy Crush Saga
YouTube
Temple Run 2
Vine
Google Maps
Snapchat
Instagram
Facebook
Pandora Radio
Despicable Me: Minion Rush

According to Instagram.com, the photo-sharing site has 150 million users as of September 6, 2013.

CHECK IT OUT !

Going Social: Mobile vs. Desktop

Social Network	Desktop	Mobile
Facebook	32%	68%
Twitter	14%	86%
Instagram	2%	98%
LinkedIn	74%	26%
Pinterest	8%	92%
Tumblr	54%	46%
Vine	1%	99%
Snapchat	0%	100%

5 Top Social Networks

As of September 2013, almost three-quarters of all adults who go online use social networking sites. More than four out of ten social network users go to multiple sites.

The top sites are:

Site	% of Online Adults Who Use
Facebook	71%
LinkedIn	22%
Pinterest	21%
Twitter	18%
Instagram	17%

Teens and Technology: Connecting 24/7

According to the Pew Research Center, 93% of young people 12–17 own or have use of a computer, and 95% of teens are online—more than any other age group except 18–29. More and more, teens are using their mobile devices to connect anytime they want.

Percent of all teens

78%	Have a cell phone
37%	Have a smartphone
23%	Have a tablet computer
74%	Occasionally go online with a mobile device
25%	Mostly go online with a mobile device

According to a survey of 13- to 17-year-olds by Commonsense Media, teens love to text and connect with friends through social media. But almost half of respondents said their favorite way to communicate is face-to-face.

Percent of respondents

90%	Have used social media
68%	Text every day
51%	Visit social network sites every day
23%	Visit at least two different social sites a day
11%	Send or receive tweets at least once a day
49%	Prefer to communicate in person
33%	Prefer to communicate by text
7%	Prefer to communicate by social networks
4%	Prefer to communicate by talking on the phone

US GOVERNMENT

Favorite First Lady

According to a 2014 poll, Eleanor Roosevelt, wife of former President Franklin D. Roosevelt, is the First Lady we admire most. In the poll, which Siena College has run five times since 1982, historians and scholars ranked each First Lady in leadership, courage, accomplishments, and other categories. Mrs. Roosevelt has won the top spot in every poll.

The nine other top First Ladies are:

- ② Abigail Adams
- ③ Jacqueline Kennedy
- ④ Dolley Madison
- ⑤ Michelle Obama
- ⑥ Hillary Clinton
- ⑦ Lady Bird Johnson
- ⑧ Betty Ford
- ⑨ Martha Washington
- ⑩ Rosalynn Carter

Eleanor Roosevelt was a writer and a lifelong champion of human rights. After leaving the White House, she became the first US delegate to the United Nations. You can visit sculptures honoring Mrs. Roosevelt at the Franklin Delano Roosevelt Memorial in Washington, DC, and in Riverside Park in New York City (pictured at left).

There have been 46 official First Ladies, but did you know that 13 women have tried for another title—Madam President? The first woman to run for president was Victoria Woodhull, in 1870. The most recent was Hillary Rodham Clinton, in 2008. As of early 2014, women occupy the highest political position in 19 countries. Why not the United States?

YOUR TURN

Find tons of information about US presidents and first ladies at archives.gov/presidential-libraries/research/alic/presidents.html.

Who was the youngest president? See (pp. 295, 297 and 299.)

The Branches of Government

Executive

The President

- Symbol of our nation and head of state
- Shapes and conducts foreign policy and acts as chief diplomat
- Chief administrator of federal government
- Commander-in-chief of armed forces
- Has authority to pass or veto congressional bills, plans, and programs
- Appoints and removes nonelected officials
- Leader of his or her political party

Legislative

The Congress:
The Senate
The House of Representatives

- Chief lawmaking body
- Conducts investigations into matters of national importance
- Has power to impeach or remove any civil officer from office, including the president
- Can amend Constitution
- The Senate is made up of 100 senators—2 from each state
- The House of Representatives is made up of 435 congressional representatives, apportioned to each state according to population

Judicial

The Supreme Court

- Protects Constitution
- Enforces commands of executive and legislative branches
- Protects rights of individuals and shields citizens from unfair laws
- Defines laws of our nation
- Can declare laws unconstitutional

US Government

Highest Federal Salaries

Official	Salary
President	$400,000
Vice President	$231,900
Speaker of the House	$224,600
Chief Justice of the Supreme Court	$223,500
Associate justices	$213,900
President Pro Tempore of the Senate	$194,400
Senate majority and minority leaders	$194,400
House majority and minority leaders	$194,400
Appeals court judges	$184,500
Senators	$174,000
Representatives	$174,000
District judges	$174,000

CHECK IT OUT!

For most of the years between 1789 and 1855, members of Congress received no yearly salary at all. Instead they were paid $6.00 to $8.00 a day when Congress was in session. Benjamin Franklin proposed that elected government officials not be paid anything for their service, but his proposal didn't win much support.

How a Bill Introduced in the House of Representatives Becomes a Law

How a Bill Originates

The executive branch inspires much legislation. The president usually outlines broad objectives in the yearly State of the Union address.

Members of the president's staff may draft bills and ask congresspersons who are friendly to the legislation to introduce them.

Other bills originate independently of the administration, perhaps to fulfill a campaign pledge made by a congressperson.

How a Bill Is Introduced

Each bill must be introduced by a member of the House. The Speaker then assigns the bill to the appropriate committee.

The committee conducts hearings during which members of the administration and others may testify for or against the bill.

If the committee votes to proceed, the bill goes to the Rules Committee, which decides whether to place it before the House.

The House Votes

A bill submitted to the House is voted on, with or without a debate. If a majority approves it, the bill is sent to the Senate.

Senate Procedure

The Senate assigns a bill to a Senate committee, which holds hearings and then approves, rejects, rewrites, or shelves the bill.

If the committee votes to proceed, the bill is submitted to the Senate for a vote, which may be taken with or without a debate.

Results

If the Senate does not change the House version of the bill and a majority approves it, the bill goes to the president for signing.

If the bill the Senate approves differs from the House version, the bill is sent to a House–Senate conference for a compromise solution.

If the conference produces a compromise bill and it is approved by both the House and Senate, the bill goes to the president for signing.

When a Bill Becomes Law

The bill becomes law if the president signs it. If the president vetoes the bill, two-thirds of both the House and Senate must approve it again before it can become law. If the bill comes to the president soon before Congress adjourns, the president may not do anything at all. If the bill is not signed before Congress adjourns, the bill dies. This is called the president's "pocket veto."

(A similar procedure is followed for bills introduced in the Senate.)

State and Federal Court Systems

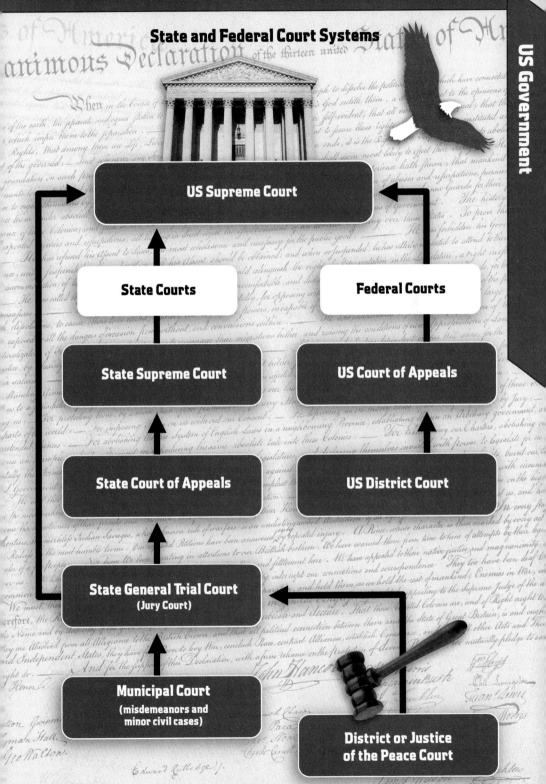

US Supreme Court

State Courts

Federal Courts

State Supreme Court

US Court of Appeals

State Court of Appeals

US District Court

State General Trial Court
(Jury Court)

Municipal Court
(misdemeanors and minor civil cases)

District or Justice of the Peace Court

The Sequence of Presidential Succession

If the president dies, resigns, is removed from office, or can't carry out his or her duties, the vice president assumes the president's duties. If the vice president dies or becomes unable to serve, who is next in line? The order of presidential replacements is below.

1. **Vice President**
2. **Speaker of the House**
3. **President Pro Tempore of the Senate**
4. **Secretary of State**
5. **Secretary of the Treasury**
6. **Secretary of Defense**
7. **Attorney General**
8. **Secretary of the Interior**
9. **Secretary of Agriculture**
10. **Secretary of Commerce**
11. **Secretary of Labor**
12. **Secretary of Health and Human Services**
13. **Secretary of Housing and Urban Development**
14. **Secretary of Transportation**
15. **Secretary of Energy**
16. **Secretary of Education**
17. **Secretary of Veterans Affairs**
18. **Secretary of Homeland Security**

Voting

Basic Laws and Requirements

- You must be 18 years of age or older before an election in order to vote in it.
- You must be an American citizen to vote.
- You must register before voting.
- You must show proof of residence in order to register.

How to Register

- Registering often only requires filling out a simple form.
- It does not cost anything to register.
- You need not be a member of any political party to register.
- To find out where to register, you can call your town hall or city board of elections.
- You can find out more about voting and registering at:

eac.gov/voter

Voter Turnout: Presidential Elections 1960-2012

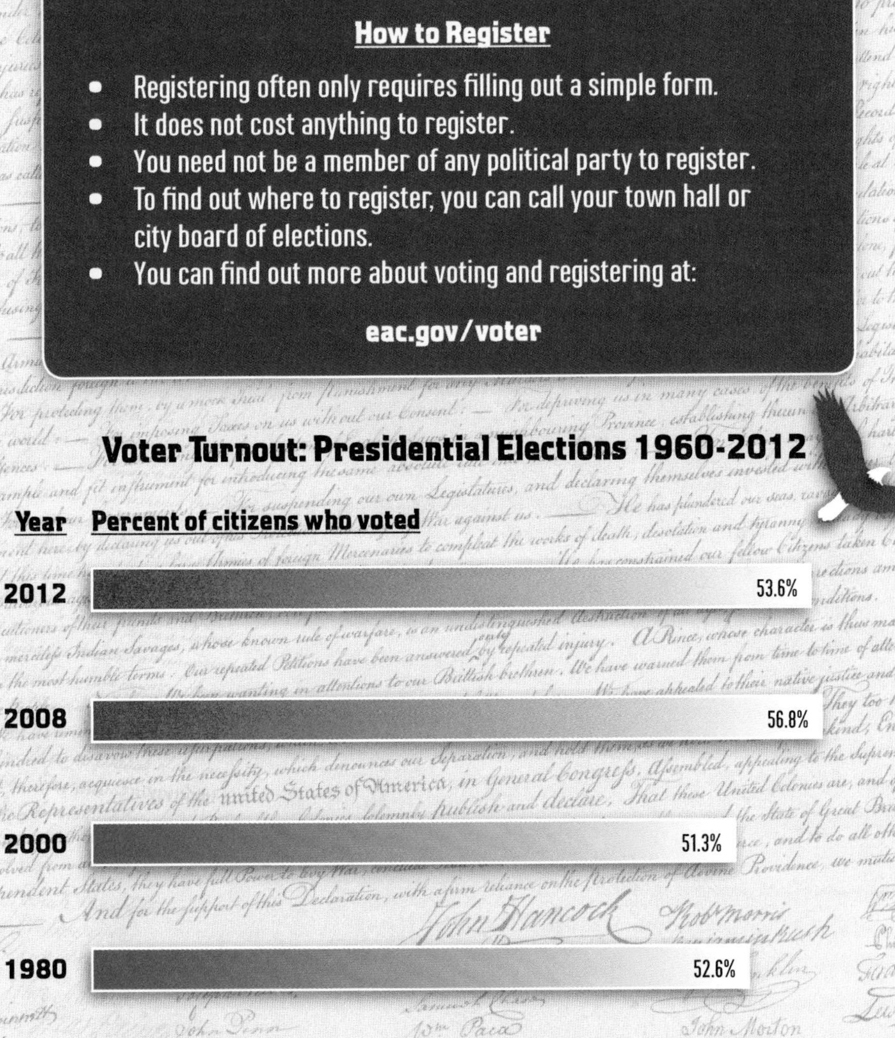

Year	Percent of citizens who voted
2012	53.6%
2008	56.8%
2000	51.3%
1980	52.6%
1960*	63.1%

The Electoral College

Although people turn out on Election Day and cast their votes for president, the president and vice president are only indirectly elected by the American people. In fact, the president and vice president are the only elected federal officials not chosen by direct vote of the people. These two officials are elected by the Electoral College, which was created by the framers of the Constitution.

Here is a basic summary of how the Electoral College works:

- There are 538 electoral votes.
- The votes are divided among the 50 states and the District of Columbia. The number of votes that each state has is equal to the number of senators and representatives for that state. (i.e., California has 53 representatives and 2 senators; it has a total of 55 electoral votes.)
- During an election, the candidate who wins the majority of popular votes in a given state wins all the electoral votes from that state.
- A presidential candidate needs 270 electoral votes to win.

You may have heard that it is possible for a presidential candidate who has not won the most popular votes to win an election. This can happen if a candidate wins the popular vote in large states (ones with lots of electoral votes) by only a slim margin and loses the popular votes in smaller states by a wide margin.

Electoral Votes for President

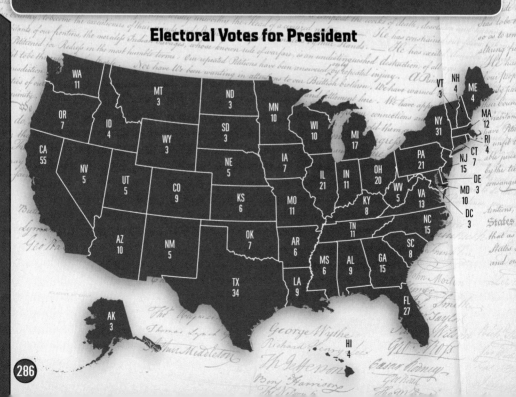

US Government

US Presidents with the Most Electoral Votes

President		Year	Number of electoral votes
Ronald Reagan	🐘	1984	525
Franklin D. Roosevelt	🐴	1936	523
Richard Nixon	🐘	1972	520
Ronald Reagan	🐘	1980	489
Lyndon B. Johnson	🐴	1964	486
Franklin D. Roosevelt	🐴	1932	472
Dwight D. Eisenhower	🐘	1956	457
Franklin D. Roosevelt	🐴	1940	449
Herbert Hoover	🐘	1928	444
Dwight D. Eisenhower	🐘	1952	442

🐘 = Republican

🐴 = Democrat

US Presidents with the Most Popular Votes

President		Year	Number of popular votes
Barack Obama	🐴	2008	69,498,000
Barack Obama	🐴	2012	62,611,000
George W. Bush	🐘	2004	61,837,000
Ronald Reagan	🐘	1984	54,167,000
George W. Bush	🐘	2000	50,465,000
George H. W. Bush	🐘	1988	48,643,000

Who Is on Our Paper Money?

$1
George Washington

$2*
Thomas Jefferson

$5
Abraham Lincoln

$10
Alexander Hamilton

$20
Andrew Jackson

$50
Ulysses S. Grant

$100
Benjamin Franklin

$500*
William McKinley

$1,000*
Grover Cleveland

$5,000*
James Madison

$10,000*
Salmon P. Chase

$100,000*
Woodrow Wilson

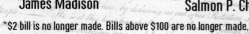

*$2 bill is no longer made. Bills above $100 are no longer made.

Who Is on Our Coins?

Dime:
Franklin D. Roosevelt

Half-dollar:
John F. Kennedy

Penny:
Abraham Lincoln

Nickel:
Thomas Jefferson

Quarter:
George Washington

Dollar:
Sacagawea

Presidents of the United States

1. George Washington
Born: Feb. 22, 1732, Wakefield, Virginia
Died: Dec. 14, 1799, Mount Vernon, Virginia
Term of office: April 30, 1789—March 3, 1797
Age at inauguration: 57
Party: Federalist
Vice President: John Adams
First Lady: Martha Dandridge Custis Washington

2. John Adams
Born: Oct. 30, 1735, Braintree (now Quincy), Massachusetts
Died: July 4, 1826, Braintree, Massachusetts
Term of office: March 4, 1797—March 3, 1801
Age at inauguration: 61
Party: Federalist
Vice President: Thomas Jefferson
First Lady: Abigail Smith Adams

3. Thomas Jefferson
Born: April 13, 1743, Shadwell, Virginia
Died: July 4, 1826, Monticello, Virginia
Term of office: March 4, 1801—March 3, 1809
Age at inauguration: 57
Party: Democratic Republican
Vice President: Aaron Burr, George Clinton
First Lady: Martha Skelton Jefferson

4. James Madison
Born: March 16, 1751, Port Conway, Virginia
Died: June 28, 1836, Orange, Virginia
Term of office: March 4, 1809—March 3, 1817
Age at inauguration: 57
Party: Democratic Republican
Vice President: George Clinton, Elbridge Gerry
First Lady: Dolley Todd Madison

CHECK IT OUT!

George Washington is the only president who was unanimously elected. He received every single vote!

5. James Monroe

Born: April 28, 1758, Westmoreland County, Virginia
Died: July 4, 1831, New York City, New York
Term of office: March 4, 1817—March 3, 1825
Age at inauguration: 58
Party: Democratic Republican
Vice President: Daniel D. Tompkins
First Lady: Elizabeth Kortright Monroe

6. John Quincy Adams

Born: July 11, 1767, Braintree, Massachusetts
Died: Feb. 23, 1848, Washington, DC
Term of office: March 4, 1825—March 3, 1829
Age at inauguration: 57
Party: Democratic Republican
Vice President: John C. Calhoun
First Lady: Louisa Johnson Adams

7. Andrew Jackson

Born: March 15, 1767, Waxhaw, South Carolina
Died: June 8, 1845, Nashville, Tennessee
Term of office: March 4, 1829—March 3, 1837
Age at inauguration: 61
Party: Democrat
Vice President: John C. Calhoun, Martin Van Buren
First Lady: Rachel Robards Jackson

8. Martin Van Buren

Born: Dec. 5, 1782, Kinderhook, New York
Died: July 24, 1862, Kinderhook, New York
Term of office: March 4, 1837—March 3, 1841
Age at inauguration: 54
Party: Democrat
Vice President: Richard M. Johnson
First Lady: Hannah Hoes Van Buren

US Government

9. William Henry Harrison

Born: Feb. 9, 1773, Berkeley, Virginia
Died: April 4, 1841, Washington, DC*
Term of office: March 4, 1841—April 4, 1841
Age at inauguration: 68
Party: Whig
Vice President: John Tyler
First Lady: Anna Symmes Harrison

10. John Tyler

Born: March 29, 1790, Greenway, Virginia
Died: Jan. 18, 1862, Richmond, Virginia
Term of office: April 6, 1841—March 3, 1845
Age at inauguration: 51
Party: Whig
Vice President: (none)**
First Lady: Letitia Christian Tyler,
Julia Gardiner Tyler†

11. James Knox Polk

Born: Nov. 2, 1795, Mecklenburg, North Carolina
Died: June 15, 1849, Nashville, Tennessee
Term of office: March 4, 1845—March 3, 1849
Age at inauguration: 49
Party: Democrat
Vice President: George M. Dallas
First Lady: Sarah Childress Polk

12. Zachary Taylor

Born: Nov. 24, 1784, Orange County, Virginia
Died: July 9, 1850, Washington, DC*
Term of office: March 5, 1849—July 9, 1850
Age at inauguration: 64
Party: Whig
Vice President: Millard Fillmore
First Lady: Margaret (Peggy) Smith Taylor

CHECK IT OUT !

William Henry Harrison had the longest inauguration speech and the shortest term of any president. After giving a speech lasting 105 minutes in the cold rain, he developed pneumonia and died 32 days later.

* Died in office, natural causes
** Vice President Tyler took over the duties of the president when William Henry Harrison died in office, leaving the vice presidency vacant.
† President Tyler's first wife died in 1842. He remarried in 1844.

13. Millard Fillmore

Born: Jan. 7, 1800, Cayuga County, New York
Died: March 8, 1874, Buffalo, New York
Term of office: July 10, 1850—March 3, 1853
Age at inauguration: 50
Party: Whig
Vice President: (none)*
First Lady: Abigail Powers Fillmore

14. Franklin Pierce

Born: Nov. 23, 1804, Hillsboro, New Hampshire
Died: Oct. 8, 1869, Concord, New Hampshire
Term of office: March 4, 1853—March 3, 1857
Age at inauguration: 48
Party: Democrat
Vice President: William R. King
First Lady: Jane Appleton Pierce

15. James Buchanan

Born: April 23, 1791, Mercersburg, Pennsylvania
Died: June 1, 1868, Lancaster, Pennsylvania
Term of office: March 4, 1857—March 3, 1861
Age at inauguration: 65
Party: Democrat
Vice President: John C. Breckenridge
First Lady: (none)**

16. Abraham Lincoln

Born: Feb. 12, 1809, Hardin, Kentucky
Died: April 15, 1865, Washington, DC†
Term of office: March 4, 1861—April 15, 1865
Age at inauguration: 52
Party: Republican
Vice President: Hannibal Hamlin,
Andrew Johnson
First Lady: Mary Todd Lincoln

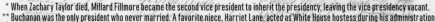

US Government

* When Zachary Taylor died, Millard Fillmore became the second vice president to inherit the presidency, leaving the vice presidency vacant.
** Buchanan was the only president who never married. A favorite niece, Harriet Lane, acted as White House hostess during his administration.
† Assassinated

292

17. Andrew Johnson
Born: Dec. 29, 1808, Raleigh, North Carolina
Died: July 31, 1875, Carter Station, Tennessee
Term of office: April 15, 1865—March 3, 1869
Age at inauguration: 56
Party: Democrat (nominated by Republican Party)
Vice President: (none)*
First Lady: Eliza McCardle Johnson

18. Ulysses Simpson Grant
Born: April 27, 1822, Point Pleasant, Ohio
Died: July 23, 1885, Mt. McGregor, New York
Term of office: March 4, 1869—March 3, 1877
Age at inauguration: 46
Party: Republican
Vice President: Schuyler Colfax, Henry Wilson
First Lady: Julia Dent Grant

19. Rutherford Birchard Hayes
Born: Oct. 4, 1822, Delaware, Ohio
Died: Jan. 17, 1893, Fremont, Ohio
Term of office: March 4, 1877—March 3, 1881
Age at inauguration: 54
Party: Republican
Vice President: William A. Wheeler
First Lady: Lucy Webb Hayes

20. James Abram Garfield
Born: Nov. 19, 1831, Orange, Ohio
Died: Sept. 19, 1881, Elberon, New Jersey**
Term of office: March 4, 1881—Sept. 19, 1881
Age at inauguration: 49
Party: Republican
Vice President: Chester A. Arthur
First Lady: Lucretia Rudolph Garfield

CHECK IT OUT!

On March 1, 1872, Ulysses S. Grant established Yellowstone as the country's first national park.

* Andrew Johnson became president when Abraham Lincoln was assassinated, leaving the vice presidency vacant.
** Assassinated

21. Chester Alan Arthur

Born: Oct. 5, 1829, Fairfield, Vermont
Died: Nov. 18, 1886, New York City, New York
Term of office: Sept. 20, 1881—March 3, 1885
Age at inauguration: 51
Party: Republican
Vice President: (none)*
First Lady: Ellen Herndon Arthur

22. Grover Cleveland

Born: March 18, 1837, Caldwell, New Jersey
Died: June 24, 1908, Princeton, New Jersey
Term of office: March 4, 1885—March 3, 1889
Age at inauguration: 47
Party: Democrat
Vice President: Thomas A. Hendricks
First Lady: Frances Folsom Cleveland

23. Benjamin Harrison

Born: Aug. 20, 1833, North Bend, Ohio
Died: March 13, 1901, Indianapolis, Indiana
Term of office: March 4, 1889—March 3, 1893
Age at inauguration: 55
Party: Republican
Vice President: Levi P. Morton
First Lady: Caroline Scott Harrison
(died in 1892)

24. Grover Cleveland

Born: March 18, 1837, Caldwell, New Jersey
Died: June 24, 1908, Princeton, New Jersey
Term of office: March 4, 1893—March 3, 1897
Age at inauguration: 55
Party: Democrat
Vice President: Adlai E. Stevenson
First Lady: Frances Folsom Cleveland

CHECK IT OUT!

Grover Cleveland is the only president elected to two nonconsecutive terms.

*Chester Alan Arthur became president when James Garfield was assassinated, leaving the vice presidency vacant.

US Government

25. William McKinley
Born: Jan. 29, 1843, Niles, Ohio
Died: Sept. 14, 1901, Buffalo, New York*
Term of office: March 4, 1897—Sept. 14, 1901
Age at inauguration: 54
Party: Republican
Vice President: Garret A. Hobart,
Theodore Roosevelt
First Lady: Ida Saxton McKinley

26. Theodore Roosevelt
Born: Oct. 27, 1858, New York City, New York
Died: Jan. 6, 1919, Oyster Bay, New York
Term of office: Sept. 14, 1901—March 3, 1909
Age at inauguration: 42
Party: Republican
Vice President: Charles W. Fairbanks
First Lady: Edith Carow Roosevelt

27. William Howard Taft
Born: Sept. 15, 1857, Cincinnati, Ohio
Died: March 8, 1930, Washington, DC
Term of office: March 4, 1909—March 3, 1913
Age at inauguration: 51
Party: Republican
Vice President: James S. Sherman
First Lady: Helen Herron Taft

28. (Thomas) Woodrow Wilson
Born: Dec. 28, 1856, Staunton, Virginia
Died: Feb. 3, 1924, Washington, DC
Term of office: March 4, 1913—March 3, 1921
Age at inauguration: 56
Party: Democrat
Vice President: Thomas R. Marshall
First Lady: Ellen Axon Wilson,
Edith Galt Wilson**

*Assassinated
**Wilson's first wife died early in his administration and he remarried before leaving the White House.

29. Warren Gamaliel Harding

Born: Nov. 2, 1865, Corsica (now Blooming Grove), Ohio
Died: Aug. 2, 1923, San Francisco, California*
Term of office: March 4, 1921—Aug. 2, 1923
Age at inauguration: 55
Party: Republican
Vice President: Calvin Coolidge
First Lady: Florence Kling De Wolfe Harding

30. (John) Calvin Coolidge

Born: July 4, 1872, Plymouth Notch, Vermont
Died: Jan. 5, 1933, Northampton, Massachusetts
Term of office: Aug. 3, 1923—March 3, 1929
Age at inauguration: 51
Party: Republican
Vice President: Charles G. Dawes
First Lady: Grace Goodhue Coolidge

31. Herbert Clark Hoover

Born: Aug. 10, 1874, West Branch, Iowa
Died: Oct. 20, 1964, New York City, New York
Term of office: March 4, 1929—March 3, 1933
Age at inauguration: 54
Party: Republican
Vice President: Charles Curtis
First Lady: Lou Henry Hoover

32. Franklin Delano Roosevelt

Born: Jan. 30, 1882, Hyde Park, New York
Died: April 12, 1945, Warm Springs, Georgia*
Term of office: March 4, 1933—April 12, 1945
Age at inauguration: 51
Party: Democrat
Vice President: John N. Garner,
Henry A. Wallace, Harry S Truman
First Lady: Anna Eleanor Roosevelt

CHECK IT OUT!

Two presidents, John Adams and Thomas Jefferson, died on the same day—July 4, 1826. Another president, James Monroe, died on July 4, 1831. A fourth, Calvin Coolidge, was born on July 4, 1872.

*Died in office, natural causes

33. Harry S Truman
Born: May 8, 1884, Lamar, Missouri
Died: Dec. 26, 1972, Kansas City, Missouri
Term of office: April 12, 1945—Jan. 20, 1953
Age at inauguration: 60
Party: Democrat
Vice President: Alben W. Barkley
First Lady: Elizabeth (Bess) Wallace Truman

34. Dwight David Eisenhower
Born: Oct. 14, 1890, Denison, Texas
Died: March 28, 1969, Washington, DC
Term of office: Jan. 20, 1953—Jan. 20, 1961
Age at inauguration: 62
Party: Republican
Vice President: Richard M. Nixon
First Lady: Mamie Doud Eisenhower

35. John Fitzgerald Kennedy
Born: May 29, 1917, Brookline, Massachusetts
Died: Nov. 22, 1963, Dallas, Texas*
Term of office: Jan. 20, 1961—Nov. 22, 1963
Age at inauguration: 43
Party: Democrat
Vice President: Lyndon B. Johnson
First Lady: Jacqueline Bouvier Kennedy

36. Lyndon Baines Johnson
Born: Aug. 27, 1908, Stonewall, Texas
Died: Jan. 22, 1973, San Antonio, Texas
Term of office: Nov. 22, 1963—Jan. 20, 1969
Age at inauguration: 55
Party: Democrat
Vice President: Hubert H. Humphrey
First Lady: Claudia (Lady Bird) Taylor Johnson

*Assassinated

37. Richard Milhous Nixon

Born: Jan. 9, 1913, Yorba Linda, California
Died: April 22, 1994, New York City, New York
Term of office: Jan. 20, 1969—Aug. 9, 1974*
Age at inauguration: 56
Party: Republican
Vice President: Spiro T. Agnew (resigned), Gerald R. Ford
First Lady: Thelma (Pat) Ryan Nixon

38. Gerald Rudolph Ford

Born: July 14, 1913, Omaha, Nebraska
Died: Dec. 26, 2006, Rancho Mirage, California
Term of office: Aug. 9, 1974—Jan. 20, 1977
Age at inauguration: 61
Party: Republican
Vice President: Nelson A. Rockefeller
First Lady: Elizabeth (Betty) Bloomer Warren Ford

39. James Earl (Jimmy) Carter

Born: Oct. 1, 1924, Plains, Georgia
Term of office: Jan. 20, 1977—Jan. 20, 1981
Age at inauguration: 52
Party: Democrat
Vice President: Walter F. Mondale
First Lady: Rosalynn Smith Carter

40. Ronald Wilson Reagan

Born: Feb. 6, 1911, Tampico, Illinois
Died: June 5, 2004, Los Angeles, California
Term of office: Jan. 20, 1981—Jan. 20, 1989
Age at inauguration: 69
Party: Republican
Vice President: George H. W. Bush
First Lady: Nancy Davis Reagan

41. George Herbert Walker Bush

Born: June 12, 1924, Milton, Massachusetts
Term of office: Jan. 20, 1989—Jan. 20, 1993
Age at inauguration: 64
Party: Republican
Vice President: James Danforth (Dan) Quayle
First Lady: Barbara Pierce Bush

CHECK IT OUT!

There have been two father-son presidential combinations: John Adams and John Quincy Adams, and George H. W. Bush and George W. Bush. In addition, President William Henry Harrison was the grandfather of President Benjamin Harrison.

*Resigned

42. William Jefferson (Bill) Clinton

Born: Aug. 19, 1946, Hope, Arkansas
Term of office: Jan. 20, 1993—Jan. 20, 2001
Age at inauguration: 46
Party: Democrat
Vice President: Albert (Al) Gore Jr.
First Lady: Hillary Rodham Clinton

43. George Walker Bush

Born: July 6, 1946, New Haven, Connecticut
Term of office: Jan. 20, 2001—Jan. 20, 2009
Age at inauguration: 54
Party: Republican
Vice President: Richard B. (Dick) Cheney
First Lady: Laura Welch Bush

44. Barack Hussein Obama Jr.

Born: Aug. 4, 1961, Honolulu, Hawaii
Term of office: Jan. 20, 2009—
Age at inauguration: 47
Party: Democrat
Vice President: Joseph R. (Joe) Biden Jr.
First Lady: Michelle Robinson Obama

President Barack Obama was born in Honolulu, Hawaii, to a white mother who had grown up in Kansas and a black father from Kenya, Africa. As a young child, Obama was one of only a few black students at his school. He became an outstanding student at college and at Harvard Law School. After law school he worked to help poor families in Chicago, Illinois, get better health care and more educational programs. In 1996, he became an Illinois state senator, and in 2004, he was elected to the US Senate. In 2008, Obama won the Democratic nomination for president and became the first African American to be elected to the highest office in the country. In 2012, President Obama defeated Mitt Romney to win reelection.

US History

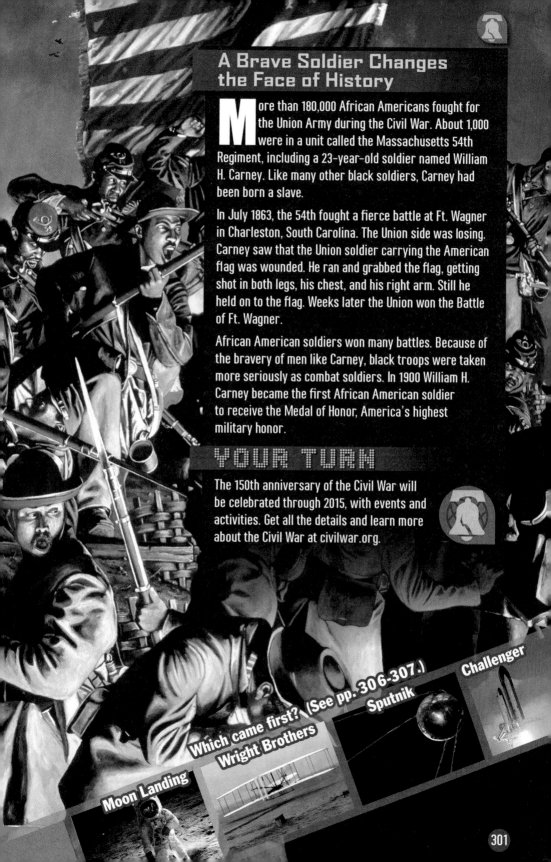

A Brave Soldier Changes the Face of History

More than 180,000 African Americans fought for the Union Army during the Civil War. About 1,000 were in a unit called the Massachusetts 54th Regiment, including a 23-year-old soldier named William H. Carney. Like many other black soldiers, Carney had been born a slave.

In July 1863, the 54th fought a fierce battle at Ft. Wagner in Charleston, South Carolina. The Union side was losing. Carney saw that the Union soldier carrying the American flag was wounded. He ran and grabbed the flag, getting shot in both legs, his chest, and his right arm. Still he held on to the flag. Weeks later the Union won the Battle of Ft. Wagner.

African American soldiers won many battles. Because of the bravery of men like Carney, black troops were taken more seriously as combat soldiers. In 1900 William H. Carney became the first African American soldier to receive the Medal of Honor, America's highest military honor.

YOUR TURN

The 150th anniversary of the Civil War will be celebrated through 2015, with events and activities. Get all the details and learn more about the Civil War at civilwar.org.

Which came first? (See pp. 306-307.)

Challenger

Sputnik

Wright Brothers

Moon Landing

US History Highlights: 1000–1700

| c.1000 | Viking explorer Leif Ericson explores North American coast and founds temporary colony called Vinland. |

| 1492 | On first voyage to America, Christopher Columbus lands at San Salvador Island in Bahamas. |

| 1513 | Juan Ponce de León discovers Florida. Vasco Nuñez de Balboa crosses Panama and sights Pacific Ocean. |

| 1520 | Ferdinand Magellan, whose ships were first to circumnavigate world, discovers South American straits, later named after him. |

| 1521 | Hernán Cortéz captures Mexico City and conquers Aztec Empire. |

| 1534–1539 | Jacques Cartier of France explores coast of Newfoundland and Gulf of St. Lawrence. Hernando de Soto conquers Florida and begins three-year trek across Southeast. |

| 1540 | Francisco Vásquez de Coronado explores Southwest, discovering Grand Canyon and introducing horses to North America. |

| 1541 | Hernando de Soto discovers Mississippi River. |

1572	Sir Francis Drake of England makes first voyage to Americas, landing in Panama.
1585	Sir Walter Raleigh establishes England's first American colony at Roanoke.
1603	Samuel de Champlain of France explores St. Lawrence River, later founds Québec.
1607	First permanent English settlement in America established at Jamestown, Virginia. Capt. John Smith imprisoned by Native Americans and saved by Pocahontas, daughter of Chief Powhatan.
1609	Henry Hudson sets out in search of Northwest Passage. Samuel de Champlain sails into Great Lakes.
1620	Pilgrims and others board *Mayflower* and travel to Plymouth, Massachusetts. They draw up Mayflower Compact.
1626	Dutch colony of New Amsterdam founded on Manhattan Island, bought from Native Americans for about $24.
1675	Thousands die in King Philip's War between New Englanders and five Native American tribes.
1692	Witchcraft hysteria breaks out in Salem, Massachusetts, leading to 20 executions.

1754	French and Indian War begins.
1763	Treaty of Paris ends French and Indian War.
1765	Parliament passes Stamp Act (tax on newspapers, legal documents, etc.) and Quartering Act (requiring housing of British soldiers in colonists' homes).
1770	Five Americans, including Crispus Attucks, perish in Boston Massacre (March 5).

1773	British Parliament passes Tea Act, leading to Boston Tea Party (Dec. 16).
1775	American Revolution begins with battles of Lexington and Concord (April 19). Second Continental Congress appoints George Washington as commander of Continental Army.

1776	Second Continental Congress approves Declaration of Independence on July 4.
1777	Congress adopts Stars and Stripes flag and endorses Articles of Confederation. Washington's army spends winter at Valley Forge, Pennsylvania.

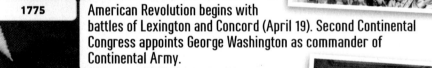

1783	Treaty of Paris signed, officially ending American Revolution (Sept. 3).
1787	Constitution accepted by delegates to Constitutional Convention in Philadelphia on Sept. 17.
1803	Louisiana Purchase from France doubles size of United States.

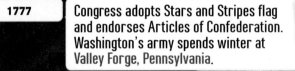

US History

1804	Lewis and Clark expedition sets out from St. Louis, Missouri. New Jersey begins gradual emancipation of slaves. Alexander Hamilton killed in duel with Aaron Burr.
1812	War of 1812 with Britain begins by close vote in Congress.
1815	War of 1812 ends.
1825	Erie Canal opens.

1846	Mexican War begins when US troops are attacked in disputed Texas territory.
1849	Gold Rush brings hundreds of thousands to California. Elizabeth Blackwell is first American woman to receive medical degree.
1860	Democratic Party splits into Northern and Southern wings. South Carolina is first Southern state to secede from Union after election of Abraham Lincoln.
1861	Civil War begins with attack on Ft. Sumter in South Carolina (April 12).

1862	Pres. Lincoln issues Emancipation Proclamation, freeing slaves in ten states.
1865	Gen. Lee surrenders to Gen. Grant at Appomattox Court House, Virginia (April 9). Pres. Lincoln assassinated by John Wilkes Booth in Washington, DC.

1870	Fifteenth Amendment, guaranteeing right to vote for all male US citizens, is ratified (Feb. 3).
1898	After mysterious explosion of battleship *Maine* in Havana harbor (Feb. 15), Spanish–American War breaks out (April 25).

1903	Orville and Wilbur Wright conduct first powered flight near Kitty Hawk, NC (Dec. 17).
1909	Expedition team led by Robert E. Peary and Matthew Henson plants American flag at North Pole (April 6). W. E. B. DuBois founds National Association for the Advancement of Colored People (NAACP).
1917	Congress declares war on Germany (April 6) and Austria–Hungary (Dec. 7), bringing United States into World War I.
1918	Armistice Day ends World War I (Nov. 11).
1920	Nineteenth Amendment establishes women's right to vote (Aug. 26).
1927	Charles Lindbergh completes nonstop solo flight from New York to Paris (May 20–21).
1929	Stock market crash on "Black Tuesday" ushers in Great Depression (Oct. 29).
1932	Amelia Earhart is first woman to fly solo across Atlantic.
1941	Japanese planes attack Pearl Harbor, Hawaii, killing 2,400 US servicemen and civilians (Dec. 7). United States declares war on Japan (Dec. 8). Germany and Italy declare war on United States (Dec. 11). United States declares war on Germany and Italy (Dec. 11).
1945	Germany surrenders, ending war in Europe (May 7). Atomic bombs dropped on Hiroshima (Aug. 6) and Nagasaki (Aug. 9); Japan surrenders, ending World War II (Aug. 14).
1950	North Korea invades South Korea, beginning Korean War (June 25).
1954	Supreme Court orders school desegregation in *Brown v. Board of Education* decision (May 17).
1958	In response to Soviet launch of *Sputnik*, United States launches *Explorer I*, first American satellite.
1962	Lt. Col. John H. Glenn Jr. is first American to orbit Earth.
1963	Dr. Martin Luther King Jr. delivers his "I Have a Dream" speech in Washington, DC (Aug. 28). Pres. Kennedy assassinated in Dallas, Texas (Nov. 22).

US History

1965	Black nationalist Malcolm X assassinated in New York City (Feb. 21). Pres. Johnson orders US Marines into South Vietnam (March 8).
1968	Dr. Martin Luther King Jr. is assassinated by James Earl Ray in Memphis, Tennessee (April 4). After winning California presidential primary, Sen. Robert F. Kennedy of New York is assassinated by Sirhan Sirhan in Los Angeles, California (June 5).
1969	Neil Armstrong and Edwin "Buzz" Aldrin of *Apollo 11* are first men to walk on Moon (July 20).
1972	Congress debates Equal Rights Amendment.
1974	Pres. Nixon resigns, elevating Vice Pres. Ford to presidency (Aug. 9).
1981	*Columbia* completes first successful space shuttle mission (April 12–13). Sandra Day O'Connor becomes first female Justice of Supreme Court.
1983	Sally Ride, aboard space shuttle *Challenger*, is first American female astronaut.
1986	Space shuttle *Challenger* explodes in midair over Florida.
1991	US sends aircraft, warships, and 400,000 troops to Persian Gulf to drive Iraq's armed forces from Kuwait in Operation Desert Storm (Jan. 17). Ground war begins six weeks later and lasts only 100 hours (Feb. 24–28).
2001	On Sept. 11, hijackers overtake four US planes, crashing two of them into World Trade Center in New York City. In all, 2,977 lives are lost.
2003	Suspecting weapons of mass destruction, United States declares war on Iraq (March 20). Official combat ends May 1.
2009	Sen. Barack Obama, first African American major presidential candidate, is inaugurated as president.
2011	Last US troops leave Iraq in December. Occupy Wall Street protest movement spreads to 100 US cities and around the world.
2012	Mass shootings in Colorado, Wisconsin, and Connecticut prompt debate about gun control.
2013	Barack Obama is inaugurated for a second term as president. Bombs at the April 15 Boston Marathon kill 3 people and injure 260. One suspect is killed and another is taken into custody, with a trial scheduled for November 2014.

DECLARATION OF INDEPENDENCE

(Phrases in red are key ideas.)

IN CONGRESS, JULY 4, 1776

THE UNANIMOUS DECLARATION OF THE THIRTEEN UNITED STATES OF AMERICA

When in the Course of human events, it becomes necessary for one people to dissolve the political bands which have connected them with another, and to assume among the powers of the earth, the separate and equal station to which the Laws of Nature and of Nature's God entitle them, a decent respect to the opinions of mankind requires that they should declare the causes which impel them to the separation.

We hold these truths to be self-evident, that all men are created equal, that they are endowed by their Creator with certain unalienable Rights, that among these are Life, Liberty and the pursuit of Happiness. —That to secure these rights, Governments are instituted among Men, deriving their just powers from the consent of the governed, —That whenever any Form of Government becomes destructive of these ends, it is the Right of the People to alter or to abolish it, and to institute new Government, laying its foundation on such principles and organizing its powers in such form, as to them shall seem most likely to effect their Safety and Happiness. Prudence, indeed, will dictate that Governments long established should not be changed for light and transient causes; and accordingly all experience hath shown, that mankind are more disposed to suffer, while evils are sufferable, than to right themselves by abolishing the forms to which they are accustomed. But when a long train of abuses and usurpations, pursuing invariably the same Object evinces a design to reduce them under absolute Despotism, it is their right, it is their duty, to throw off such Government, and to provide new Guards for their future security. —Such has been the patient sufferance of these Colonies; and such is now the necessity which constrains them to alter their former Systems of Government. The history of the present King of Great Britain is a history of repeated injuries and usurpations, all having in direct object the establishment of an absolute Tyranny over these States. To prove this, let Facts be submitted to a candid world.

He has refused his Assent to Laws, the most wholesome and necessary for the public good.

He has forbidden his Governors to pass Laws of immediate and pressing importance, unless suspended in their operation till his Assent should be obtained; and when so suspended, he has utterly neglected to attend to them.

He has refused to pass other Laws for the accommodation of large districts of people, unless those people would relinquish the right of Representation in the Legislature, a right inestimable to them and formidable to tyrants only.

He has called together legislative bodies at places unusual, uncomfortable, and distant from the depository of their public Records, for the sole purpose of fatiguing them into compliance with his measures.

He has dissolved Representative Houses repeatedly, for opposing with manly firmness his invasions on the rights of the people.

He has refused for a long time, after such dissolutions, to cause others to be elected; whereby the Legislative powers, incapable of Annihilation, have returned to the People at large for their exercise; the State remaining in the mean time exposed to all the dangers of invasion from without, and convulsions within.

He has endeavoured to prevent the population of these States; for that purpose obstructing the Laws for Naturalization of Foreigners; refusing to pass others to encourage their migrations hither, and raising the conditions of new Appropriations of Lands.

He has obstructed the Administration of Justice, by refusing his Assent to Laws for establishing Judiciary powers.

He has made Judges dependent on his Will alone, for the tenure of their offices, and the amount and payment of their salaries.

He has erected a multitude of New Offices, and sent hither swarms of Officers to harrass our people, and eat out their substance.

He has kept among us, in times of peace, Standing Armies without the Consent of our legislatures.

He has affected to render the Military independent of and superior to the Civil power.

He has combined with others to subject us to a jurisdiction foreign to our constitution, and unacknowledged by our laws; giving his Assent to their Acts of pretended Legislation:

For Quartering large bodies of armed troops among us:

For protecting them, by a mock Trial, from punishment for any Murders which they should commit on the Inhabitants of these States:

For cutting off our Trade with all parts of the world:

For imposing Taxes on us without our Consent:

For depriving us in many cases, of the benefits of Trial by Jury:

For transporting us beyond Seas to be tried for pretended offences:

For abolishing the free System of English Laws in a neighbouring Province, establishing therein an Arbitrary government, and enlarging its Boundaries so as to render it at once an example and fit instrument for introducing the same absolute rule into these Colonies:

For taking away our Charters, abolishing our most valuable Laws, and altering fundamentally the Forms of our Governments:

For suspending our own Legislatures, and declaring themselves invested with power to legislate for us in all cases whatsoever.

He has abdicated Government here, by declaring us out of his Protection and waging War against us.

He has plundered our seas, ravaged our Coasts, burnt our towns, and destroyed the lives of our people.

He is at this time transporting large Armies of foreign Mercenaries to compleat the works of death, desolation and tyranny, already begun with circumstances of Cruelty & perfidy scarcely paralleled in the most barbarous ages, and totally unworthy the Head of a civilized nation.

He has constrained our fellow Citizens taken Captive on the high Seas to bear Arms against their Country, to become the executioners of their friends and Brethren, or to fall themselves by their Hands.

He has excited domestic insurrections amongst us, and has endeavoured to bring on the inhabitants of our frontiers, the merciless Indian Savages, whose known rule of warfare, in an undistinguished destruction of all ages, sexes and conditions.

In every stage of these Oppressions We have Petitioned for Redress in the most humble terms: Our repeated Petitions have been answered only by repeated injury. A Prince whose character is thus marked by every act which may define a Tyrant, is unfit to be the ruler of a free people.

Nor have We been wanting in attentions to our Brittish brethren. We have warned them from time to time of attempts by their legislature to extend an unwarrantable jurisdiction over us. We have reminded them of the circumstances of our emigration and settlement here. We have appealed to their native justice and magnanimity, and we have conjured them by the ties of our common kindred to disavow these usurpations, which, would inevitably interrupt our connections and correspondence. They too have been deaf to the voice of justice and of consanguinity. We must, therefore, acquiesce in the necessity, which denounces our Separation, and hold them, as we hold the rest of mankind, Enemies in War, in Peace Friends.

We, therefore, the Representatives of the united States of America, in General Congress, Assembled, appealing to the Supreme Judge of the world for the rectitude of our intentions, do, in the Name, and by Authority of the good People of these Colonies, solemnly publish and declare, That these United Colonies are, and of Right ought to be Free and Independent States; that they are Absolved from all Allegiance to the British Crown, and that all political connection between them and the State of Great Britain, is and ought to be totally dissolved; and that as Free and Independent States, they have full Power to levy War, conclude Peace, contract Alliances, establish Commerce, and to do all other Acts and Things which Independent States may of right do. And for the support of this Declaration, with a firm reliance on the protection of divine Providence, we mutually pledge to each other our Lives, our Fortunes and our sacred Honor.

THE BILL OF RIGHTS
(Phrases in red are key ideas.)

THE FIRST 10 AMENDMENTS TO THE CONSTITUTION
(The first 10 amendments, known collectively as the Bill of Rights, were adopted in 1791.)

AMENDMENT I
Congress shall make no law respecting an establishment of religion, or prohibiting the free exercise thereof; or abridging the freedom of speech, or of the press; or the right of the people peaceably to assemble, and to petition the Government for a redress of grievances.

AMENDMENT II
A well regulated Militia, being necessary to the security of a free State, the right of the people to keep and bear Arms, shall not be infringed.

AMENDMENT III
No Soldier shall, in time of peace be quartered in any house, without the consent of the Owner, nor in time of war, but in a manner to be prescribed by law.

AMENDMENT IV
The right of the people to be secure in their persons, houses, papers, and effects, against unreasonable searches and seizures, shall not be violated, and no Warrants shall issue, but upon probable cause, supported by Oath or affirmation, and particularly describing the place to be searched, and the persons or things to be seized.

AMENDMENT V
No person shall be held to answer for a capital, or otherwise infamous crime, unless on a presentment or indictment of a Grand Jury, except in cases arising in the land or naval forces, or in the Militia, when in actual service in time of War or public danger; nor shall any person be subject for the same offence to be twice put in jeopardy of life or limb; nor shall be compelled in any criminal case to be a witness against himself, nor be deprived of life, liberty, or property, without due process of law; nor shall private property be taken for public use, without just compensation.

AMENDMENT VI
In all criminal prosecutions, the accused shall enjoy the right to a speedy and public trial, by an impartial jury of the State and district wherein the crime shall have been committed, which district shall have been previously ascertained by law, and to be informed of the nature and cause of the accusation; to be confronted with the witnesses against him; to have compulsory process for obtaining witnesses in his favor, and to have the Assistance of Counsel for his defence.

AMENDMENT VII
In Suits at common law, where the value in controversy shall exceed twenty dollars, the right of trial by jury shall be preserved, and no fact tried by jury, shall be otherwise re-examined in any Court of the United States, than according to the rules of the common law.

AMENDMENT VIII
Excessive bail shall not be required, nor excessive fines imposed, nor cruel and unusual punishments inflicted.

AMENDMENT IX
The enumeration in the Constitution, of certain rights, shall not be construed to deny or disparage others retained by the people.

AMENDMENT X
The powers not delegated to the United States by the Constitution, nor prohibited by it to the States, are reserved to the States respectively, or to the people.

Some Important Supreme Court Decisions

Marbury v. Madison (1803)
The Court struck down a law "repugnant to the Constitution" for the first time and set the precedent for judicial review of acts of Congress.

Dred Scott v. Sanford (1857)
Dred Scott, a Missouri slave, sued for his liberty after his owner took him into free territory. The Court ruled that Congress could not bar slavery in the territories. This decision sharpened sectional conflict about slavery.

Plessy v. Ferguson (1896)
This case was about the practice of segregating railroad cars in Louisiana. The Court ruled that as long as equal accommodations were provided, segregation was not discrimination and did not deprive black Americans of equal protection under the Fourteenth Amendment. This decision was overturned by *Brown v. Board of Education* (1954).

Brown v. Board of Education (1954)
Chief Justice Earl Warren led the Court to decide unanimously that segregated schools violated the equal protection clause of the Fourteenth Amendment. Efforts to desegregate Southern schools after the Brown decision met with massive resistance for many years.

Miranda v. Arizona (1966)
The Court ruled that Ernesto Miranda's confession to certain crimes was not admissible as evidence because he had been denied his right to silence and to legal counsel. Now police must advise suspects of their "Miranda rights" when they're taken into custody.

Roe v. Wade (1973)
In a controversial decision, the Court held that state laws restricting abortion were an unconstitutional invasion of a woman's right to privacy.

Chief Justices of the US Supreme Court

Chief Justice	Tenure	Appointed by
John Jay	1789–1795	George Washington
John Rutledge	1795	George Washington
Oliver Ellsworth	1796–1800	George Washington
John Marshall	1801–1835	John Adams
Roger B. Taney	1836–1864	Andrew Jackson
Salmon P. Chase	1864–1873	Abraham Lincoln
Morrison R. Waite	1874–1888	Ulysses S. Grant
Melville W. Fuller	1888–1910	Grover Cleveland
Edward D. White	1910–1921	William H. Taft
William H. Taft	1921–1930	Warren G. Harding
Charles E. Hughes	1930–1941	Herbert Hoover
Harlan F. Stone	1941–1946	Franklin D. Roosevelt
Fred M. Vinson	1946–1953	Harry S Truman
Earl Warren	1953–1969	Dwight D. Eisenhower
Warren E. Burger	1969–1986	Richard M. Nixon
William H. Rehnquist	1986–2005	Ronald Reagan
John G. Roberts Jr.	2005–	George W. Bush

WEATHER

America the Popsicle

There was one word to describe winter 2014 in the United States: Br-r-r-r. Bitter cold air and gusting winds brought record low temperatures to many parts of the country. In Minnesota and North Dakota, it got cold enough to cause frostbite in five minutes on unprotected skin. On January 7, temperatures dropped below freezing in all 50 states—including Hawaii. Ice covered 92.2 percent of the Great Lakes in March, the most in any recorded time except for February 1979. The photo at left shows ice on a lighthouse at Lake Michigan.

What kept much of the country in a deep freeze was something called the polar vortex. This is a swirling system of frigid air that usually stays put around the North Pole. This year, though, the winds spilled farther south than usual. Some scientists say the unusual movement of the polar vortex, like other types of extreme weather, could be a side effect of global warming.

YOUR TURN

When dangerously cold temperatures strike, stay inside! If you have to go outside, know how to protect yourself:

- ▶ Don't leave any skin exposed.
- ▶ Wear a hat and a scarf.
- ▶ Dress in layers. Wear mittens so your fingers can keep each other warm.
- ▶ Use lip balm to keep your lips from drying out from the cold and wind.
- ▶ If you get wet, go inside right away.

Astoria, OR, holds a US record for what kind of weather? (See p. 314.)

US Weather Extremes

The numbers below are based on 30-year averages of temperature, wind, snowfall, rainfall, and humidity at weather stations in the 48 continental states (not Alaska and Hawaii).

5 Driest Places

Location	Annual Precipitation
Yuma, AZ	3.01 in. (7.65 cm)
Las Vegas, NV	4.49 in. (11.40 cm)
Bishop, CA	5.02 in. (12.75 cm)
Bakersfield, CA	6.49 in. (16.48 cm)
Alamosa, CO	7.25 in. (18.41 cm)

5 Wettest Places

Location	Annual Precipitation
Mount Washington, NH	101.91 in. (258.85 cm)
Quillayute, WA	101.72 in. (258.37 cm)
Astoria, OR	67.13 in. (170.51 cm)
Mobile, AL	66.29 in. (168.38 cm)
Pensacola, FL	64.28 in. (163.27 cm)

5 Coldest Places

Location	Average Temperature
Mount Washington, NH	27.2°F (−2.66°C)
International Falls, MN	37.4°F (3.00°C)
Marquette, MI	38.7°F (3.72°C)
Duluth, MN	39.1°F (3.94°C)
Caribou, ME	39.2°F (4.00°C)

5 Hottest Places

Location	Average Temperature
Key West, FL	78.1°F (25.61°C)
Miami, FL	76.7°F (24.83°C)
Yuma, AZ	75.3°F (24.05°C)
West Palm Beach, FL	75.3°F (24.05°C)
Fort Wayne, FL	74.9°F (23.83°C)

CHECK IT OUT !

The line where cold and warm air masses collide is called a front. A cold front occurs when cold air pushes warm air out of its way. Cold fronts can bring stormy and even severe weather. A warm front occurs when warm air pushes away cold air, and it can bring gray, drizzly weather. (On a weather map, a cold front is indicated by a blue line with triangles below. Warm fronts are shown as red lines with half-circles above.)

Weather

Worldwide Weather Extremes

Highest Recorded Temperatures by Continent

Temperature	Continent	Location	Date
131°F (55°C)	Africa	Kebili, Tunisia	July 7, 1931
134°F (56.7°C)	North America	Death Valley, California, United States	July 10, 1913
129.2°F (54°C)	Asia	Tirat Tsvi, Israel	June 21, 1942
123°F (50.5°C)	Australia	Oodnadatta, South Australia	January 2, 1960
120°F (48.9°C)	South America	Rivadavia, Argentina	December 11, 1905
118.4°F (48°C)	Europe	Athens, Greece (and Elefsina, Greece)	July 10, 1977
59°F (15°C)	Antarctica	Vanda Station	May 1, 1974

Lowest Recorded Temperatures by Continent

Temperature	Continent	Location	Date
-129°F (-89.4°C)	Antarctica	Vostok Station	July 21, 1983
-90°F (-67.8°C)	Asia	Oimekon, Russia	February 6, 1933
-90°F (-67.8°C)	Asia	Verkhoyansk, Russia	February 5 and 7, 1892
-81.4°F (-63°C)	North America	Snag, Yukon Territory, Canada	February 3, 1947
-72.6°F (-58.1°C)	Europe	Ust-Shchugor, Russia	December 31, 1978
-27°F (-32.8°C)	South America	Sarmiento, Argentina	June 1, 1907
-11°F (-23.9°C)	Africa	Ifrane, Morocco	February 11, 1935
-9.4°F (-23.0°C)	Australia	Charlotte Pass, New South Wales	June 29, 1994

Highest Average Annual Precipitation by Continent

Amount	Continent	Location
467.4 in. (1,187.2 cm)	Asia	Mawsynram, India
405.0 in. (1,028.7 cm)	Africa	Debundscha, Cameroon
354.0 in. (899.2 cm)	South America	Quibdo, Colombia
316.3 in. (803.4 cm)	Australia	Bellenden Ker, Queensland, Australia
276.0 in. (700.0 cm)	North America	Henderson Lake, BC, Canada
183.0 in. (464.8 cm)	Europe	Crkvica, Bosnia and Herzegovina

Lowest Average Annual Precipitation by Continent

Amount	Continent	Location
0.03 in. (0.08 cm)	South America	Arica, Chile
0.08 in. (0.20 cm)	Antarctica	Amundsen–Scott South Pole Station
0.10 in. (0.25 cm)	Africa	Wadi Halfa, Sudan
1.20 in. (3.05 cm)	North America	Batagues, Mexico
1.80 in. (4.57 cm)	Asia	Aden, Yemen
4.05 in. (10.28 cm)	Australia	Mulka (Troudaninna), South Australia
6.40 in. (16.26 cm)	Europe	Astrakhan, Russia

WEIGHTS & MEASURES

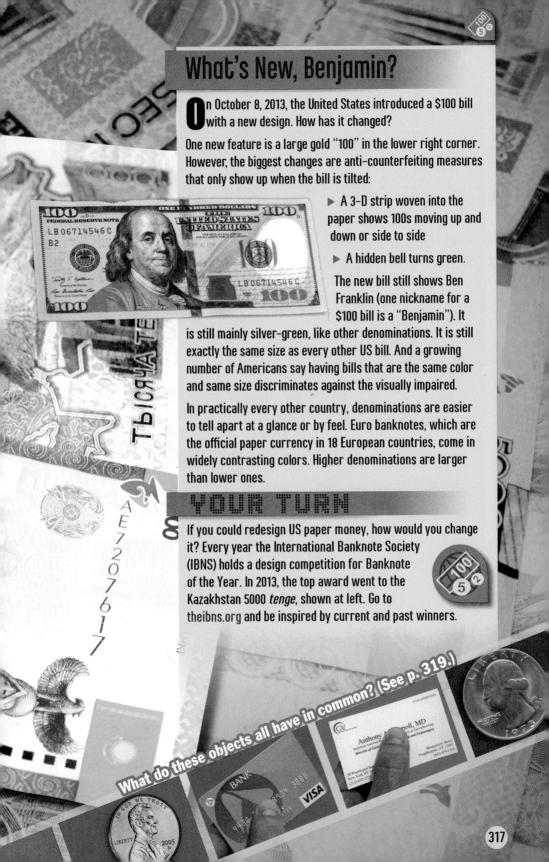

What's New, Benjamin?

On October 8, 2013, the United States introduced a $100 bill with a new design. How has it changed?

One new feature is a large gold "100" in the lower right corner. However, the biggest changes are anti-counterfeiting measures that only show up when the bill is tilted:

▶ A 3-D strip woven into the paper shows 100s moving up and down or side to side

▶ A hidden bell turns green.

The new bill still shows Ben Franklin (one nickname for a $100 bill is a "Benjamin"). It is still mainly silver-green, like other denominations. It is still exactly the same size as every other US bill. And a growing number of Americans say having bills that are the same color and same size discriminates against the visually impaired.

In practically every other country, denominations are easier to tell apart at a glance or by feel. Euro banknotes, which are the official paper currency in 18 European countries, come in widely contrasting colors. Higher denominations are larger than lower ones.

YOUR TURN

If you could redesign US paper money, how would you change it? Every year the International Banknote Society (IBNS) holds a design competition for Banknote of the Year. In 2013, the top award went to the Kazakhstan 5000 *tenge*, shown at left. Go to theibns.org and be inspired by current and past winners.

What do these objects all have in common? (See p. 319.)

Simple Metric Conversion Table

To convert	To	Multiply by
centimeters	feet	0.0328
centimeters	inches	0.3937
cubic centimeters	cubic inches	0.0610
degrees	radians	0.0175
feet	centimeters	30.48
feet	meters	0.3048
gallons	liters	3.785
grams	ounces	0.0353
inches	centimeters	2.54
kilograms	pounds	2.205
kilometers	miles	0.6214
knots	miles/hour	1.151
liters	gallons	0.2642
liters	pints	2.113
meters	feet	3.281
miles	kilometers	1.609
ounces	grams	28.3495
pounds	kilograms	0.4536

Converting Household Measures

To convert	To	Multiply by
dozens	units	12
baker's dozens	units	13
teaspoons	milliliters	4.93
teaspoons	tablespoons	0.33
tablespoons	milliliters	14.79
tablespoons	teaspoons	3
cups	liters	0.24
cups	pints	0.50
cups	quarts	0.25
pints	cups	2
pints	liters	0.47
pints	quarts	0.50
quarts	cups	4
quarts	gallons	0.25
quarts	liters	0.95
quarts	pints	2
gallons	liters	3.79
gallons	quarts	4

Temperature Conversions

Fahrenheit	Celsius
475	246.1
450	232.2
425	218.3
400	204.4
375	190.6
350	176.7
325	162.8
300	148.9
275	135.0
250	121.1
225	107.2
212	100.0
110	43.3
105	40.6
100	37.8
95	35.0
90	32.2
85	29.4
80	26.7
75	23.9
70	21.1
65	18.3
60	15.6
55	12.8
50	10.0
45	7.2
40	4.4
35	1.7
32	0.0
30	−1.1
25	−3.9
20	−6.7
15	−9.4
10	−12.2
5	−15.0
0	−17.8
−5	−20.6
−10	−23.3
−15	−26.1
−20	−28.9
−25	−31.7
−30	−34.4
−35	−37.2
−40	−40.0
−45	−42.8

Weights & Measures

Fractions and Their Decimal Equivalents

1/2	0.5000	2/7	0.2857	5/9	0.5556
1/3	0.3333	2/9	0.2222	5/11	0.4545
1/4	0.2500	2/11	0.1818	5/12	0.4167
1/5	0.2000	3/4	0.7500	6/7	0.8571
1/6	0.1667	3/5	0.6000	6/11	0.5455
1/7	0.1429	3/7	0.4286	7/8	0.8750
1/8	0.1250	3/8	0.3750	7/9	0.7778
1/9	0.1111	3/10	0.3000	7/10	0.7000
1/10	0.1000	3/11	0.2727	7/11	0.6364
1/11	0.0909	4/5	0.8000	7/12	0.5833
1/12	0.0833	4/7	0.5714	8/9	0.8889
1/16	0.0625	4/9	0.4444	8/11	0.7273
1/32	0.0313	4/11	0.3636	9/10	0.9000
1/64	0.0156	5/6	0.8333	9/11	0.8182
2/3	0.6667	5/7	0.7143	10/11	0.9091
2/5	0.4000	5/8	0.6250	11/12	0.9167

Length or Distance
US Customary System

1 foot (ft.)	=	12 inches (in.)				
1 yard (yd.)	=	3 feet	=	36 inches		
1 rod (rd.)	=	5½ yards	=	16 ½ feet		
1 furlong (fur.)	=	40 rods	=	220 yards	=	660 feet
1 mile (mi.)	=	8 furlongs	=	1,760 yards	=	5,280 feet

An international nautical mile has been defined as 6,076.1155 feet.

Six Quick Ways to Measure If You Don't Have a Ruler

1. Most credit cards are 3⅜ inches by 2⅛ inches.
2. Standard business cards are 3½ inches long by 2 inches tall.
3. Floor tiles are usually manufactured in 12-inch squares.
4. US paper money is 6⅛ inches wide by 2⅝ inches tall.
5. The diameter of a quarter is approximately 1 inch, and the diameter of a penny is approximately ¾ of an inch.
6. A standard sheet of paper is 8½ inches wide and 11 inches long.

WORLD HISTORY

"Take Action, Inspire Change."

Nelson Mandela was a South African who fought courageously to change the racially unfair policies of his government, called apartheid. For his activism, he spent 27 years in jail. He slept on the floor in a cell with no toilet. He suffered brutal punishments that permanently damaged his lungs, eyes, and hearing. Yet he was so encouraging to fellow prisoners and taught them so much that they called the jail "Nelson Mandela University."

Thanks in large part to Mandela's efforts, apartheid was finally abolished. He was released from jail and became the first black president of South Africa. Later he remained a devoted champion for peace and social justice in his own nation and around the world. He died on December 5, 2013, at the age of 95.

YOUR TURN

July 18, Nelson Mandela's birthday, is Nelson Mandela International Day. Its motto is "Take Action, Inspire Change." Nelson Mandela spent his whole life working for positive change. Mandela Day supporters ask others to honor his memory by giving a little time to help their communities.

Here are four things you can do. However, you don't have to wait until next July 18. Start today to start changing the world!

1. Make a new friend from a different culture.
2. Read to someone visually impaired.
3. Help clean up your neighborhood or school.
4. Help feed the hungry in your area.

Ask your teachers, friends, and parents about other ways you can bring about positive change. Find more project suggestions at MandelaDay.com.

Which woman discovered radium? (See p. 329.)

Ancient History Highlights

Date	Event
4.5 billion BCE	Planet Earth forms.
3 billion BCE	First signs of life (bacteria and green algae) appear in oceans.
3.2 million BCE	*Australopithecus afarensis* roams Earth (remains, nicknamed Lucy, found in Ethiopia in 1974).
1.8 million BCE	*Homo erectus* ("upright man"). Brain size twice that of *australopithecine* species.
100,000 BCE	First modern *Homo sapiens* live in east Africa.
4500–3000 BCE	Sumerians in Tigris and Euphrates valleys develop city-state civilization. First phonetic writing.
3000–2000 BCE	Pharaonic rule begins in Egypt with King Menes. Great Sphinx of Giza constructed. Earliest Egyptian mummies created.
2000–1500 BCE	Israelites enslaved in Egypt.
1500–1000 BCE	Ikhnaton develops monotheistic religion in Egypt (circa 1375 BCE). His successor, Tutankhamun, returns to earlier gods. Moses leads Israelites out of Egypt into Canaan. Ten Commandments. End of Greek civilization in Mycenae with invasion of Dorians.
800–700 BCE	First recorded Olympic Games (776 BCE). Legendary founding of Rome by Romulus (753 BCE).
700–600 BCE	Founding of Byzantium by Greeks (circa 660 BCE). Building of Acropolis in Athens by Solon, Greek lawmaker (630–560 BCE).
600–500 BCE	Confucius (551–479 BCE) develops philosophy of Confucianism in China. Siddhartha Gautama or Buddha (563–483 BCE) founds Buddhism in India.
300–241 BCE	First Punic War (264–241 BCE). Rome defeats Carthaginians and begins domination of Mediterranean. Invention of Mayan calendar in Yucatán (more exact than older calendars). First Roman gladiatorial games (264 BCE). Archimedes, Greek mathematician (287–212 BCE).
250–201 BCE	Construction of Great Wall of China begins.
149–146 BCE	Third Punic War. Rome destroys Carthage.
100–4 BCE	Julius Caesar (100–44 BCE) invades Britain and conquers Gaul (France). Spartacus leads slave revolt against Rome (73 BCE). Birth of Jesus (variously given 7 BCE to 4 BCE).

People of Ancient History

Lucy

In 1974, in Hadar, Ethopia, scientists discovered a nearly complete skeleton of an *Australopithecus afarensis*, or early human being, which they named Lucy. The skeleton provided scientists with critical insight into the history of humans.

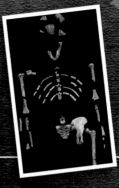

Tutankhamun

Tutankhamun, or King Tut, was one of the most famous pharaohs, or rulers, of ancient Egypt. He began ruling at age 10 and died at 19. There are no written records about his life. Until recently, most of the information known came from what Howard Carter discovered in King Tut's tomb in 1922. In 2010, results of a two-year study including DNA tests and CT scans of King Tut's mummy revealed the probable cause of his death as a leg injury complicated by bone disease and malaria.

Confucius

Confucius was a thinker and educator in ancient China. His beliefs and teachings about the way a person should live and treat others greatly influenced the Chinese culture and inspired the Ru school of Chinese thought. Later his beliefs spread to other parts of the world, and his type of belief system came to be known as Confucianism.

Buddha

Siddhartha Gautama was born the son of a wealthy ruler in what is modern-day Nepal. One day he was confronted with the suffering of people outside his kingdom, and he left his life of privilege. Siddhartha searched for enlightenment through meditation and eventually found his own path of balance in the world. He earned the title Buddha, or "Enlightened One," and spent the rest of his life helping others to reach enlightenment.

Julius Caesar

As a great politician, military leader, and dictator, Julius Caesar expanded the Roman Empire. He led Rome in conquering Gaul (France), ended the civil war, and instituted many social reforms. His rule ended with his assassination by many of his fellow statesmen on March 15, the Ides of March.

World History Highlights: 1–1499 CE

Date	Event
1–49 CE	Crucifixion of Jesus Christ (probably 30 CE).
312–337	Under Constantine the Great, eastern and western Roman empires reunite and new capital, Constantinople, is established.
350–399	Huns (Mongols) invade Europe (circa 360).
622–637	Muhammad flees from Mecca to Medina. Muslim empire grows (634). Arabs conquer Jerusalem (637).
c. 900	Vikings discover Greenland.
c. 1000	Viking raider Leif Ericson discovers North America, calls it Vinland. Chinese invent gunpowder.
1211–1227	Genghis Khan invades China, Persia, and Russia.
1215	King John of England forced by barons to sign Magna Carta, limiting royal power.
1231–1252	Inquisition begins as Pope Gregory IX creates special court to locate and punish heretics. Torture used (1252).
1251	Kublai Khan comes to prominence in China.
1271–1295	Marco Polo of Venice travels to China.
c. 1325	Renaissance begins in Italy.
1337–1453	English and French fight for control of France in Hundred Years' War.
1347–1351	About 25 million Europeans die from "Black Death" (bubonic plague).
1368	Ming dynasty begins in China.
1429	Joan of Arc leads French against English.
1452	Leonardo da Vinci, painter of *Mona Lisa* and other masterpieces, born near Florence, Italy.
1492–1498	Columbus discovers Caribbean Islands and Americas, returns to Spain (1493). Second voyage to Dominica, Jamaica, Puerto Rico (1493–1496). Third voyage to Orinoco (1498).
1497	Vasco da Gama sails around Africa and discovers sea route to India (1498). John Cabot, employed by England, explores Canadian coast.

World History

People of 1–1499 CE

Constantine

Known as Constantine the Great, he served as the emperor of Rome from 312 to 337. He created a "new" Rome by bringing religious tolerance to the empire and laying a foundation for Western culture. He moved the center of the empire from Rome to the Greek colony of Byzantium, which he renamed Constantinople.

Muhammad

As a prophet from Mecca, Muhammad worked to restore the faith of Abraham. He spread the religion of Islam and the belief in one true God, Allah. His teachings were recorded in the Koran. As his teachings spread, many aristocrats in Mecca began to oppose him. Muhammad fled to Medina, an event that marks the beginning of the Muslim calendar. In 629, he won over his opposition in Mecca. By the time he died in 632, most of the Arabian Peninsula followed his political and religious ideas.

Genghis Khan

Born around 1162 in Mongolia, Genghis Khan was a warrior and ruler who united the tribes of Mongolia and founded the Mongol Empire. He spent his life establishing and increasing his empire by conquering China, Russia, and parts of Persia.

Joan of Arc

At the age of thirteen, Joan of Arc heard the voices of saints telling her to help the French king defeat the English. She presented herself to the king and led the French army to victory at Orléans, forcing the English out of the region. She was later captured by the English, accused of heresy, and burned at the stake. Joan of Arc was hailed as a hero in France for her bravery and made a saint.

Leonardo da Vinci

Italian-born Leonardo da Vinci was one of the most farsighted, multitalented, and relentless thinkers of the time. He was a great artist, inventor, engineer, mathematician, architect, scientist, and musician whose works and insights influenced generations.

World History Highlights: 1500–1899

Date	Event
1509	Henry VIII becomes king of England.
1513	Juan Ponce de León explores Florida and Yucatán Peninsula for Spain.
1517	Martin Luther pins his 95 theses on door of Wittenberg Castle Church in Wittenberg, Germany, starting Protestant Reformation.
1520	Ferdinand Magellan discovers Strait of Magellan and Tierra del Fuego for Spain.
1547	Ivan IV, known as Ivan the Terrible, crowned czar of Russia.
1558	Elizabeth I, Henry VIII's daughter, becomes queen of England.
1585–1587	Sir Walter Raleigh's men reach Roanoke Island, Virginia.
1588	Spanish Armada attempts to invade England and is defeated.
1609	Henry Hudson explores Hudson River and Hudson Bay for England.
1632	Italian astronomer Galileo Galilei is first person to view space through a telescope and confirms belief that Earth revolves around Sun.
1687	Sir Isaac Newton publishes his theories on gravity and his laws of motion.
1721	Peter I, known as Peter the Great, crowned czar of Russia.
1756	Seven Years' War breaks out, involving most European countries.
1778	James Cook sails to Hawaii.
1789	Parisians storm Bastille prison, starting French Revolution.
1804	Scottish explorer John Ross begins expedition to find Northwest Passage in Arctic.
1821	Mexico gains its independence from Spain.
1845	Irish potato crops are ruined by blight, or fungus, creating famine that causes millions to starve to death or emigrate to America.
1859	Charles Darwin publishes *On the Origin of Species*.
1898	Spanish-American War begins.

People of 1500–1899

Ferdinand Magellan

As a Portuguese explorer, Magellan sailed under both the Portuguese and Spanish flags. To find a route to India by sailing west, he sailed around South America to the Pacific Ocean, discovering the Strait of Magellan along the way. Although he was killed in the Philippines and did not complete the journey, his ships made it back to Spain and were the first to circumnavigate the globe.

Elizabeth I

Queen Elizabeth I ruled England, leading her country through war with wisdom and courage. She was a beloved queen who brought prosperity and a rebirth of learning to England, making the country a major European power. For this reason, the era in which she ruled became known as the Elizabethan Age.

Galileo

Galileo Galilei was a great Italian thinker whose contributions in philosophy, astronomy, and mathematics shaped the way we view the world. He helped develop the scientific method and establish the mathematical laws of falling motion. He advanced the development of the telescope to the point where he could use it to view objects in space and prove that Earth revolved around the Sun. His findings and beliefs were radical at the time and led to his excommunication from the Catholic Church.

Sir Isaac Newton

The contributions of this English physicist and mathematician laid the foundation of many modern sciences. Newton's discovery of white light and its composition of colors paved the way for studies in modern optics. His laws of motion gave a basis to modern physics and his law of universal gravity created a framework for classic mechanics.

Peter the Great

Crowned czar of Russia at the age of ten, Peter ruled jointly with his half brother until his brother's death. As sole ruler, Peter expanded the Russian empire to reclaim access to the Baltic Sea and establish trade with Europe. He reorganized government, founding the city of St. Petersburg as the new capital of Russia and creating the Russian army and navy.

World History Highlights: 1900–Present

Date	Event
1905	Albert Einstein formulates his theory of relativity.
1911	Marie Curie wins Nobel Prize for chemistry.
1914	Archduke Franz Ferdinand, heir to Austrian-Hungarian throne, assassinated in Sarajevo, setting off events that lead to World War I.
1918	Massive worldwide flu epidemic kills more than 20 million people.
1919	Treaty of Versailles signed, ending World War I.
1927	American Charles Lindbergh is first to fly solo across Atlantic Ocean.
1939	Germany invades Poland, sparking World War II. Britain and France declare war on Germany. United States remains neutral.
1941	Japan attacks United States by bombing American ships at Pearl Harbor, Hawaii. United States declares war on Japan and enters World War II.
1945	Germany surrenders. United States drops atomic bombs on two Japanese cities, Hiroshima and Nagasaki. World War II ends. United Nations, international peacekeeping organization, formed.
1948	Israel proclaims its independence. Gandhi, nonviolent leader of Indian Nationalist movement against British rule, assassinated.
1950	North Korea invades South Korea, starting Korean War.
1964	United States begins sending troops to Vietnam to assist South Vietnam during Vietnamese civil war.
1973	Paris Peace Accords signed, ending Vietnam War.
1989	Chinese army shoots and kills protestors in China's Tiananmen Square. Berlin Wall, separating East and West Germany, torn down.
1991	President Frederik Willem de Klerk negotiates to end apartheid in South Africa. Union of Soviet Socialist Republics (USSR) dissolved into independent states.
1994	Nelson Mandela elected president of South Africa in first free elections.
1997	Mother Teresa, champion of poor in Calcutta, India, dies.
2006	Iraqi dictator Saddam Hussein captured and killed for crimes against humanity.
2011	Protests in Tunisia, Egypt, and Libya lead to the removal or death of longtime dictators. US forces in Pakistan kill Osama bin-Laden, Al-Qaeda leader and mastermind of the September 11, 2001, attacks.
2012	Egyptians voted in the country's first-ever democratic election.
2013	Prince George Alexander Louis, third in line to be King of England, is born to the Duke and Duchess of Cambridge.

World History

Albert Einstein

Called the greatest scientist of the 20th century, physicist Albert Einstein developed revolutionary theories about how the world works, especially the connection between matter and energy. Einstein's knowledge was applied to the development of the atomic bomb, which he said saddened him. Today calling somebody an "Einstein" means that he or she is a genius. However, young Albert Einstein didn't get good grades in every subject. His problems mastering French caused him to fail a college entrance examination.

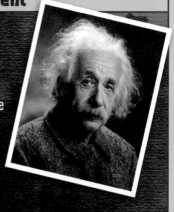

Marie Curie

Polish-French chemist Marie Curie is best known for discovering the radioactive element radium, for which she won a Nobel Prize. She also discovered an element called polonium, named for her birthplace, Poland. Although radium is used to treat and diagnose diseases, repeated or excessive exposure can cause serious illness and even death. After years of working with radium, Marie Curie died in 1934 from radiation poisoning.

Mohandas Gandhi

To the people of India, Mohandas Gandhi was the Mahatma, or Great Soul. Gandhi believed in tolerance for all religious beliefs. He led peaceful protests to bring about social change and freedom from British rule. India was granted freedom in 1947, but fighting between Hindus and Muslims continued. Gandhi spoke out against the fighting, angering many and resulting in his assassination. In America, Dr. Martin Luther King Jr. modeled his nonviolent strategy of fighting racism on Gandhi's methods.

Mother Teresa

Born Agnes Gonxha Bojaxhiu, Mother Teresa was a Roman Catholic nun who became known as the "Saint of the Gutters" for her work with poor people. She founded a religious order in India to provide food, schools, health care, and shelters for the poor, sick, and dying. Mother Teresa received numerous awards for her work, including the Nobel Peace Prize. In 2003, Pope John Paul II approved the first step toward declaring Mother Teresa a saint in the Roman Catholic Church.

Homework Helpers

Use the tips, guides, definitions, examples, and ideas on the next four pages to help you ace spelling, writing, and every homework assignment.

Parts of Speech

Picking Up the Pieces

Pieces of a jigsaw puzzle need to be correctly connected to form a complete picture. Words need to be correctly connected to form a sentence. The part each word plays in a sentence is called its part of speech.

Part of Speech	Definition	Example
Noun	A person, place, or thing	kids, plates, spaghetti, meatballs
Pronoun	A word that replaces a noun	they
Adjective	A word that modifies a noun (*A*, *an*, and *the* are special types of adjectives called articles)	the, hungry
Verb	An action word	devoured, exclaimed
Adverb	A word that modifies a verb, adjective, or other adverb	quickly, loudly
Conjunction	A word like *but* or *and* that joins together groups of words or sentences	and
Preposition	A word like *in* or *of* that shows the relationship between one noun and another noun, verb, or adverb	of
Interjection	An exclamation, usually a short part of speech that shows emotion or emphasis	Yum!

The hungry kids quickly devoured plates of spaghetti and meatballs. "Yum!" they exclaimed loudly.

Tip: A proper noun is a word for a particular person, place, or thing. Always use capital letters for proper nouns. Examples: Abraham Lincoln, Australia, Fourth of July

Vocabulary

Prefixes

A prefix is a group of letters that starts a word. If you know common prefixes, you can figure out meanings of new words and expand your spoken and written vocabulary. (Some prefixes have more than the one meaning given below.)

Prefix	Meaning	Example
anti–	against	antibacterial
circum–	around	circumnavigate
co–	with	copilot
dis–	not	disappear
ex–	away from	expel
in–	not	incomplete
inter–	between	intersection
micro–	small	microchip
pre–	before	prefix
sub–	under	submarine
trans–	across	transform

Roots

Hidden within many words are parts of words called roots, which come from the Greek and Latin languages. Word roots can appear at the beginning, middle, or end of a word, but they always mean the same thing.

Root	Meaning	Example
audi	hear	audition
auto	self	automatic
bene	good	benefit
bio	life	biology
chrono	time	chronicle
dict	say	dictate
phil	love	philosophy
port	carry	portable
spec	see	spectacle
terr	earth	terrain

Spelling
Sounds Wrong to Me

Homophones are words that sound the same but have different spellings and meanings, like *know* and *no* and *bare* and *bear*. Avoid making these common homophone mistakes.

There Their They're

There is an adverb meaning a place.

Their is a pronoun that shows possession.

They're is a contraction that stands for "they are."

They're riding *their* bikes over *there*.

To Too Two

To is a preposition that shows direction.

Too is an adverb meaning "also."

Two is a number.

You *two* can come *to* the party, *too*.

Its It's

Its is a pronoun that shows possession.

It's is a contraction of "it is" or "it has."

It's a road known for *its* dangerous curves.

Punctuation
Use Your Comma Sense

Teachers say using commas incorrectly is the mistake students make most frequently. Here are three rules to remember:

1. Don't use a comma between the subject and verb.

Wrong:
Jennie, picked some flowers for her grandma.

Right:
Jennie picked some flowers for her grandma.

2. Use a comma before a conjunction to join two complete thoughts (independent clauses).

Jennie picked some flowers for her grandma, and then she put them in a vase.

3. Use commas around extra information (nonrestrictive clauses).

Jennie picked some flowers for her grandma, who was visiting, and then she put them in a vase.

Research and Study Skills
Book It

Got a report to write? The help you need to craft a perfect paper is as near as the library.

- Use an atlas to find maps of continents, countries, states, or cities.
- Use encyclopedias and almanacs for facts, figures, stats, and other information.
- Use a dictionary to find out a word's meaning and pronunciation, its origin, and its part of speech.
- Use a thesaurus to find synonyms (words that mean the same as other words) and antonyms (words that mean the opposite of other words).
- Ask a librarian (nicely, of course) for help if you get stuck. Librarians know a tremendous amount of information and are eager to point kids in the right direction.

Cool Tools Online

Dictionaries, thesauruses, and other reference materials are available online as well as in book form. In fact, you can find out almost anything you want to know online—the catch is, not all the information is correct. You can trust the information on these websites to be accurate, up to date, and especially good for kids.

Site: ipl.org
What you'll find: Information about almost everything, from animals to sports to school cancellations! Plus a chance to e-mail a librarian or connect with other kids

Site: nal.usda.gov/awic/pubs/scifair.htm
What you'll find: Science fair topics

Site: kids.gov
What you'll find: Information about US history, government, the states, and more

Site: nasa.gov/audience/forstudents/index.html
What you'll find: Information on the planets, the stars, space research, and missions

Site: scholastic.com/kids/homework
What you'll find: Tips on writing, research, test-taking, and study skills

Site: ala.org
What you'll find: Keyword "great websites for kids" for a terrific assortment of sites, reviewed and selected by librarians

Tip: Don't copy and paste material directly from the Internet. Rewrite it in your own words to avoid plagiarism, which is using someone else's ideas and words as your own. Another tip: Use more than one source whenever you do research.

WHAT'S NEXT?

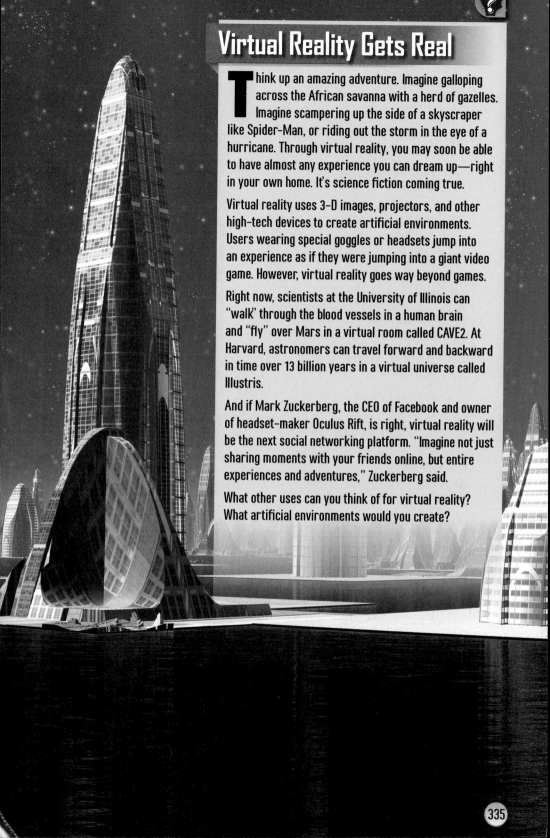

Virtual Reality Gets Real

Think up an amazing adventure. Imagine galloping across the African savanna with a herd of gazelles. Imagine scampering up the side of a skyscraper like Spider-Man, or riding out the storm in the eye of a hurricane. Through virtual reality, you may soon be able to have almost any experience you can dream up—right in your own home. It's science fiction coming true.

Virtual reality uses 3-D images, projectors, and other high-tech devices to create artificial environments. Users wearing special goggles or headsets jump into an experience as if they were jumping into a giant video game. However, virtual reality goes way beyond games.

Right now, scientists at the University of Illinois can "walk" through the blood vessels in a human brain and "fly" over Mars in a virtual room called CAVE2. At Harvard, astronomers can travel forward and backward in time over 13 billion years in a virtual universe called Illustris.

And if Mark Zuckerberg, the CEO of Facebook and owner of headset-maker Oculus Rift, is right, virtual reality will be the next social networking platform. "Imagine not just sharing moments with your friends online, but entire experiences and adventures," Zuckerberg said.

What other uses can you think of for virtual reality? What artificial environments would you create?

Hands off My Computer!

Not long ago, computers were too big to carry. Now they are so small we can wear them. As computers get smaller, hands-free "wearable technology" will become a bigger and bigger part of everyday life.

Smartwatches and wristbands track heart rate, distances run or walked, calories burned, and other physical activity. Some smartwatches send texts and location-specific tips, such as the nearest pizza place, at the flick of a wrist.

A company called **Cuff** makes products that look like jewelry but are really personal security devices. Wearers in sudden danger press a bracelet or necklace to send a signal to a smartphone preprogrammed with emergency contact numbers. The phone sends a message giving the wearer's location.

Hands-free cameras let you move around freely while they take pictures or videos of everything you see. Some are small enough to pin on clothing.

Smart earbuds track a wearer's heartbeat while playing music. If the beat is too slow or too fast, the device plays charge-up or calm-down music.

(Some of these devices are available now. Others are still in development.)

Eyes on Medicine

Most people with diabetes test their blood glucose levels by pricking themselves at least once a day, which is painful and inconvenient. Now Google is developing a soft contact lens that can measure glucose levels painlessly, through the eyes' natural fluids—tears.

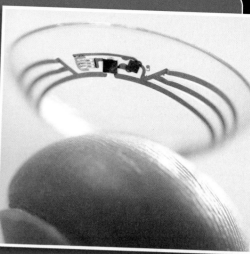

Meanwhile, some surgeons are wearing special glasses with a patient's medical data embedded inside when they operate. The glasses let them see important information, such as whether the patient is allergic to certain medications, without turning away to look at a computer. Every minute saved can be a matter of life or death.

Robots Ready to Lend a Hand

Experts say robots will take over many ordinary and extraordinary functions in the future. A team in Switzerland has developed a robotic arm that can catch flying objects in a fraction of a second. The arm may be used in the future to snag space debris before it crashes into satellites and space stations.

Index

Index

Index

Answers

Animals: Turtles—bales; goats—trip; cows—drove; kangaroos—troop; **Birthdays:** Mark Foster's birthday is February 29, which only takes place in a Leap Year (every four years); **Books:** *Hard Luck* (Diary of a Wimpy Kid #8); **Buildings & Landmarks:** Mona Lisa--The Louvre; Rosetta Stone--British Museum; *Starry Night*—Museum of Modern Art; **Calendars & Holidays:** Thanksgiving; **Crime:** They are all related to the case of hijacker D.B. Cooper; **Disasters:** Hurricane Katrina; **Environment:** Styrofoam; **Flags & Facts: Countries of the World:** Red and white are the two most popular colors, followed by blue; **Flags & Facts: States of the United States:** The northern cardinal; **Games:** Candy (Candy Crush Saga); **Geography:** From left, Bryce Canyon, Redwood Forest, Yellowstone, Crater Lake; **Health & Wellness**: skin; **Inventors & Inventions:** piano; **Languages:** Please; **Math:** They are all polygons; **Military:** Distinguished Flying Cross; **Movies & TV:** Jim Parsons; **Music:** Justin Timberlake; **Plants:** They are all dicotyledons, a class of flowering plants; **Population:** Florida; **Religion:** Christianity, symbolized by the cross; **Science:** Phosphorus (P); **Signs & Symbols:** C-O-O-L; **Space:** Ganymede, third from the left, is a moon of Jupiter; **Sports:** 3 times; **Technology:** China; **US Government:** Theodore Roosevelt was the youngest president. (John F. Kennedy was the youngest *elected* president); **US History:** Wright Brothers; **Weather:** Heat; **World History:** Marie Curie, third from the left, discovered radium.

Photo Credits

Nyong'o, © Evan Agostini/Invision/AP Images; Ariana Grande, © Rich Polk/AMA2013/ Getty Images; Selena Gomez, © DFree/Shutterstock; Jim Parsons, © Dan Steinberg/ Invision/AP Images; p. 212: Lupita Nyong'o, © Evan Agostini/Invision/AP Images; p. 213: Robert Downey Jr., © s_bukley/Shutterstock; Jennifer Lawrence, © Featureflash/ Shutterstock; p. 214: Jim Parsons, © Dan Steinberg/Invision/AP Images; p.215: Selena Gomez, © DFree/Shutterstock

Music pp. 216-217: Lorde in concert, © Jon Furniss/Invision/AP Images; p. 217: Bruno Mars, © Mark Humphrey/AP Images; pp. 217 and 218: Justin Timberlake, © Antonio Scorza/Shutterstock; p. 217 and 219: Demi Lovato, © John Shearer/Invision/AP Images; p. 218: Bruno Mars onstage, © Mark Humphrey/AP Images

Plants pp. 220-221: Green caterpillar, © Balashova Ekaterina/Shutterstock; p. 221: bananas, © Maks Narodenko/Shutterstock; peanuts, © Maks Narodenko/Shutterstock; cabbage, © Thanamat Somwan; tulip, © atiger/Shutterstock

Population pp. 224-225: Weeki Watchee mermaids, © Sang Tan/AP Images; p. 226: penguin on ice floe, sxc.hu, © Jan Will; Holy See (Vatican City), © Banauke/Shutterstock; p. 229: Los Angeles, CA, © Andrewy Bayda/Shutterstock; p. 231: Miami, FL, © Songquan Deng/Shutterstock

Religion pp. 232-233: Basilica of St. Peter, © avarand/Shutterstock; Harley-Davidson motorcycle, © Andrey Armyagov/Shutterstock

Science pp. 236-237: Jet Man, © Katsuhiko Tokunaga/Breitling for Photopress via AP Images

Signs & Symbols pp. 244-245: Smoking skull, © Dynamicfoto/Shutterstock

Space pp. 248-249: NASA

Sports pp. 258-259: © John Froschauer/AP Images; p. 260: Malcolm Smith, © Damian Strohmeyer/AP Images; p. 261: James Winston, © Julio Cortez/AP Images; p. 263: David Ortiz, © Jeff Roberson/AP Images; p. 265: Shabazz Napier, © David J. Phillip/AP Images; p. 266: Meryl Davis and Charlie White, © Diego Barbieri/Shutterstock; p. 267: Sochi skier, © Iurii Osadchi/Shutterstock

Technology & Computers pp. 268-269: Facebook solar drone, © Titan Aerospace/ AP Images; p. 275: girl with mobile phone, © Denix Kuvaev/Shutterstock; p. 276: social networks icon, © gst/Shutterstock; social media network connection concept, © Cienpies Design/Shutterstock; p. 277: © gezzeg/Shutterstock

US Government pp. 278-279: Eleanor Roosevelt statue, © Ron Leighton Design; p. 280: Supreme court, © Mesut Dogan/Shutterstock; p. 283: gavel, © Neamov/Shutterstock

US History pp. 300-301: Battle of Ft. Wagner, Rick Reeves/Wikipedia ; p. 301: First flight at Kitty Hawk, Library of Congress

Weather pp. 320-321: Frozen Lake Michigan pier, © Tim Komoelje/Shutterstock; p. 313: snow falling, © LilKar/Shutterstock; rain on water, © Sukit Hanphayak/Shutterstock; windy palm, © underworld/Shutterstock; orange sun in sky, © Jaromir Chalabala/Shutterstock

Weights & Measures pp. 316-317: money of Kazakhstan, © Redko Evgeniya/Shutterstock; money of Kazakhstan background, © schankz/Shutterstock; new $100 bill, © Andrey Lobachev/Shutterstock

World History pp. 320-321: Nelson Mandela Memorial Service, © AP Images

Homework Helpers p. 332: flowers in a vase, © Africa Studio/Shutterstock

What's Next? pp. 334-335: Oculus headset, © Barone Firenze/Shutterstock: cybercity background, © diversepixel/Shutterstock; p. 336: girl reading, © Paul Hakimata Photography/Shutterstock; smartwatch, © Denys Prykhodov/Shutterstock; man jumping, © imagedb.com/Shutterstock; p. 337: smart contact, © Rex Features via AP Images; artificial hand, © Ociacia/Shutterstock; asteroids, © Paul Fleet/Shutterstock